AUSTIN CLARKE:

ESSAYS ON HIS WORKS

ESSENTIAL WRITERS SERIES 38

**Canada Council   Conseil des Arts
for the Arts   du Canada**

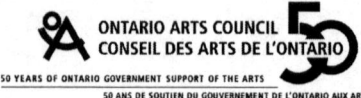

ONTARIO ARTS COUNCIL
CONSEIL DES ARTS DE L'ONTARIO

50 YEARS OF ONTARIO GOVERNMENT SUPPORT OF THE ARTS
50 ANS DE SOUTIEN DU GOUVERNEMENT DE L'ONTARIO AUX ARTS

Guernica Editions Inc. acknowledges the support of
the Canada Council for the Arts and the Ontario Arts Council.
The Ontario Arts Council is an agency of the Government of Ontario

We acknowledge the financial support of the Government of Canada
through the Canada Book Fund (CBF) for our publishing activities.

AUSTIN CLARKE:

ESSAYS ON HIS WORKS

Edited by
Camille A. Isaacs

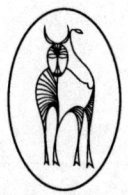

GUERNICA
TORONTO—BUFFALO—BERKELEY—LANCASTER (U.K.)
2013

Camille A. Isaacs, editor
Michael Mirolla, general editor
Joseph Pivato, series editor
Book Design by Jill Ronsley
Guernica Editions Inc.
P.O. Box 76080, Abbey Market, Oakville, (ON), Canada L6M 3H5
2250 Military Road, Tonawanda, N.Y. 14150-6000 U.S.A.

Distributors:
University of Toronto Press Distribution,
5201 Dufferin Street, Toronto (ON), Canada M3H 5T8
Gazelle Book Services, White Cross Mills, High Town, Lancaster LA1
4XS U.K.

First edition.
Printed in Canada.

Legal Deposit—First Quarter
Library of Congress Catalog Card Number: 2012953444
Library and Archives Canada Cataloguing in Publication
Austin Clarke : essays on his work / Camille A. Isaacs, editor.

(Essential writers series ; 38)
Includes bibliographical references.
Also issued in electronic format.
ISBN 978-1-55071-723-5

1. Clarke, Austin, 1934- --Criticism and interpretation.
I. Isaacs, Camille A. (Camille Andrea) II. Series: Writers
series (Toronto, Ont.) ; 38

PS8505.L38Z57 2013   C811'.54   C2012-907652-X

Contents

Introduction

CAMILLE A. ISAACS

I first came to appreciate the work of Austin Clarke through a desire to understand what it would have been like for my mother, one of many Caribbean immigrants who came to Toronto in the 1950s and 1960s, to be part of the first large-scale, post-war wave of West Indian immigration to Canada. My mother told wondrous stories (much like Bernice does in *The Meeting Point*) of the first black girl who managed to get a job working on the shop floor of Eaton's Department Store. Many of those in the current generation have no first-hand experience of Eaton's, nor understand the significance of seeing the epitome of white, Protestant capitalism infiltrated by a West Indian aesthetic. It would be difficult for them to comprehend the significance of that first black hire or what it would have been like to live in such times, where every accomplishment had to be fought for and then lauded. This historical reckoning is, in part, the significance of Austin Clarke's work. I can think of no other Canadian author writing at the time who documented the West Indian immigrant's condition not only for West Indian immigrants themselves and their descendants, but also for white Canadians, so that they could see the racist and discriminatory manner in which those immigrants were treated.

Although his first published novels were set in Barbados, Clarke became known to Canadians primarily as a result of his successful Toronto trilogy, regularly reprinted and the work for which there now exists the most scholarship. Clarke has been writing and publishing in Canada for almost 50 years (he was first published in 1964) and has created a formidable body of work. This critical edition, which includes new and previously published articles on everything from his memoirs to his novels and short stories, is long overdue. Regardless of the genre of his writing, there are some consistent themes that show themselves regularly in his work, the most common of which are a response to injustice and marginalization. More often than not, Clarke's fiction highlights a character or characters who are fighting some form of systemic unfairness. The characters of *The Survivors of the Crossing* (1964) and *Amongst Thistles and Thorns* (1965) rail against the after-effects of colonialism, themes which are revisited in *The Polished Hoe* (2002) and the memoir *Growing Up Stupid Under the Union Jack* (1980). His immigrant narratives describe discrimination in employment and a lack of acceptance from the larger Canadian society. Clarke's middle novels, *The Origin of Waves* (1997), and *The Question* (1999) and the reminiscences in *A Passage Back Home* (1994) highlight the importance of friendship. That he wrote two culinary memoirs, *Pig Tails 'n Breadfruit* (2001) and *Love and Sweet Food* (2004), suggests how central cooking is in Clarke's life. His nonfiction books and pamphlets, *Public Enemies* (1992) and *The Confessed Bewilderment of Dr. Martin Luther King* (1968), both contend with violence in the black community. Clarke is a man who has dedicated himself for decades to the downtrodden and under-represented figures in the communities with which he has had contact.

The forms in which he details these very themes match the issues he discusses. What better way to give voice to the thousands of undocumented workers, domestics, underemployed men, and aging, overlooked women than through well-drawn character sketches where they detail their plight in their own voices. So many of his short stories, and long sections of many of his novels, showcase a lone man or woman expounding what it is like to live on a day-to-day basis, often ruminating on their condition with no one to listen to their troubles, or no one able to do anything about it even if they are willing to listen. Stream-of-consciousness, then, becomes the form for these unheard voices. Dating back to the Toronto trilogy, Clarke has long used this narrative structure to allow his characters to think out loud, as it were—often in dialect. While that may be considered normal and even expected nowadays, we have to remember that Clarke was using Bajan dialect at a time when many Canadians would have had scant access to, or even knowledge of, Bajan speech patterns.

Yet the often-depressing subject matter does not prevent Clarke from injecting humour into his tales of woe. One may sympathize with Boysie's and Henry's inability to find work in *The Meeting Point*, but one also laughs at the many escapades in which they find themselves. So many of his characters land in outlandish situations, in part as a response to some difficulty. Their "solutions" to the problems they find themselves in may cause the reader to either guffaw or weep. This humour is also evident in Clarke's many memoirs, which showcase some of his best writing. In many ways, Clarke is an historian, documenting the education system in his youth, or how Barbadian women made a feast out of meagre provisions. His memoirs and nonfiction writing excel not only because of the personal reminiscences he calls to mind, but as a result of the context in which he places them. He details the very British education he received and the many beatings that accompanied it, and also elaborates on how colonialism shapes him and others for the rest of their lives. Beneath the many humorous episodes in his work, however, there is often a thinly veiled anger at work, anger at the manner in which so many characters and people have been treated. One laughs, but one simmers as well.

While Clarke has been celebrated for his use of Bajan dialect, his methods of capturing the immigrant experience, and his characterization of marginalized figures, he has also been criticized for the manner in which he has brought many of these characters to life. The stream-of-consciousness narrative style so central to giving the under-represented figure a voice results in long-winded and often repetitive sections. There is no self-editing button when one is contemplating one's status, no one to interject and say: "You said that already." Clarke has also been criticized for what he, or perhaps some of his characters, exhibits as an elitist or classist stance in the very British snobbishness that he both displays and critiques. It appears that some of his characters cannot shake the very colonialism and conservatism that entrap them. The prolific nature of Clarke's output, with a major work appearing every few years, has caused one biographer to describe his body of work as "of uneven quality" (Algoo-Baksh 66). Clarke is also a controversial figure for his polemical writing about many Canadian institutions that he, often quite rightly, labels as racist. It does not make one popular to draw to nice, polite Canadians' attention the racism and discrimination they would rather sweep under the carpet of multiculturalism. Algoo-Baksh also points out that some of Clarke's portrayals of women could be seen as "misogynistic" (162). But she urges readers, in order to get a more balanced view, to consider how women appear in the entirety of his writing.

Whatever your take on Clarke, as supporter or critic, the articles in this volume offer a wide range of opinions on the merits of his work. In "Austin Clarke's Extra-Curricular Bajan Education," Linda MacKinley-Hay considers the colonial education that Clarke received and writes about in *Growing Up Stupid Under the Union Jack*, and as evidenced in *The Survivors of the Crossing* and *Amongst Thistles and Thorns*. But she also highlights the influence of teacher and writer Frank Collymore on Clarke's work.

Several articles in this volume examine Clarke's Toronto trilogy, the body of his work on which there is the most scholarship, which also highlights its importance to the literature of Toronto. In "Nationalism in Austin Clarke's Toronto Trilogy," Marquita R. Smith discusses the role of the Civil Rights and Black Power movements in the trilogy and how blackness shows itself in Clarke's work. Batia Boe Stolar, in "Afro-Caribbean Immigrant Experiences in the White City," looks at the how the city of Toronto is constructed in the literary imagination and the role immigrants play in depictions of the city, in particular the way gender affects one's approach to the space. How Jewishness is represented is the focus of Sarah Phillips Casteel's article, "Experiences of Arrival." She shows how Jewishness vacillates between racial and ethnic constructions in Clarke's work. Michael A. Bucknor, in "'Voices Under the Window' of Representation," considers how Clarke uses memory to filter the experiences of various characters in the trilogy, in what he calls "body-memory poetics."

Clarke's short stories have been widely anthologized, so it is not surprising that there is also a significant amount of scholarship related to this genre and the collections in which they were originally published. Several critics comment not just on *Nine Men Who Laughed*, but also on Clarke's introduction to the volume, where he discusses the despair behind the laughter in the male characters in that collection. In "'Playin' 'Mas,' Hustling Respect," Daniel Coleman examines how masculinity shows itself in two of those short stories; while in "Clarke versus Clarke," George Elliott Clarke considers Austin Clarke's elitism, comparing him to the James Bond character by Ian Fleming. Smaro Kamboureli examines the role of laughter as a means of self-reflexivity in "Signifying Contamination." In comparison, Victor Ramraj compares Clarke's and Sam Selvon's senses of humour in "Philosophize or Indict." He comes to the conclusion that Clarke's sense of humour is much more militant than Selvon's, which he describes as lighter in tone.

Clarke's nonfiction writing is the subject of Brinda Mehta's article, "The Mother as Culinary Griotte," in which Mehta considers how food is used to transfer cultural memory. She argues that Clarke's detailed descriptions of various Barbadian staples, such as pudding and souse, are so much more than informal recipes, and she displays how he uses the various female family members he describes to intertwine cultural and culinary history. Finally, "Caribbean-Canadian *Reifungsroman*," my article on Clarke's later fiction (*More* and *The Polished Hoe*), questions the genre of the *Reifungsroman* ("literature of ripening"), as is it currently configured. Clarke's work shows us that the literature of female senescence must take into consideration the way that race and class affect the aging process.

As a bonus, this volume also includes a review of Clarke's latest literary offering, the long poem, *Where the Sun Shines Best*. In this poem Clarke returns to his roots, describing the circumstances of a murder in Moss Park. In her review, "'A Plea of Love and Blood,'" Maggie Quirt shows how Clarke's focus comes full circle with this volume through his continued interest in social justice.

Despite the extent of scholarship in this collection, there are still gaps that need to be filled. There is a dearth of academic material on Clarke's middle novels, *The Prime Minister*, *Proud Empires*, *The Origin of Waves*, and *The Question*. Clarke actually considers *The Prime Minster*, *Proud Empires*, and *Growing Up Stupid* as a kind of second trilogy (Algoo-Baksh 166). It would be interesting to see a critical response to these texts as a body of work to be considered together, or in comparison to his earlier trilogy. Clarke also has numerous unpublished manuscripts, which can be found at the Austin Clarke Papers at McMaster University in Hamilton. He seems to keep everything, and there are drafts of these novels that were never published, as well as various manifestations of texts that were published. Many a doctoral dissertation is waiting to be written in the numerous boxes that make up this collection. Finally, Clarke's nonfiction writing has been under-represented in scholarly articles. In several cases, the ideas shown in the columns, diatribes, reviews, letters, and interviews that he conducted, many of them dating back to the 1960s, resurface in his fiction. It would be interesting to trace the evolution of his ideas from nonfiction to fiction and from novel to short story.

Clarke continues to write. When last I spoke to him in the spring of 2013, he had completed another novel, was revising his memoirs, and considering returning to the long-poem format, all as he prepares to become an octogenarian in 2014. This collection of essays should not be considered the end of a meritorious career, nor as a finite commentary on his work. There is a wealth of material still to be explored, especially if he sustains his prolific output.

Work Cited

Algoo-Baksh, Stella. *Austin C. Clarke: A Biography.* Toronto: ECW Press, 1994. Print.

Brief Biography

CAMILLE A. ISAACS

Austin Ardinel Chesterfield "Tom" Clarke was born on July 26, 1934, in St. James, Barbados. His parents, Gladys Irene Clarke and Kenneth Trotman, were not married and the "stain" of his illegitimacy caused him a great deal of anguish in his formative years. Although his mother later married Fitz Herbert Luke, his stepfather was often absent due to his work, and Gladys assumed the roles of both mother and father. In several of his works, including *Pig Tails 'n Breadfruit*, Austin Clarke writes lovingly of his relationship with his mother and other female relatives who helped raise him. After primary school at St. Matthias Boys' School, where corporal punishment was the norm, Clarke went on to Combermere School, where he was in part under the tutelage of writer Frank Collymore. In 1950, he entered Harrison College, one of the most highly respected boys' schools in Barbados and, in 1952, he received his Cambridge and Oxford higher school certificates. He began his first forays into writing poetry and short stories at this stage. Prior to emigrating to Canada in 1955, he taught at a rural high school in Barbados and later worked in a factory to earn money for his journey.

Clarke arrived in Toronto on September 29, 1955, with little money, but with several bottles of rum and a great deal of attitude. His studies in economics and political science at the University of Toronto did not last, in part due to a lack of interest, but also because Clarke felt his classes fostered a "high school environment" (Algoo-Baksh 35). Although he withdrew from academics in 1957, he did find some success with his writing, winning a $5 prize for five poems he submitted to a Trinity College competition (Algoo-Baksh 37). This was the same year he met and married his wife, Betty Reynolds, a nursing supervisor. Clarke grew increasingly frustrated at this stage of his life in his inability to find work suitable to his tastes and education, and he often relied on his wife, who had a more stable income. In addition to various manual labour positions, Clarke eventually landed on his feet through his pen, working as a journalist in Northern Ontario and later at the CBC. His daughter Janice was born in 1958, followed by Loretta in 1960.

Clarke's writing career took off in the 1960s and has continued almost unabated ever since, with major publications every few years. *The Survivors of the Crossing* (1964) and *Amongst Thistles and Thorns* (1965) were co-published by McClelland & Stewart and Heinemann. In addition to his Toronto trilogy (1967-1975), these novels solidly established Clarke on the Canadian literary scene and enabled him to make a living through his writing. His literary success and increased hours of work, however, led to a separation from his wife, although the two remain amiable. Clarke would eventually have two more daughters and a son.

Despite personal setbacks, Clarke has had a long and varied career. He taught at several American universities in the late 1960s and 1970s. He was cultural attaché to the Barbadian Embassy in Washington in 1973 and then returned to Barbados in 1975 to be acting general manager of the Caribbean Broadcasting Corporation, a position for which he was terminated due to differences of opinion about the direction in which the channel should proceed. Clarke returned to Canada and dabbled in politics, running as a Progressive Conservative candidate in 1977 and in the 1980s working at the Ontario Board of Censors. He also served on the Immigration and Refugee Board of Canada in the late 1980s and early 1990s.

Throughout these varied pursuits, Clarke continued to write, to date amassing eleven novels, six collections of short stories, four memoirs, two nonfiction pieces, and a volume of poetry. This list does not include numerous articles, interviews, and unpublished material. This prolific output has garnered Clarke numerous prizes and awards, including the Casa de la Americas literary prize in 1980 for *Growing Up Stupid Under the Union Jack*; the Rogers Communication Writers Trust Prize in 1998; Order of Canada in 1998; and the W.O. Mitchell Literary Prize in 1999. In 2002, he received his most prestigious award, the Giller Prize for fiction for *The Polished Hoe*, which also won the Commonwealth Writers' Best Book Award. Most recently, he was awarded the 2012 Harbourfront Festival Prize. As he approaches his 80th year, Clarke continues to write; he is currently working on another memoir and a novel, and is considering returning to the long-poem format.

Work Cited

Algoo-Baksh, Stella. *Austin C. Clarke: A Biography*. Toronto: ECW Press, 1994. Print.

Still Angry: An Interview with Austin Clarke

CAMILLE A. ISAACS

The following interview was conducted in April 2013 at Austin Clarke's home in Toronto.

Camille Isaacs [CI]: As you have aged, your protagonists have aged.

Austin Clarke [AC]: Oh, really?

CI: Well, I've noticed that both Idora and Mary-Mathilda are older women. In many ways, Idora could be seen as an older Bernice or Dots, and if we had followed the characters of *The Survivors of the Crossing* into older age, you seem to be revisiting that theme, or revisiting that place, with older protagonists in *The Polished Hoe*. So I'm curious about your own aging and how it's been for you and your interest in what I see are aging protagonists, usually female.

AC: Well, I'm not aware of picking up certain women at later ages than when I first introduced them to the readers. I suppose you could say that I am an autobiographical writer. I deal with what is around me. And the poem, *Where the Sun Shines Best*, is set right across the street from where I live.

CI: Were you here the evening that [murder] took place?

AC: I was in the house, but I didn't hear about it until the next day.

My own aging has taken me by surprise [he laughs], because of arrogance, the West Indian or Barbadian arrogance. Although I was brought up by people who were old, they had passed the average age of bearing children, that you have in this country. So I was brought up by grandmothers, great-aunts. So I've seen that aspect. Having said that, I'm amazed that you would point this out because it was not in my mind when I was writing the story. Of course, if I was analyzing the story, I would have to concede that flashes back to people in the book who are old or getting old is a reflection of what you might say I am experiencing now. I don't think I'm old. I've never thought of life in that respect. I can't help but express my alarm at that. I would have to tell you. I wrote a short story, which I think is the best short story I have written. It's called "They Didn't Tell Me," meaning, they didn't tell me how to get old, or what would happen. To me, the disintegration of the body is not only alarming, but interesting because I was an athlete. I was a sprinter and in that kind of activity one never looks past the present race. And I doubt whether many athletes think of old age.

CI: Well, I think young people don't think of old age, generally.

AC: Yes. And I'm becoming more alarmed and interested, from a writer's point of view, at the organization or the reorganization of families in a house in which most of them grew up, where the house is now divided into sections to deal with age and aging.

[...]

CI: You said you were surprised by your own aging, arrogant perhaps. Is it that you didn't expect it to happen to you now? You didn't expect it to happen to you like this?

AC: Well, the short story I wrote, "They Didn't Tell Me," talks about some of the things that I have experienced because I have to have an operation that is not serious. It is a man's disease. [...] They assure me that it is not anything so dramatic, that I have to say my rosary or anything. Still, it's the doctor's knife, which can slip. So, it's about that, and the man [in the story] can't remember the names of the street on which he lives and the names of friends. And there all these calls coming. And what is so interesting and frightening at the same time, after a certain time in his life, living in the same place, having the same friends, he is greeted almost every morning by friends on the telephone. Sometimes he cannot remember the voice. But they say the same thing, "Guess who dead?" [laughter] And they tell him who dead. So that brings him back to his own reminisces of youth. There's one other aspect. Living on this street, where I see parades of men who look as if they're broke and homeless. I sort of look at them and say: "My God, I hope not to be like that." Not that I hope not to be ever sick, but I hope to not be sick and have no facilities to ameliorate ...

CI: You're lucky you have this [house].

AC: Right. And it's very interesting. There comes a time where you doubt where you are. And you regard yourself as a patient or a sufferer of the disease of poverty that you see parading in front your house. And then it takes a while to say: "Well, nobody can bring me home. I'm already home." You see that kind of vague mind that comes before you. So that's the situation. There's one other reason, too, that I find very fascinating. When my mother died at the age of 92, in Brooklyn, when I came home from the funeral, there was a time when, living in this house alone, I would feel, in a physical sense, my mother sleeping in the same bed, right? And it was so life-like, that I would call her name. And I would be very scared that there was nobody there. I've lived in this house for 15 years alone. [...]

I had [medical] problems and, all of a sudden, they [Clarke's daughters] decided to be very concerned about the stairs, which I have been climbing for 15 years and was still climbing. So, when I was in the hospital, they took the opportunity to reorganize my house. For weeks, I couldn't find one damn thing [laughter]. It seems as if I was bringing into reality an aspect of fiction that I had written about. But it is a serious thing. I detest it.

CI: But what is it that you detest, though? Aging, or being dependent on people?

AC: I detest being dependent on people. Aging I can do nothing about. I have to accommodate aging, like most of us. The physical aspect of that accommodation as me now, going upstairs during the day, to sit in my study ... And the idea that I'm sitting in my study, and they have made a kind of study for me down here, is a bit disconcerting. So I have two studies ...

CI: Yes, but you always did, right at the back there, no?

AC: Yes. I promised that my last two books would be written on the IBM Selectric Typewriter on which I wrote *More*. I dug it up from the basement and it works. But then the problem was what would happen when the present ribbon runs out. And then it came to me that a friend of mine who knew when I was converting from the thing upstairs to the typewriter had given me a box of ribbons, which I had never opened. And it came to me and I moved from the chair in which I was sitting and picked up the first box and there it was. And it is a very interesting feeling of companionship when you could hear the keys banging against the ribbon. That is the thing.

CI: You reference this story, "They Didn't Tell Me," but the story that I see some similarities, but not a lot, is "Leaving This Island Place," where you talk about visiting your father before you left Barbados. I realize the situation is different in that he was in an alms house, but in a sense, age doesn't discriminate. And when you talk about what you detest the most, the dependence, right? That's the similarity there.

AC: Yes, and the whole idea of, which I think might be clinically incorrect, the whole idea of putting my body in the body of a young man or a young woman who walks with a stride of elegant health. And I remember winning the athletic championship at Harrison College for the second time and at Combermere for the fourth time. So I am being very unfair and astonished in trying to pull the body from the car or the street and put the best of that body in my body, which is aging. But that is the writer talking about it. I don't think that I'm so obsessed by it. It has become part of life. It is still an object of a situation that I can compare and perhaps draw a lesson from because, being reasonably intelligent, I know that the only thing that can take the virility of a body from its present functioning is witchcraft.

CI: So, you talk about having people come in to cook for you now. Do you miss cooking because, of course, cooking was so important to you, central to you, at one point? Are you still able to do any cooking for yourself?

AC: Oh, yes. [...] I miss that aspect of my life because I like cooking. But I still cook. I wouldn't cook as lavish a meal or for as many people, but I still cook. I get a bit tired. [...]

CI: So, are you still writing or are you able to? I know the last time I was here you were hoping to be working on your memoirs. Are you doing that at all?

AC: Well, I've finished the first draft of the memoirs. My publisher, meaning the publisher of my most recent book, showed some interest, but he needs a more, as we would say, a "vulgarization" of the memoir.

CI: "Vulgarization," what does that mean?

AC: He wants the memoirs to deal with ordinary things, to be vulgar.

CI: I imagine you wrote your life.

AC: Well, he's saying I did not write the whole of my life. I'm holding back.

CI: I see. He wants the details, the juicy details.

AC: And I resent that, the position of the invasion of people's character and all that. He made the point that struck me like a spear in my heart, that I did not even mention my wife.

CI: Well, it's funny because you're so open in so many different ways, like your papers at McMaster. I mean, that's very personal. You have your professional work, but you also have a lot of personal information, even things like some of your kids' childhood drawings are there, your finances are there. I can see your publisher's point in that a scholar could easily go to McMaster, get all this personal information, and write about it. Perhaps what he's asking is for you to give your side of it.

AC: Yeah, I'm not, still, too keen on that. It's interesting because one of the young writers who knew that I finished this first draft asked if he could introduce it into seminar. So they read the first 20 pages and I could see from listening that I need to inject a stronger personal presence in the memoir.

CI: Do you want to, not necessarily set the record straight, but leave your side of things, your account, so that somewhere down the line, some researcher doesn't go to McMaster and write the story as they saw it? Do you want to leave that account, your side? You don't feel the need or the desire to tell your side of things?

AC: No. I have always felt that the personal side of things should be kept personal. I know the possibility of invention on the part of researchers. That doesn't bother me because anyone who is a better researcher would understand the need for balance. So that doesn't bother me. I'll be dead. Let them wrestle over the bones.

CI: I guess because you've been so autobiographical in your writing, I think the tendency might be, and I'm not saying good or bad, to read the personal in your work, to try and pull autobiographical details out of your writing.

AC: That would be a great flaw in the critical ability of the graduate student.
[...]

CI: I want to take you back a little bit, to when you first came to Canada and what it was like. I think it was Mordecai Richler who referred to you as "Canada's angriest black man." Do you remember that?

AC: Yes.

CI: And I read many of your articles as they showed up in "Dissent" the column you used to write. That was in the *Toronto Telegram*. You were often quite critical, and rightly so, of Canada's stance toward immigration and the way immigrants were treated once they were here. So, I'm wondering, are you still angry?

AC: Yes, angrier, but more silent. Silent anger. [...]

CI: So you don't think things have improved?

AC: No. And the new thing now, the new interpretation by the press, was violence, black violence. Because if there is no serious attention given to these incidents, as tragic as they are, the time will come when we will go back to the 1960s in America.

[the telephone rings]

CI: Where were we? You said you're still angry and I'm surprised because, in some ways, you seem to have mellowed.

AC: I have mellowed only through my silence.

CI: But what makes you silent?

AC: Being fed up with the situation not changing.

CI: So, you don't think there's hope?

AC: There is no hope that the black man will get his righteous amount of dignity in this city.

CI: Ever? You don't think?

AC: Well, ever? How many years must you wait? [...]

CI: We create new "others" every day. I see your point. Things haven't gotten better. Every day there is going to be a new "other" created. But I do think on the whole, certainly, some of the discrimination is better.

AC: It's less visible.

CI: Do you not think there are more opportunities for blacks in the city, than there were, say, in the 1950s and 1960s when you first came?

AC: Well, I don't like the comparative aspect of your statement.

CI: Why?

AC: Because you are suggesting to me that there could be a limit on decency.

CI: No, but I do think things are better than they were then.

AC: Well, things are better because, I would think, it had to be better, since it was so bad in the beginning. [...] As racism becomes respectable in its presentation not only by whites to blacks, but by blacks to blacks, there will be, necessarily, new techniques of presenting this racism, which might delude some people who have been here not so long as I have that there's this real progress.
    [...]

CI: I see your point. I have a four-year-old son myself. And I think back to when my mom came to this country (She came in 1962. She was a nurse—my family is Guyanese, by the way), not that the possibilities are endless—I don't think that Canada's ready for a black Prime Minster, for example—but I want my son to know, I want him to be able to pursue whatever's in his heart, whatever position, field, dream—whatever he wants to pursue, and I think that while things are still not where they should be, it is better than it was.

AC: I couldn't argue against that.

    [...]

We have allowed the aroma of racism to stick on our clothes without attention because we are going over, pages turn with equal efficiency than many years ago. [...]

    At this stage in time, the fact of hiring another black man is not so declaratively an aspect of progress. This is a late payment and we must not be deluded by that.

    [...]

I've noticed this: I haven't been mixing socially too well recently because of my preoccupation with my own work. The time will come when the bell will ring for the last time. And I shall, like Dylan Thomas' advice, "do not go gently into that good night" and I'm not sure that I will respect that adjective "good." But realizing that I was, I suppose, anti-social, to some extent ...

    A whole bunch of them [black leaders] died around the same time. There's Jan Carew, then Charlie Roach. And all of them seemed just to disappear around the same time and that had a very serious effect on me because ... I even thought of writing a short story in which the main character, from a telephone call one morning, with the same question, "Guess who dead?" And the fellow says: "Austin Clarke" [laughter]. But I still feel very badly that I did not spend time ...

    [...]

CI: What do you have left to write? What more do you want to write?

AC: I have a responsibility as a writer to do the best work I can in order for people to see another point of view. I feel very strongly about that. So my responsibility [...] is to produce the books and let the readers decide. I'm not going to do anything to guide their apprehension of ... I'm not going to give them a hint that is there. So, it is the revision of the memoirs, which is in one of those three boxes there; another novel called "So, What?", that my publisher didn't like and said so. But he didn't like *More* either. [...] So that is what I hope to do. I think I'd like to write some more long poems.

CI: In some ways you're going back to your youth because your earliest writing was poetry in Barbados. Is it a more manageable form or is it just the space you're in right now?

AC: I always thought that poetry was a trumpet played by clearer notes. I was brought up on Eliot, Keats, and Milton. And I went through the same, apparently contradictory positions expressed by Derek Walcott in his poetry. [...] So, they have remained with me and certain plays by Shakespeare. [...]

CI: So, now, when you look back on your career, and your life, are there things you would have done differently in either your writing or your life? What are your greatest joys and what are your greatest sorrows?

AC: Well there was no doubt that I would not fit in on the Canadian scene because I went to school in Barbados at a time when Canada was considered a third-rate country. [...] So I wonder if that was one of the mistakes I made [in not going to England].

CI: But I read your work and you said—because you did go later and you interviewed several writers, including Sam Selvon. And you said at the time that you didn't feel the same—I think you said you felt much more affiliated with the civil rights movement of the United States than you felt for what was going on in England at the time at Notting Hill, etc .

You're still wondering what it would have been like if you had gone to England?

AC: Yes. I would have been a barrister. I know it.

CI: And would that have been a good thing?

AC: Yes, I would have been a barrister dealing with murder cases or, or what? Or a businessman, buying houses and selling them.

CI: Well, I'm glad you came here. I think Canada would have had a great loss had you gone to England.
    [...]

AC: But I had always said that my responsibility to those four children [his four daughters] was to cover their university, even if they were to postpone and postpone and postpone. I would still pay.

CI: So, are they your greatest joy then?

AC: Yes, they are beautiful. They take after their mother.

CI: So, when you think about your legacy, it's not necessarily just your writing, it's your family?

AC: I would think so. And I look at this as such a natural ending of a life. [...]

CI: So what do you think of the Canadian or Toronto literary scene? Are you able to do any reading? Do you think it's robust?

AC: I was never too impressed with Toronto's literary scene. I was more impressed with the Toronto literary scene that included blacks because I think if this activity of writing had taken place in England, there would have been more acclaim prescribed to it. And it would by now have been regarded as Canadian writing. The English have been able to do this. Not that I'm comparing situations. It might appear contradictory. I'm here sitting down with you in a house which because of circumstances, I myself could not afford to buy now. It might appear churlish to make any comment about that, but I still do not ... especially when the brothers start shooting and killing one another. I certainly don't feel comfortable. And sometimes I feel, the thought comes to me, not seriously of course, but I shouldn't say that ... the thought comes to me seriously, have I paid enough respect to this phenomenon by marching in the black community? What will I suggest to them? Peace. Understanding. And the blacks will shoot me. So there is no peace, understanding. How could you offer peace and understanding to people who are treated so badly?

CI: So you're still concerned with injustice?

AC: Oh, yes. If I should ever cease to be concerned, well, take me out and whip or kill or something. And, of course, when you live alone, that adds to your anxiety, I think, because there's nobody, at the moment, with whom you could discuss these things to see if you're going crazy or you're fair in your criticism.

CI: I think that's Idora in *More*. The three days that she's locked up in her basement apartment in an area very much like this ...

AC: It's downstairs.

CI: ...Yes, I know—she has no one to share her ideas with, nobody to talk to, nobody to see, as you say, if her ideas are just.

AC: So she becomes explosive ... and her ignorance is expressed in her dreaming about killing the policeman.

CI: Well, I won't keep you any more. I thank you so much for your time. It has been lovely chatting with you.

AC: No problem.

Austin Clarke's Extra-Curricular Bajan Education

LINDA MACKINLEY-HAY

What is well known in Canadian literary circles is that Barbadian-born Austin Clarke is Canada's "first major black writer" (Algoo-Baksh, Preface 9). Less referenced is that he is "the first black West Indian-Canadian novelist published [simultaneously] in Canada and in Britain" (62). Known to only a select few is that Clarke's fearless satirical treatment of the Barbadian education system, specifically in his second published novel and his first volume of autobiography, owes much of its impetus not only to his exported British education at Combermere Boys School in Bridgetown but also to the generous extra-curricular instruction by a teacher there. This teacher's tutelage during Clarke's adolescent years and following his departure to Canada will be examined in the following pages.

In order to fully appreciate the heady juxtaposition of the curricular and extracurricular instruction that shaped Austin Clarke during and following his years at Combermere, it is necessary to first understand the Barbadian educational legacy. First, the island of Barbados can claim a longer connection with England than any of the other West Indian islands.

Geographically situated further to the east than the others, it became "the natural point of call from the mother-country" (Lucas 201). It was settled as early as 1627 by Englishmen accompanied by Negro slaves, and when the island turned to sugar production, a powerful expatriate plantocracy emerged (Algoo-Baksh, Notes 197). Owing to the topography of the island with its flat, cultivable land, its good water and healthy climate (dryer and less malarious), Barbados was a place where the English came to live and not simply to trade (Lucas 202).

Because no aboriginal race was encountered on the island by the original English settlers—F.A. Hoyos, in his definitive work, *Barbados: A History from the Amerindians to Independence,* reports that the reason for the disappearance of the Caribs found in Barbados early in the sixteenth century by Spaniards is their transportation to Espaniola as slaves (12), Barbados was unarguably "purely British from the first" (173). John Hearne's appraisal that "[h]istory Englished" the Barbadian differently from the way it did either the Jamaican or the Trinidadian helps to justify the following special consideration of Austin Clarke's English schooling and his consequent testimony of the exile of the colonial schoolchild from both the island community and the centuries-old traditions represented by the British educational design and generally safeguarded by teachers in colonial schools.

One of the abovementioned teachers, Frank Appleton Collymore, was a Barbadian-born educator, writer, editor, painter, actor, and lexicographer who left his mark on generations of boys who attended Combermere, and significantly on Austin Clarke. As both pupil and teacher for more than sixty years at Combermere, Collymore rose to the position of Deputy Headmaster, though it is speculated that his mixed blood may have prevented him from attaining Headmaster status in class-conscious Barbados. As Edward Baugh explains, the school's designation as a second-grade school by an Education Act of 1878 was "based on considerations of class and colour," and "very few Blacks" were even appointed to the teaching staffs of first-grade schools before the 1950s (6). Teaching primarily English and French to Fifth Formers from 1909 onwards (Barratt and Sander), Collymore did so within an educational system criticized for being overly reliant upon pupil-teacher recruitment, inappropriate curricula, and irregular student attendance (Ramchand 21-2).

In his review of education in the British Caribbean, Kenneth Ramchand notes that elementary educational standards in the islands were generally poor during the nineteenth and twentieth centuries and that Reading, one of the "three compulsory subjects," was most problematic (24). Typically taught in parts of the Caribbean for almost half a century (Brydon 48) by way of Nelson's *Royal Readers*, reading instruction involved mere coaching and parroting. Adding to the ineffectiveness of the "laborious memorization drills," Ramchand ascertains, was the "obligation to stand and deliver when the inspector came" (24). And Clarke witnesses this in *Amongst Thistles and Thorns* as his protagonist is therefore moved to play truant from his colonial school. Continuing his investigation into Britain's educational export to the Caribbean, Ramchand notes that the seemingly compensatory schemes by which poor and illegitimate children could compete for free places in secondary institutions pointed rather to the inadequacy of elementary education and the inhumane and often simply ridiculous program of training for these exhibitions to enter high schools.

In this regard, F.A. Hoyos, who comments in his autobiography, *The Quiet Revolutionary*, on "the supreme advantage of working at Combermere with Frank Collymore" and of attempting to "model [...] his style and approach to young people" (144), also notes that at the approach of examination day the cane was applied for failure to meet progressively higher targets until only the ninety-percenters escape reprimand (23). In his own autobiography, Austin Clarke also alludes to this practice as he catalogues the eating of raw eggs to "fertilize the brain, to sharpen the retentive capacities" (*Growing Up Stupid* 182). But this training is perhaps best satirized by Trinidadian V.S. Naipaul in *A House For Mr. Biswas* (1961). In this novel, the son of the protagonist is placed on a special brain-food diet of milk and prunes while he lives "a life of pure work":

> Private lessons were given in the morning for half an hour before school; private lessons were given in the afternoon for an hour after school; private lessons were given for the whole of the Saturday morning. Then in addition to all these private lessons from his class teacher, Anand began to take private lessons from the headmaster, at the headmaster's house from five to six. He ate. Then he did his school homework; then he prepared for all his private lessons. (463)

This competition for the Exhibition Scholarship to attend secondary school, the winning of which provides access to "all there really is to know" (Collymore, "Voici la plume de mon oncle" l. 40), plays so large a part in the life of the Caribbean schoolchild that it comprises a distinctive feature of the literature of the British West Indies (Sunitha 293). And Austin Clarke joins his teacher in witnessing to its importance as he scrutinizes his own schooling in both novel and memoir.

The aforementioned poem by Collymore colloquially echoes the cant of such English public school standards as Donald Hughes' "The Short Cut," while at the same time it satirizes the Tom Brown education model "benignly" exported to the colonies and its subsequent appropriation by West Indian society. Enumerated in the poem are the age-old traditions of public school: parents' unshaken faith in education, segregation by sex, rote-learning, caning, religion, moral training, the Classics, English nationalism, "gentlemanly" dress and deportment, games, paramilitarism—in short, preparation of the colonial student for "a status that's secure" (l. 20).

In his biography of Frank Collymore, Edward Baugh illuminates the social history of colonial Barbados during the opening half of the twentieth century while examining the life and work of his colourful and ambivalent subject. On the one hand, Baugh quotes the Headmaster of Combermere School in his admiration of "a trusted colleague, and an outstanding Schoolmaster" (82). On the other, the biographer finds some carefully articulated views of teaching in his diary entries that suggest a less-than-conventional Tom Brown approach to school-mastery. Baugh's discovery of Collymore's rejection of flogging as counter-productive is represented by a diary entry for 15 April 1940:

> I think I've written enough to show that since the object of teaching is to bring about improvement or progress in some form or other, and this through

> the free working of the intellect, the main purpose is
> to implant a desire for improvement in the mind of
> the boy; hence recourse to "fear and trembling" in
> the guise of flogging and threats and all the mumbo-
> jumbo of severity and power would have no part in
> my programme. (qtd. in Baugh, Lecture 7)

Collymore's preference for developing the mind and
personality of his charges over the imparting of expertise
in the subjects taught is corroborated by Hoyos, his colleague at Combermere:

> Above all he succeeded because, it seemed to me,
> his philosophy as a teacher was based on that of
> St. Francis of Assisi. He sought not so much to be
> understood as to understand, not so much to be loved
> as to love, not so much to be respected as to respect
> the thousands of boys who passed through his hands.
> (*The Quiet Revolutionary*, 45)

It is perhaps relevant that, in spite of the constant floggings at St. Matthias Boys' Elementary where Clarke was
enrolled at four years of age, he received no beatings,
despite his education-supporting mother having directed
the headmaster "who reigned in militaristic fashion" to
flog him when necessary to advance the learning (Algoo-
Baksh 20).

Continuing his review of education in the British
Caribbean, Ramchand notes that after secondary school
the island scholars selected from those who got the best
results in the Cambridge Local Examinations could
study law or medicine in Britain, returning "stamped
like an envelope with what they called the culture of the
Mother Country" (Lamming, *Castle* 19) and with a profession and salary that guaranteed great social privilege
and independence (30). Attesting to the achievement of

these "been tos" as a result of "[t]his fuss of education" as Collymore satirically views it (l. 5), is "a marble cross" planted precisely "six inches" in the West Indian sod from which they, if not their ancestors, sprang (l. 48).

To return to Ramchand's review, these graduates of secondary schools who were denied the social mobility afforded them through training abroad were recruited for the "limited privilege" accorded by the teaching profession or government or commercial offices (30). In his assessment, this accounts for the emergence of a black middle class in the Caribbean "jealously" holding on to their restricted advantage, alienated from an educational structure that they slavishly perpetuate—a sort of "hegemony" through "consent" (Gramsci, as translated by Hoare, et al 170)—which preoccupies both George Lamming and Austin Clarke in their counter-discursive texts.

Of his education in Barbados the writer under investigation has had a great deal to say, both to his reading public and eventually to his Trinidadian-born biographer. Born in 1934 to a poor mother in the village of St. Matthias near Bridgetown, Austin Ardinel Chesterfield Clarke is not hesitant to credit both Frank Collymore and George Lamming for the encouragement to write from the West Indian margins about the effects of colonialism on a poor black (Algoo-Baksh 15). As he chronicles in fictional and biographical form the individual's sense of dislocation at the hands of both church and school, he criticizes the educational system while crediting one of its teachers with whom he developed a long-standing relationship.

Because he is less pensive, more caustic, and plainly more hyperbolic than George Lamming in his narrative assessment of the impact of education on the individual West Indian, Clarke's first novels, *The Survivors of the Crossing* and *Amongst Thistles and Thorns,* and biographical memoir, *Growing Up Stupid Under the Union Jack,* have more of a satiric thrust. This strategy immediately recalls Collymore's poem, "Voici la plume de mon oncle," with its emphasis on the material benefits of the standard colonial education. Clarke's technique, which involves the extensive use of the "Bajan" (Barbadian) dialect, also owes much to the advice offered by Collymore (concerning some of Clarke's early short story attempts) some twelve years after the student left Combermere:

> The dialogue should not be too West-Indianized, especially as to spelling ... The best thing is to try to suggest most of it by speech rhythms ... and of course the ignored auxiliary and the floating participle— these all make for the raciness of the speech. (qtd. in Algoo-Baksh 51)

This advice presumes an audience unfamiliar with "Bajan" speech—a "metropolitan" audience that will not tolerate anything "too West-Indianized"—and is a reminder of the constraints imposed by the colonial relationship, and most especially in literary resistance. And by heeding his former teacher's editorial expertise (outside his teaching duties Collymore was publisher and editor of the literary magazine *Bim* from the 1940s to the 1970s) and personal interest in Barbadian dialect, Clarke demonstrates the lessons learned and his continuing respect for this particular Combermere alumnus and teacher, if not for the colonial schooling otherwise offered at such institutions. Perhaps ironically, it is Clarke the student who is lauded for his "great achievement with Bajan speech" (Baugh

139). Additionally, it is suggested that Clarke's proficiency may have been further stimulated by Collymore's correspondence to him in Bajan (Baugh, Lecture 16). The teacher's own compilation of a small book on the Barbadian vernacular entitled *Notes for a Glossary of Words and Phrases of Barbadian Dialect*, published the year Clarke emigrated to Canada and five years after he left Combermere for two years of Sixth Form at Harrison College, was regarded as "a pioneering work" that had four subsequent editions up to 1970 (Gafoor 5).

Whereas fellow Barbadian author George Lamming's first novel reflects his own childhood, Clarke's is content merely to skewer the agencies of colonialism. Categorized by its author as "a novel of nostalgia and remembering" (qtd. in Algoo-Baksh 63), *The Survivors of the Crossing* is set in 1961 and populated by a group of underpaid cane-cutters on a Barbados plantation involved in an abortive revolt. However, a hint of what is to flow from Clarke's pen subsequent to 1964 is found in the considerable space devoted to the portrayal of the local schoolmaster.

Dickensian with a marginal twist, Mr. Whippetts' moniker suggests Collymore's "playfulness with names" (Clarke, "Colly," 125) as well as the "physical abuse that often substituted for sound education in colonial schools" (Brown 43). Alienated from his village by virtue of his own colonial education, he belongs to a generation that has been schooled to revere everything British: he mimics the speech and the dress of his white superiors, and for twenty-four hours every day he represents the colonial education that essentially denigrates that which is indigenous or black. As the novel's "really tragic isolate" (Brown 43), this black man in a white linen suit and white straw hat cannot entirely conceal "the island's broad dialect[...] beneath the artificial English [he] always used in the company of his inferiors" (Clarke, *Survivors* 23). Believed by the protesting villagers to be in league with the plantation owners, but dismissed by his white superiors for suspected sympathy with the striking workers, the doubly exiled teacher recalls the head teacher at G's school in *In the Castle of My Skin* with his divided loyalties and "limbo" status.

His own precarious position notwithstanding, it is British-style education rather than political independence that Mr. Whippetts attempts to convince the villagers is the "door-opener" to a better life. This education, he argues, is guaranteed to release its subscribers from the "tyrannies o' slavery." Less schooled but more enlightened than Lamming's "history-challenged" schoolboys, Rufus, the illiterate instigator of the revolt against the plantation owners, reminds the teacher in this instance that, while open slavery has indeed been abolished, "'they forget to abolish the next kind'" (24). This would also seem to echo Kenyan Ngugi wa Thiong'o's charge against the Centre for its artful training in colonial subjectification.

However, while acknowledging his own powerlessness to overthrow the prevailing structure and to establish a more egalitarian regime in rural Barbados, Rufus' continuing dream that his two children will attend Harrison College and Queen's College respectively is that of parents everywhere for a better life for their children.

In terms of the importance of *The Survivors of the Crossing* to Clarke's body of work to date, Stella Algoo-Baksh concludes in her 1994 biography that his first novel functions as a practice run: it allows Clarke to externalize his own "initial blindness" about the impact of colonialism on Barbadian society, and that he is able to "confront" and "come to grips" [from afar] with the damage both he and his people have sustained in his later narratives of struggle "against white society in general" (65-66). And so, mentored and shaped by Frank Collymore, given the [standard English] language and form for expressing the contempt he harbours for having been "Union-Jacked" by his schooling, Austin Clarke extends his reach with his next novel.

In *Amongst Thistles and Thorns*, published a year later in both Canada and Britain (Algoo-Baksh 66), Clarke follows Lamming's lead and makes use of an adult narrator-protagonist who casts an examining eye on the various youthful experiences that have shaped his character and his future. Incorporating elements of his own life and naming such familiar territory as the Garrison Savannah and Gravesend Beach, Clarke presents a world thoroughly informed by personal experience. And as Lamming does in *Castle*, Clarke scrutinizes the Barbadian child's exposure to the forces of colonialism, reserving his fullest disdain for the school system with its "criteria established by the white elite [...] against which all men [sic] must be measured" (Algoo-Baksh 77). Instead of allowing himself, and by extension his narrator, to be tested against these normative standards and found "substandard," through his "alter ego" Clarke turns about-face and assumes what has come to be regarded as a typically postcolonial stance: he examines the examiners.

It is evident from the opening scene that not only is the author going to concern himself with the general experience of growing up, but that he is also determined to expose the way in which colonial schooling figures in the coming-of-age of the West Indian. Collymore's poetic ironic justification for corporal punishment within the

British school—"There's a road to the brain through the backside by blows" (l. 16)—is illustrated here by the nine-year-old Standard One narrator. It is doubtless significant that he is being punished for looking away from the copying of "Manners maketh man" in penmanship class. An errant sixpence rolling under the bench fuels the boy's active imagination until "a large shoe" covers the bare foot covering the coin, and Clarke's examination of the colonial school—by way of its personnel—is underway.

Reminiscent of G's headteacher at Groddeck's Boy School, the colonial functionary here is named Joshua Blackman (doubtless to implicate the Christian religion in the colonial school enterprise). The delight he takes in exacting servitude from his barefoot charges is highlighted by the caricaturish proportions in which he is drawn by the narrator: "a large, cruel man" with "four yellowish teeth[...] standing guard" over the mouth where [s]aliva and remnants of his lunch of soda biscuits and cheese" sputtered "from the spaces" (5). In this particular context he arms himself with both the local hard yellowish tamarind tree and the authority of centuries of British imperialism. The near-epic description of his whipping of the protagonist for such a minor infraction exposes the grotesquerie of the situation:

> ... fifteen ... sixteen. He was almost completely out of breath now. With each lash, he gave off a heavy, laboured exhaust, as if something inside him was going to collapse. Eighteen ... nine ... (4-5)

The village school over which the bicycle-riding Joshua Blackman dutifully presides with a voice "like a plantation overseer's" (97), employs four assistant masters. The narrator notes that the four doors and six windows of the structure are draped in Union Jacks, and portraits of English royalty line the walls. As with children throughout the Empire, the narrator and his classmates are instructed in the "glories of Britannia":

> Britannia, who, or what or which [the relative pronoun being such an elusive entity], had brought us out of the ships crossing over from the terrible seas from Africa, and had placed us on this island, and had given us such good headmasters and assistant masters, and such a nice vicar to teach us how to pray to God—and he had come from England; and such nice white people who lived on the island with us, and who gave us jobs watering their gardens and taking out their garbage, most of which we found delicious enough to eat [...] Britannia, who, or what or which had ruled the waves all these hundreds of years [...] and had kept us on the island, happy—the island of Barbados (Britannia the Second), free from all invasions. (12)

Within the island context and amongst benches, desks, and slates (perhaps a sly suggestion of the most treacherous "thistles and thorns" of daily life in the colonies), the narrator notes that the colonial schoolchildren—"little black Britons" all (13)—are persuaded that learning is their only escape from the backwardness of life on the periphery. Like the "Island Scholar" godson of the headmistress of the girls' school, the protagonist can also progress to Oxford or Cambridge, if only he will aspire to something other than servant status or hereditary example (his father is a well-known layabout). Encouraged to despise what the school disparages, the villagers also do their part to supplement, both at home and on the streets, the institutional instruction (the Bath Corner of Clarke's youth figures as prominently in his boyhood memoir as does the "stand-pipe" in the village of *Thistles*). A "marginal" Greek chorus, they function extra-curricularly to impress upon their youthful audience the benefits of being, if not white (like God), then educated. As they display their "outsider/insider status" in relation to the colonial culture of the colonizer (Brown 18), they give their implicit approval to the "MADE IN ENGLAND" school.

Not content to make the schoolteacher (the co-opted type whom Collymore credits with "dish[ing] out the stuff" at the typical colonial school (l. 9) the only butt of his satire, Clarke offers up for his reader's inspection a white school inspector. While a comparison with Lamming's "sacrificial lamb" obviously reveals the commonality of their creators' experience, it also highlights the differences in the two writers' approaches to their theme. Described by Clarke's narrator as being "a world away" from the schoolboys he oversees (174), this inspector, unlike his predecessor in *Castle*, is clad in the "white of colonial power." However, the clear-sighted Milton Sobers discovers an underbelly, and so there is an edgier, more discerning quality to his description of a

> [W]hite shirt with the short sleeves exposing the copper-wire sprigs of hair on his bony arms; white cork hat with green undersides, white short pants with white three quarter stockings and white leather shoes which he never cleaned.

Emitting a "smell of whiteness and richness" (173), the British-born inspector examines colonial ears for wax and heads for lice, and pontifically disregards the head teacher's rules against eating within the school by munching on wafer-thin (cucumber?) sandwiches from an embossed English tin and drinking white lemonade in full view of the hungry children. Where Lamming's inspector is guilty of benign detachment from the daily reality of colonial schooling, Clarke's is a more explicit throwback to his slaver ancestors as he coldly applies the whip to their black backsides.

After he pats his white cork hat (with its telltale underside) in place and drives off, the boys receive conflicting messages as they view the head teacher venting his rage at having his own blackness cast up to him by "a blasted white man" (176). His fetching of the inspector's lunch from a white shop puts into sharp relief the "inferiority" of his own fried dolphin and bread repast, and like G's head teacher, Joshua Blackman is relegated to being a mere pawn in the chess game of empire: he is accorded limited forward mobility from his "black" starting point, but he is denied full acceptance by the "white" playmakers who control the game as well as the white side of the board. And so, doubly exiled, he is incisively drawn by Clarke as a "cultural schizoid" (Algoo-Baksh 147), an opportunist who takes advantage of his position within the community for personal gain. In Collymore's phraseology, "[he] has learnt to use both edges of the Golden Rule" (l. 36). In reality, any "advantage" he can take is negligible, and he has sold his birthright for a very small mess of pottage indeed.

Initially dragged to the village school by his illiterate mother [Clarke's biographer reports that his mother enrolled him at St. Matthias Boys' Elementary School for the indispensable education when he was a mere four years of age (18)], Clarke's nine-year-old protagonist is expressly one of Collymore's "wayward" students (l. 17). Milton, son of Ruby Sobers, is a reluctant scholar, privately subversive and authority-resistant. As the thematic centre of the novel, Milton's consciousness recalls that of G in *Castle*, reflecting both his basic belonging to the village culture and his marginalization from it as schooling intervenes. His imaginative transformation of the "sterile literacy" of the classroom into the flogging orgy by the head teacher (Brown 170), and his periodic running of "private, silent races" with the horses "around the racecourse" of his mind (130) are preludes to his actual running away from both the school with its sadistic head teacher and his mother with her dream of having a son at Harrison College.

Milton Sobers' three-day truancy represents his alienation from both the traditions represented by the colonial school system and the "clutter of poverty and shacks" from which he has sprung (36). By literally going "underground," he is instructed in the limitations of religious worship and village life just as earlier, hidden in the school's toilet, he has discovered the head teacher's betrayal of the education he represents by arranging for the sale of the roses from the school garden for his own gain. While not mature enough at this stage to put into words the full implications of all of this sensory input, Milton trusts his instincts to resist both Blackman and eventually his parents' bullying. And, as though he has Clarke's protagonist in mind in *The Pleasures of Exile*, George Lamming alludes to that subversive spirit with which the colonial "transforms the colonizer's language from the badge of subordination to the tool of subversion and rebellion" (qtd. in Brown 48). And, while at the conclusion of the novel the prodigal is ostensibly back in the fold of home and village, he is still resentful of his "second class" treatment both at home and at school. As Lamming's novel does, Clarke's ends at a crucial juncture: Milton's formal education in the classroom is to be replaced, beginning the next day, by work in the limestone quarry. However, his ex-centric three days have exposed the reality of the colonial Caribbean, and the "thistles and thorns" of his existence, experienced in full measure, have stiffened his resolve. Armed "with a new courage" (182) after "playing hooky" on the margins, Milton Sobers, like John Milton's Samson (to whom Blackman earlier draws a less-than-deft comparison), now dares to question the status quo. Within these three days there has obviously been a kind of growth.

Milton has had his eyes opened to the "colonial brainwashing" of both the self-loathing head teacher and the self-effacing villagers (Brown 45). And Milton Sobers' spirit resolutely and independently rejects both in favour of a more life-respecting world tomorrow.

In the third early prose piece of Clarke's to reveal the influence of Frank Collymore's mentorship, his boyhood memoir subversively entitled *Growing Up Stupid Under the Union Jack*, the theme of double exile is again introduced. By guiding the reader back and forth throughout the key incidents in his elementary and secondary school years at St. Matthias and Combermere before stepping across the "Maginot Line" to Harrison College, "that old, time-honoured and timeless bastion of higher learning, higher snobbery" (Clarke, "Harrison" 31), Clarke paints a picture of life and education and the resultant "stupidity" on the margins of empire.

Serving as a frame for his autobiographical treatment of schooling is an article by Clarke that appeared in the Barbadian Independence issue of *New World Quarterly*. In it he looks "back over the snapshots of [his] youth in

Barbados" to find in it a "freedom restricted by the history of that parallelogram of life drawn[...] many years ago by the English." The top and parallel sides of the figure represent for him the colonizer; the "hard bottom line" (31) the Barbadian, "shackled by colonialism and ignorance and hunger" (32). To his way of thinking, the use made of the school in the colonial enterprise assures the fixed nature of the figure's three sides; it is this that Clarke proceeds to examine in his autobiography.

From the opening sentence of this episodically structured narrative, Clarke documents the complicating factor of transplanted British education in the lives of Barbadians:

> I was admitted to Combermere School, a secondary school in Barbados, on Roebuck Street, in Town, in September 1944, and placed in the "L2D," the Lower Second Form, with thirty other boys. (5)

As does Eric Williams in his autobiography entitled *Inward Hunger: The Education of a Prime Minister*, Clarke here criticizes the "total disregard of the environment" by the British colonial education model in which the staff was "English by birth, training, sympathy, or all three" (Williams 35). Again, just as Williams confesses that he "could not see the value of study unless there was that connection" with the surroundings (43), Clarke notes that the externally set and marked examination questions, though they contained "educated" questions, obviously reflected the interests of the examiners and had "nothing to do with the way we saw ourselves." Yet these exams "would determine our lives in Barbados" (*Stupid* 183). If unsuccessful in secondary school, students "languished and starved" on small salaries as elementary school teachers, and like those figures portrayed in both Clarke's and Lamming's coming-of-age narratives, they took out their "anger and disappointment on the small frightened boys in those dark, steamy and underequipped school rooms" (181). As an additional insult to the local populace, they also collected a pension for their pains.

As Clarke presents his case against the Centre, he reviews the pedagogical methods employed in colonial schools of the West Indies: the exported education model stressed "acquisition" of certain subjects—most often by memorization. According to the editors of *The Post-Colonial Studies Reader*, this internalization (learning by heart) of the English text and its reproduction before audiences of other colonials served a dual purpose: it taught the English language of the colonizer, and it implanted in the colonial the "moral, spiritual, and political" lessons to be learned ("Introduction" 426). The implication here is that inhabitants of the colonies are "in need of change to meet English standards" (Brydon, "Daffodils" 6), and Clarke captures this prevailing attitude as he reports the often-heard ultimatum: "you'll remain the savages you are if you don't read the English poets" (*Stupid* 48). And so Barbadian students "acquire" lines from the Acts of the Apostles, a catalogue of the countries and capitals of the British Empire, and details "about a man with 'resolution and independence' who walked beside a sea and picked up seashells" (49). Clarke counters this enforced induction into white culture by recalling that the master who taught Scripture was an "atheist," that instead of seashells, Barbadians picked "welts and 'sea beefs'," and that instead of having poems written about them, these dotards were "committed to the Jenkins mental hospital" (49). In this regard, the "teacher who had taken a special interest in Clarke at Combermere" (Algoo-Baksh 51) and who later urged his former student to find his literary subjects in the West Indian community cannot be dismissed when considering Clarke's own pedagogical creativity: he evidently required Fifth Form English Literature students at Coleridge and Parry Secondary School in rural Barbados to "translate the [prescribed] text into Barbadian dialect" (28).

In the same vein, the copying of the prohibitively priced texts which Clarke and those like him are obliged to do during vacation would seem to suggest a further reinforcement of the ethnocentric lessons contained between the covers. In Clarke's case, however, this enforced familiarity with *The Merchant of Venice* results in his identifying with Shylock, "a small man, a brilliant man, an illegitimate man" who broke his bonds and spoke out against injustice. Shylock's proclamation of independence encourages the student to rebel himself "against the authorities, against [some of] the assistant masters at Combermere" (50), and eventually, one might add, to "write back" about the flaws in the exported schooling of the "Master." The subversive use which he and other resistant students make of the texts selected for export to the colonies may suggest that the cultural product supported by British education is not as mono-lithic as teaching methods might imply, and that it is the built-in "fault lines" that actually enable graduates to critique the system.

In addition to the texts in use in British West Indian schools, the personnel also come under scrutiny, and this becomes apparent when Clarke moves from elementary to Combermere Secondary at age ten. There is no ques-tion of the daily inspection of hands and ears which both G and Milton Sobers undergo at primary school and which Lamming and Clarke witness in their respective novels. This associative "cleanliness and godliness" is left behind for well-ordered classes in which "Cawmere" (Combermere) boys are trained to become "Little black Englishmen" (*Stupid* 52). "[C]oached to be discriminating" and "trained" to be snobs, Clarke and his peers prefer "a cuppa toy" to one of rich, locally produced chocolate, and unknowingly mimic "working-class London fish-sellers' speech" (53). Because "believing" in English superiority "was a part of [one's] education in the colonies" (167), that which was MADE IN ENGLAND is the product of choice—if not of suitability for those on the margins.

Clarke enumerates the profusion of consumer symbols of British power and influence with the by-now expected assertion of "otherness":

> The clothes we wore; the books we read; the pencils we wrote with; the Quink ink; the book bags; the combs made from tortoise-shell, which were too fine-toothed for our thick, nappy hair [...] and the Brilliantine which made our heads shine, slicked back, concealing the African kink in our hair. Rule Britannia. (51)

What the author is pointing to here are the dangers of unconscious over-identification with the colonizer's value system, a practice which is inevitably at the expense of one's own (in this case racial) identity.

Illustrative of the danger of whole-hearted acceptance of the superiority of everything British is the application by the Barbadian schoolboys of the "Manners maketh man" adage from which Milton Sobers is distracted in the opening scene of *Thistles*. The English sailors who arrive on their shores fail to display a textbook correctness. Instead, this "strange tribe of economizing men" kick the village boys (50), cheat the local prostitutes, and generally disregard the rules of the playing field of the English public school. Following these, author Thomas Hughes believes, ultimately prepares one for "correct behaviour" both in life and in the colonies.

Operating on a system of demerits for various offenses, and with house captains and prefects who could be straight out of Tom Brown's Rugby, the Combermere of George Lamming and Austin Clarke in the 1940s is headed by a recently demobilized British Army Major—a veritable "drill sergeant of a man" (42). And during the war years, the school, as Clarke describes it, becomes "a regiment," and public floggings the order of the day. Ransome's *History of England* is at the core of the history curriculum, and Clarke intones, "I knew all about the Kings; the Tudors, Stuarts and Plantagenets; and the Wars of the Roses," ending with the searing indictment: "nothing was taught about Barbados" (72). Barbadian-born Keith Sandiford concurs with Clarke's assessment here as he writes of his own secondary schooling: "Our school system was still patterned on nineteenth-century Eton and Winchester and the emphasis was still then very much on the four C's: Cricket, Christianity, Classics and the Cane." He, too, concludes his description in the following way: "No one instilled in us any pride in our own past or heritage" (qtd. in Algoo-Baksh 24). One is reminded here of Frank Collymore's "enlightened" schoolmastery: his dislike of flogging, his turn to agnosticism under the influence of Bertrand Russell and Aldous Huxley (Baugh, Lecture 3), his encouragement of wide extra-curricular reading by way of his own extensive library holdings (Lamming, Interview 5), and exposure to local theatre in which he was active by way of arranged ushering duties (Baugh, Lecture 7).

The literary emphasis given in the British West Indies secondary school curriculum is again alluded to as Clarke continues to regale his reader with details about Combermere and the instruction in resistance gained there. Keats, Shakespeare, Defoe constitute the "daily intellectual fare" at the school (137), while such classic English texts as *Robinson Crusoe* "naturalise" for the students "black/white and empire/colony relations" (Brydon and Tiffin 49).

Analyzing the supposedly "universal aspects" of British literature, Clarke undercuts the myth of British superiority in all things in two ways: he relocates the revered English author of *Paradise Lost* to the West Indian island of Barbados and specifically to "a boy in my village who did not know about paradise lost and regained, and who was not blind, and who [furthermore] was an expert at killing lizards and ground doves" (48); secondly, he makes a case for alterity as he presents a dialogue between himself and a non-"Cawmere" boy regarding Robert Herrick's poem "Fair Daffodil":

> "What is a daffodil, though? They have daffodils at Cawmere?|
>
> "A daffodil? A daffodil is only the name of a flower, man!"
>
> "But we got flowers growing all over the place, wild flowers and good flowers. In the school garden and *out the front road.*" (56)

In a context where "appearance" is valued—a point Collymore himself satirically makes in the poem "Voici la plume de mon oncle" in the line: "See how nicely his tie sits underneath his collar" (l. 31)—and where the entire school system revolves around the production of "island scholars," Clarke recalls that Quink-ink-stained fingers, Cathedral choir membership, and glasses are highly respected. The reality is that the forbidden ball points are still used—"to write love letters to the girls at St. Michael's Girls' School and Queen's College" (148)—the English-made tortoise-shell spectacles are widely worn, though "not manufactured to accommodate the flatness and broadness of [black] noses," and choir boys "slept and sometimes snored" during the Church of England service (109).

This demonstration of "native ingenuity," which Clarke smilingly notes that "England did not tolerate" (81), is also evident in this counter-discursive text in the terminology that mixes dialect form with standard English—no doubt a credit to Collymore's earlier lexicographical advice. The effect of this interplay is subversive, and in satirizing the school with its middle-class value system, Clarke uses the juxtaposition to full advantage. The "Cawmere" sense of style as portrayed by the author reflects both the Barbadian's respect for and suspicion of education. Being "smart and well-educated" is to be a "fool," and so his classmates are identified as Latin, science, and mathematics fools. In his book on Clarke's fiction, Lloyd Brown explains that, although the standard meaning of "fool" suggests a dupe, Creole usage implies "awesome expertise," thus invigorating while still deferring to the colonizing culture (15). However, Clarke's subsequent mention of these "slightly mad" boys who were "'spraining' their brains by always reading" and who were "going mad because of the things learned in books but [...] not discuss[ed] with sister, brother [...] mother and father" (69-70) also suggests that, with the imposition of British-style education on the youth of the community, "something strange and dangerous" is happening (70)—a double exile is being effected.

Having chronicled for the reader his disdain for both the acquisition of foreign knowledge and its regulation through team play, Clarke does not surprise when he admits to the choice of "a more acceptably aggressive way of fighting back" than finishing first in Latin. He further explains his choice of athletics: in individual sport he could be "in front, alone, in victory" (34), and applauded for it. And so he becomes a "running fool [...] to run for [his] glory, like no one had ever run" (80).

At the Speech Day that closes the school year of every Combermere throughout the empire, the British Governor himself—the "King pin" of the Caribbean colonial system, according to Lamming (*Exile* 46)—presides. The grand finale is the inspection of the requisite Cadet Guard of Honour, "Overseas, Dominion and Colonial" (156), decked out in their stiff khaki, regulation discipline, and "all the paramilitary trappings of an up-and-coming elite." Despite the cadets' "carefully nurtured conformity with the dominant colonial class values," the flies which swarm from the nearby canals to the cadets' faces, and the pervasive dialectic of the street vendors announce the life of the community, a life the educated elite can never entirely erase from their memory. And so, as critic Lloyd Brown so correctly puts it, these graduate student-soldiers have essentially acquired outsider-insider status. As "fully-formed fools" whose education will serve to alienate them from their roots by placing them in leadership roles, they will also be excluded from the white traditions to which they have conformed (19). As Clarke learns from the nameless rich of Belleville Avenue in Bridgetown, Barbados, British-style schooling notwithstanding, "you would never pass any examination big enough to land you beside them" (168).

Concluding the relation of his Combermere experience with a direct nod to George Lamming –"you left Carrington's Village with the slime of poverty, left the people living in the castles of their skins" (167), Clarke moves on to Harrison College. There he will spend two years of Sixth Form studies, honing his "aggression and ambition" (Clarke, "Harrison" 34) before turning to teaching and writing, like Collymore and Lamming before him (Algoo-Baksh 24).

Though a commission was appointed to consider the problems of the educational system in Barbados and other West Indian islands as early as 1931 with its concerns regarding irrelevant curricula and unqualified personnel (Williams, "Education" 149), it was not until the 1950s that West Indians began to document their youthful experience of being doubly exiled as a result of their Union Jack-ing. One can merely speculate on the reason for the empowerment of "black Britons" to respond as they do and to counteract the powerful whitewashing of a colonial education. In the case of both George Lamming and Austin Clarke, the catalyst seems to be Frank Collymore, M.A., O.B.E. A white Barbadian with "a dash of colour" and a passion for reading from an early age (Baugh 139-40), he continued to teach at Combermere, while indulging his love for painting, writing, and acting. But just what the source was of Collymore's own independence from the strictures of a grammar school education can again only be conjecture. The fact that he was invited to join the staff at Combermere after his own seven years there as a student might suggest that he had so impressed the headmaster with his academic and sports prowess that he was an ideal candidate for modelling the standards represented by the institution. But the fact that he was largely self-taught beyond secondary—the M.A. was an honorary degree conferred by the University of the West Indies in 1968 (148)—suggests rather that his approach to schoolmastery was a less hardened one.

F.A. Hoyos remarks on both personality and methods that were "peculiarly his own" (*Quiet* 45), and, in the biography that appeared seven years before his death, Edward Baugh points to the "treasury of ["reverently autographed"] West Indian first editions" that line the shelves of his library at Woodville as proof of Frank Collymore's creative influence on generations of Caribbean youth (148). One might safely speculate that *The Survivors of the Crossing* and *Amongst Thistles and Thorns*, Austin Clarke's first narratives, stand beside those others that also valorize the Caribbean experience and subvert "the New Order" that colonial schooling promised ("Voici" l.12)—and that Frank Collymore personally delivered.

Works Cited

Algoo-Baksh, Stella. *Austin C. Clarke: A Biography.* Toronto: ECW, 1994. Print.

_____. Notes on Chp. 1. *Austin C. Clarke: A Biography* Toronto: ECW, 1994. 197. Print.

_____. Preface. *Austin C. Clarke: A Biography.* Toronto: ECW, 1994. 7-13. Print.

Ashcroft, Bill, Gareth Griffiths, and Helen Tiffin, eds. *The Post-Colonial Studies Reader.* London: Routledge, 1995. Print.

Barratt, Harold, and Reinhard Sander, eds. Biographical Note. *The Man Who Loved Attending Funerals And Other Stories.* By Frank Collymore. London: Heinemann, 1993. Print.

Baugh, Edward. "The Blossoming of Caribbean Literature: The Life and Work of Frank Collymore." The Walter Rodney Lecture. University of Warwick, 18 Mar. 2010. Web. 19 Nov. 2010.

_____. *Frank Collymore: A Biography*. Kingston: Ian Randle, 2008. Print.

Brown, Lloyd W. *El Dorado and Paradise: Canada and the Caribbean in Austin Clarke's Fiction* . London, ON: U of Western Ontario P, 1989. Print.

Bryden, Diana. "Wordsworth's Daffodils: A Recurring Motif in Contemporary Canadian Literature." *Kunapipi* 4.2 (1982): 6-14. Print.

Bryden, Diana, and Helen Tiffin. *Decolonising Fictions*. Sydney: Dangeroo, 1993. Print.

Clarke, Austin. *Amongst Thistles and Thorns*. 1965. Toronto: NCL, 1984. Print.

_____. "Colly." *Bim: Arts for the 21st Century.* 2.1 (Nov. 2008-Apr. 2009): 125. Print.

_____. *Growing Up Stupid Under the Union Jack* . Toronto: McLelland, 1980. Print.

_____. "Harrison College and Me." *New World Quarterly,* Barbados Independence Issue 3-4 (1966): 31-4. Print.

_____. *The Survivors of the Crossing*. London: Heinemann, 1964. Print.

Collymore, Frank. "Voici la plume de mon oncle." *Caribbean Voices. An Anthology of West Indian Poetry.* Vol 2. London: Evans, 1970. 91-3. Print.

Gafoor, Ameena. Rev. of *Frank Collymore: A Biography,* by Edward Baugh. Kingston: Ian Randle, 2008. Kaieteur News, 20 Mar. 2010. Web. 05 Dec. 2012.

Hearne, John. "What the Barbadian Means To Me." *New World Quarterly*. Barbados Independence Issue 3-4 (1966): 6-9. Print.

Hoyos, F.A. *Barbados: A History from the Amerindians to Independence*. London: MacMillan Education, 1978. Print.

_____. *The Quiet Revolutionary*. London: Macmillan, 1984. Print.

Hughes, Donald. "The short cut." *The Games Ethic and Imperialism: Aspects of the Diffusion of an Ideal*. By J.A. Mangan. Markham, ON: Penguin, 1986. 7. Print.

Lamming, George. "Interview with George Lamming." *Kas-Kas: Interviews with Three Caribbean Writers in Texas*. Eds. Ian Munro and Reinhard Sander. Austin: U of Texas, 1972. 5-22. Print.

_____. *In the Castle of My Skin*. 1953. Harlow, Eng.: Longman, 1987. Print.

_____. *The Pleasures of Exile*. London: Michael Joseph, 1960. Print.

Lucas, C.P. *A Historical Geography of the British Colonies. Vol II. The West Indies*. 2nd ed. Oxford: Clarendon, 1905. Print.

Naipaul, V.S. *A House For Mr. Biswas*. 1961. London: Penguin, 1969. Print.

Ramchand, Kenneth. *The West Indian Novel and its Background*. 2nd ed. London: Heinemann, 1983. Print.

Sunitha, K.T. "The theme of Childhood in *In the Castle of My Skin* and *Swami and Friends*." *WLWE* 27.2 (Autumn 1987): 291-96. Print.

Williams, Eric. "Education in the British West Indies." *Consequences of Class and Colour: West Indian Perspectives*. Eds. David Lowenthal and Lambros Comitas. New York: Anchor, 1973. 148-66. Print.

_____. *Inward Hunger: The Education of a Prime Minister*. London: Deutsch, 1969. Print.

"The Whole Damn World Is the Same All Over" … Or Is It?: The Relevance of Black Nationalism in Austin Clarke's Toronto Trilogy

MARQUITA R. SMITH

Austin Clarke's Toronto trilogy, which features the novels *The Meeting Point* (1967), *Storm of Fortune* (1971), and *The Bigger Light* (1975), highlights the integral role racism has played in shaping the Canadian experience of Caribbean-born immigrants to Canada. Though Clarke's focus is on the condition of Caribbean immigrants, his writing potentially holds wider implications for black Canadians. The politically tumultuous period of the late 60s and early 70s—with the rise of the Civil Rights and Black Power Movements in the United States—greatly influenced Clarke and his work. *The Meeting Point*, the first of the trilogy, was published during Canada's centennial year and mounted a significant challenge to the nation's seemingly favourable treatment of minorities.

Despite this open challenge, Clarke's work was not taken up in Canadian literary criticism until the 1980s and 1990s, leaving many aspects of his writing unexplored.

Clarke's Toronto trilogy demonstrates how particular models of blackness rooted in black American experiences cannot be readily employed within a Canadian context. Beginning with *The Meeting Point*, this essay will explore the limits of American 'blackness'—a politically and socially defined subjectivity—as textually represented through Clarke's questioning of the usefulness or relevance of the Nation of Islam's black nationalism rhetoric as a socio-political tool for Canadian-based Caribbean peoples. This endeavour will explore one part of a development of consciousness that exemplifies Clarke's engagement with both larger, international social issues and topics that remain relevant to contemporary Canadian society.

The Toronto trilogy deftly explores what Rinaldo Walcott calls the "interstitial space" (41) of blackness and highlights what he also views as the incapability of black American models to represent the locality of black Canadian political concerns (38). By revisiting Clarke's Canadian imagining of American race relations, which highlights the shared demands for equality by black people across national borders, this essay will demonstrate how Clarke makes literary use of elements of American-derived black nationalist rhetoric as potentially valuable tools of resistance for black Canadians. The characters of the Toronto trilogy all, to varying degrees, consider the relevance of various models of blackness. Many of the Caribbean or black Canadian characters in the trilogy reference black American models of subjectivity as guides for maintaining blackness in a country where, as George Elliott Clarke notes, such blackness is often assumed to be absent (35). Paradoxically, these characters cannot escape their blackness even when it is treated as a spectre within a predominantly white national identity.

My approach to Austin Clarke's 1967 novel *The Meeting Point* pays particular attention to the framework of the Nation of Islam's (hereafter the NOI) rhetoric of black nationalism within its doctrine. The presence of black nationalist rhetoric, though seemingly minimal, is brought forth by the protagonist Bernice's careful consideration of its possible uses in her new home of Toronto. Bernice, a Barbadian woman in Canada under the domestic worker scheme, must find a way to reconcile her desires for equal treatment with the realities of living in a multicultural Canadian society. She undergoes a process of learning and critique and later emerges as a more critical member of her community who is able to see the merits and disadvantages of the NOI's brand of black nationalism—much like Austin Clarke himself.

Similarly, Walcott views black American models of blackness as possibly critical parts of transnational political identifications (33). Walcott and G.E. Clarke both acknowledge the importance of American blackness for black Canadians but also advocate for critical engagement that takes seriously the locality of Canadian blackness and highlights its uniqueness. In *Odysseys Home: Mapping African-Canadian Literature*, G.E. Clarke argues that there is no model blackness and his analysis strives to view African-Canadian literature outside of the shadow of African-American literature and culture. Although G.E. Clarke is quite critical of some of Austin Clarke's literary tendencies in representations of class, the Toronto trilogy appears to work toward the same goal of *Odysseys Home*. The trilogy demonstrates how the particular model of blackness rooted in black American experiences cannot be generically situated with a Canadian context.

In *The Meeting Point*, Bernice's initial encounter with black Muslims in Harlem sets the stage for her ongoing, often private consideration of the use value of such ideology as a black woman in Canada. The appeal of black nationalist ideology for both Clarke and his characters must be understood within the historical specificity of the United States' tumultuous political and cultural climate of racial politics in the 1960s in contrast to Canada's lack of a galvanizing, politicized black movement at the time. In the trilogy black American experience serves as a reference point for black Canadians seeking a way to maintain an existence that is not consumed by the dominant white culture and instead celebrates blackness.

Early in his career in 1963, before his first publication as a writer, Clarke interviewed Malcolm X in New York for CBC radio. Although he initially sought to interview James Baldwin, Clarke was convinced by some local Harlem residents to interview the NOI leader in lieu of the literary figure. The popularity of Malcolm X—due to a variety of his characteristics but especially his oratory skills—made him a captivating figure. For example, historian Jeffrey Ogbar notes that membership for the NOI doubled after a 1959 CBS news special appearance by the spokesman (21). Clarke's own perception of Malcolm X, as he shared in a 1965 CBC radio broadcast after his assassination, was that he was a sincere man. Clarke's respect and moderate admiration for him was clear but, at the time, Clarke favoured Martin Luther King Jr.'s non-violent approach over the by-any-means-necessary attitude of Malcolm X. Clarke was expressly displeased with the highly publicized manner in which Malcolm X's attacks on MLK were made to the detriment of a unified black front which Clarke saw as an essential political need given the pressing racial politics. Clarke was wary of the rhetoric of the NOI and stated that its "moral and social ambivalences provided the failure of the Muslim movement as a well-thought-out theology" ("Malcolm X" 3-4). This was largely due to the ambivalence within the NOI's doctrine, which Clarke saw as teetering dangerously close to making the mistake of viewing one man as god. In addition to the issue of deification, Clarke was very critical of what he called Elijah Muhammad's doctrinaire racism ("Malcolm X" 10).

However, by 1968, shortly before King's assassination, Clarke had changed his views of King's approach. In a pamphlet entitled "The Confessed Bewilderment of Martin Luther King, Jr." published in February 1968, just months before King's death and soon after the publication of *The Meeting Point*, Clarke lambasted King for attempting to appeal to "white conscience and white morality" (3), both of which he claims were lacking to begin with. Clarke, apparently no longer invested in the non-violent approach of MLK and the maintenance of a unified black front, described King's idealism as "the basic madness of unreality" (4). Clarke also remained skeptical of the political potential of black nationalism. As he put it: "It will not be the Black Panther, and other nationalist-oriented forces, that will bring out this destruction. It will be American intransigence" (13). Along with his newfound skepticism, Clarke takes up a decidedly separatist (racially and politically) stance in which he questions the logic of multi-ethnic alliance:

> In America, the great ineffectiveness, among other weakness of the non-violent movement, is that it is not only integrated along racial lines, but also political lines, (some are moderates, some conservatives), and moreover, its orientation and its direction is non-black.

> For more than 50 years of the existence of the NAACP,
> (the leading force behind Dr. King's moral non-violent
> tactics), the president has been a Jew. It is conceivable
> therefore, that such a movement would contain
> conflict: both with the real and other white liberals
> who sing, "We shall overcome someday." Would these
> Jews and white liberals overcome themselves, or their
> relations, to give Dr. King and other black people, their
> freedom? ("The Confessed Bewilderment of Martin
> Luther King, Jr." 7-8)

Clarke implies that multi-ethnic coalition possesses some
measure of futility in terms of what can ultimately be
accomplished for liberation movements. This view of
Jewishness reads it as a part of the dominant, oppressive
structure of whiteness and casts doubt on (to borrow
from black lesbian feminist Audre Lorde), the ability of
the master's tools to dismantle the master's house.[1]

It is likely that Clarke's knowledge of the NOI's
movement and a measure of admiration for its most
visible spokesman, alongside Canada's tendency to
compare itself to its southern neighbour, influenced his
characterization of Bernice's attraction to the NOI. As
G.E. Clarke highlights, Canada, though close in proximity to the United States, assumed itself to hold a place
of moral superiority for its more favourable treatment of
racial minorities despite its own history of discreet racism
(30). Clarke questions this standing of moral superiority
through the pseudo-liberal character Mrs. Burrmann,
Bernice's employer. Despite their conception of themselves as progressive, equality-advocating anti-racists, the
Burrmanns expose and subject her to some of the most
intimate and disturbing racist encounters in her new
home. Upon reviewing Sarah Phillips Casteel's article on

the exploration of connections between Jewish and black identities in *The Meeting Point,* David Chariandy points to the importance of class in the relationships between Bernice and her employers (154). Mr. Burrmann, who grew up Jewish and poor as opposed to his wife's rich upbringing, has a familiarity with blackness that calls attention to both the heterogeneity of whiteness and the questionability of equating Jewishness with whiteness. Mrs. Burrmann shares with Bernice her perception of the supposed advanced racial politics in Canada compared to the civil rights challenges taking place in the United States, promulgating what G.E. Clarke calls the tendency of popular Canadian usage of African-American experience to "paint Canada as a tolerant 'Peaceable Kingdom' in contrast to the blood-splattered, gun-slinging, lynch-'em-high Republic" (31).

Bernice's experience as a Caribbean domestic worker in 1960s Canada inevitably pushes her to find a way of understanding the precariousness of her place in Canadian society. However, the racism she faces is not always of the overt or direct kind. Though Bernice makes no comment in response to her employer's inane moral superiority, her silence should not be read as acquiescence to Mrs. Burrmann's depiction of Canadian society. When Bernice attempts to feed the Burrmann children and their guests she is mercilessly attacked by a young white boy who demonstrates the racism he has learned at home by hurling racist epithets at her as she goes about her job. The Burrmann daughter attempts to defend Bernice against the boy's racist tirade but once confronted with the viciousness of racism, Bernice cannot bring herself to distinguish the two children beyond race. Bernice fails to differentiate the young girl who knows and attempts to protect her from "one of four white children" (25). This interchangeability spills over into her perception of others as she declares the *"whole damn world is the same all over,"* and enables her hate for the racist white child to "[become] a corporate hate" (25).

This encounter with blatant racism early in the narrative highlights the significance of racism in the lives of the trilogy's characters. Bernice's collection of reading materials from the NOI, notably their official newspaper *Muhammad Speaks*, and her recollection of time spent in Harlem enable her to turn to the black American resources to understand the challenges she faces and how, possibly, to resolve them. The rhetoric of the NOI intersects with the hate Bernice comes to feel for white people "all over" with its universal declaration of the deviltry of white people and embraces all people of colour as "black" as an inversion of the doctrine of white supremacy (Ogbar 3). Bernice, moving from an experience like the one she had with the children, initially finds these elements of the Nation's doctrine appealing. In this case, the hate of the white child begets hate from Bernice. The Nation's leader Elijah Muhammad articulates in the list "What the Muslims Want" (which was published in each issue of *Muhammad Speaks* until 1975) its demands for equality in law and justice, education, and employment opportunity (Lee 109-10). Someone in Bernice's precarious position could certainly find such demands agreeable. However, the NOI's potentially violent method of approach to obtain the desired changes turns out to not be as palatable for Bernice.

Another important feature of the NOI's rhetoric is the notion of a black community irrespective of national boundaries. In addition to Bernice's ocassional longings for Harlem, Henry—who joyfully adopts black American slang—also feels a sense of connection to the city. G.E. Clarke nicely articulates the nuances of Canadian usage of black American style in the following passage:

> [O]ne culture's borrowing of ideas, personalities, and goods from another culture can serve to structure its own sense of itself, as well as to objectify the source culture. Hence, African-Canadian appropriations of African Americana enact a version of Edward Said's Orientalism: that is to say, Black America is, for Black Canada, an exotic *Other*. African Canadians construct their own *African-Americanism* to suit their own cultural and psychological needs. (39)

This notion of African-Canadians reconstructing and, I suggest, discarding of aspects of 'African Americana' to suit their place-specific needs is one that is well explored in the trilogy. As G.E. Clarke observes, Canada's black communities reside in disparate parts of the nation (48). Therefore, the notion of a racial community with far reaches could serve the interests of black people at distances beyond a particular city and even country limits. Black immigrants to Canada, at least in the novel, attempt to form their own communities outside of their work to provide a space for communing and support. Having a sense of belonging to a community larger than the immediate one (which, as G.E. Clarke suggests, may be lacking) is an integral part of subjectivity formation. The complexities of diasporic movements and inheritances must figure into understandings of cross-cultural and transnational identifications.

Bernice's appropriation of "African Americana" manages to avoid romanticism by confronting the realities of circumstances in the United States with reference to her own experience in Harlem. She does consider the possibility of moving from Toronto to somewhere else—possibly Harlem, but never Africa. Nevertheless, she decides that she is "as happy as she could be (as a black woman)" on Marina Boulevard as anywhere else in North America (*The Meeting Point* 132). Although Bernice seems to greatly appreciate the energy and people of Harlem, she does not ultimately envisage it as a viable option for an improved living situation. Perhaps this resignation to be happy where one is can be better understood in light of Clarke's own experience in Harlem in 1963. On his trip to the city in pursuit of the Baldwin interview, Clarke says he felt the elation of being in the epicentre of black empowerment but it soon proved to be too taxing for him. In "We Want a Black Poem" Clarke writes:

> Harlem was too intense in offering what it had to offer [...] The watching of men and women on the street corner was too intense. It was no longer a diversion. The soapbox speakers were proclaiming doom. And doom was too quick and instant for a life not yet lived [...] Harlem was preparing for a twentieth-century exodus back to Africa. ("We Want a Black Poem")

In a semi-autobiographical account of experience, Bernice finds the energy of Harlem to be both overwhelming and a source of "serious knowledge" (48), which she recommends to her friend and fellow domestic Dots. Dots recommends reading for Bernice—tabloid weeklies *Flash* and *Hush*—in an attempt to redirect her attention away from the "race books" to what Dots refers to as the Canadian-based "history books" (*The Meeting Point* 266) concerned with revealing "injustice and hypocrisy with the establishment" to "serve the interests of the general public" (Shaw). The notion of history, or what gets read as history, is central to this narrative exchange and Clarke's legacy as a black Canadian writer. In a conversation among fellow black Canadian writers Karina Vernon notes the historical impetus of most black Canadian authors. Vernon says: "I think until recently many black authors, at least those in Canada, felt that part of their job was to be historians, so that black Canadian history wouldn't get erased from the public imagination" (qtd. in Compton). The either/or approach to issues of general injustice and racism leading to the privileging of the "interests of the general public" runs the risk of minimizing the very real problem of racism in Canadian society. Being conscious of injustice on a personal level must also be balanced with awareness of injustices as they exist in the wider context to avoid being blind to just how much the concerns of publications like *Flash*, *Hush*, and—to an extent—*Muhammad Speaks* intertwine.

The radical black nationalism Bernice learns about and the stories Brigitte, the German domestic worker, shares with her about Nazism are eerily similar in their propagation of hate leading to murderous action. While the two women do share a superficial laugh about these parallels, Bernice has trouble finding much humour in such hateful rhetoric. Given the fact that the Burrmanns are Jewish, this connection to the atrocities of the Holocaust rings far too true for Bernice. She seriously questions the doctrine of the NOI in its call for her "spiritually and morally, to kill the white devil nearest her" (166). This call shakes Bernice so much "that she started to fold the newspaper in half, with the front page hidden, and to file it under her chesterfield" (166). This act, though seemingly trivial, may be the strongest moment of resistance Bernice displays; without a listener, reader, or follower the rhetoric becomes powerless and the doctrine cannot be disseminated. This scene elucidates Clarke's conceptual work to frame the NOI brand of black nationalism in a way that unmasks the potential violence and aggressiveness that seems particularly unappealing within the Canadian context. As Black Canadian author Wayde Compton notes, Afrocentrism is often fascistic and "cannot be assailed with rational argument, because it usually rejects rationalism, in an essentialist or religious way." *The Meeting Point* brings this rejection of rationality into view by fictively placing the rhetoric into the realm of possible action to demonstrate the implausibility of such an aggressive black nationalism in a Canadian context.

After becoming disenchanted with the NOI, Bernice turns to different religious publications, namely *Awake* and *The Watchtower* of the Jehovah's Witness faith, but these do not fulfill her spiritual and material needs. Though she does find some solace in them, she feels the papers do not provide real solutions (166). Although Bernice is not content with any of the religious doctrines she has been exposed to she is critical enough of the NOI to distance herself from its rhetoric, which is full of ambivalence, as Clarke highlights in his 1965 radio broadcast. This follows what G.E. Clarke notes as a defining aspect of African-Canadian nationalism. He writes:

> Even though Canadian realities promote a racial ambivalence, they also stimulate, for many African Canadians, a *compensating black nationalism*. This nationalism enacts a counter-influence to the pervasive identification of Canada as a northern,

white, wanna-be empire, a pseudo-imperial self-image which reduces blackness to the status of problematic and pitiable *Other*. But while African-Canadian cultural nationalism makes common cause with African-American symbols, styles, leaders, and ideas, it also *deviates from them sharply*. (Emphasis added, 45)

Bernice (and others in her circle) may not find all aspects of American black nationalism useful but by encountering it the members of the African-Canadian community are able to see possibilities for solidifying an identity that is both acknowledged and valued. This is a more nuanced approach to the complex issues of the racial histories of the U.S. and Canada. Racial politics in the U.S. historically lacked the "civility" of invisible violence and such an openly vicious environment set the unfortunate precedent for desires of retributive violence for black people who have often been victimized in the American context. For Bernice, the turning point after the meeting point comes with the realization that impersonalized, race-based violence in response to larger systemic and social injustices is not the solution she seeks.

The initial attractiveness of radical liberation ideology such as the black nationalism of the NOI wanes by the close of *The Meeting Point* and, although the novel is highly critical of the NOI, it is not a complete dismissal of this particular model of blackness. *Storm of Fortune*, the second novel in the trilogy, has less of a focus on the revolutionary slant of the NOI and from this point the trilogy becomes more critical of black American models of subjectivity. Dots has not forgotten Bernice's dabbling in Islam and questions her principles in terms of friendship and adherence to her religious tenets. She asks:

"Well, tell me now, Bernice, what kind o' Black Muslim, or black nationalist-woman you walking 'bout Toronto telling people you is, what kind o' conscience-thinking woman you admit yourself to be, to me, that you would leave me, a friend, the same black woman as you, and go 'cross that road there, and present your problems to a woman like Brigitte? [...] You think that because the same Brigitte smiles with you today, that tomorrow morning you have any guarantee she is going to smile again with you? Bernice, do you call that wisdom?" (*Storm of Fortune* 21)

Dots takes issue with Bernice confiding in Brigitte instead of her, especially in light of the black national-ist tendency to privilege shared racial bonds. As Dots explains, she and Bernice are not just two black women, they are friends; therefore this slight is not just about a failed bonding over shared racial membership, but more so of a genuine friendship with cultural and ethnic shared history. Bernice's response to this criticism implores Dots to see Brigitte not as a white woman but as a friend, demonstrating exactly what is problematic for her about the black nationalist impulse to focus singularly on race. Bernice later returns to consider a Judeo-Christian out-look after reading from Mr. Burrmann's "strange Bible" whose message she likes even though she "disliked the way it was written" (*Storm of Fortune* 114). She then takes this message as a personal order and vows to reread the passage in "the right Bible-language" (114).

Henry, one of the characters most interested in black American culture, has also changed in his respect for the culture. Henry launches into an anti-black American rant after being picked on by a black American man in a bar for being West Indian and goes as far as using the racial epithet "nigger" (176), which holds a distinctly derogatory connotation in the American context—a significance Henry seems acutely aware of. Henry's reactionary response to this particular encounter seems to go beyond this specific instance and exposes his own racist sentiments as he explains to Boysie: "'I hate them American negroes more than I hate white people, you don't know that? [...] I prefer to be a fucking American *Indian* than to be an American negro'" (176). Henry taps into existing racist discourse that places black Americans on the lowest end of the American racial hierarchy and attempts to justify their ill-treatment. This moment is one of narrative let-down. Throughout the trilogy thus far Henry has been representative of a hoped-for unity in blackness, but his disillusionment points to the potential of ethnicity divides within blackness to become insurmountable barriers to much needed solidarity. Concurrently, it points to an important particularity in terms of the non-homogeneity of blackness. While momentary strategic essentialism may serve an important function in anti-racist coalition, ethnic differences that may temporarily be masked by this essentialism do not disappear.

With Henry now a cynical figure, the rest of the group suffers from the lack of his good-spiritedness. Boysie especially feels the effects of not having Henry's knowledge at hand. Being more conservative and much less interested in "blackness" generally, Boysie often depends on Henry to fill in these knowledge gaps. When visiting Henry and Agatha's apartment he takes note of the wall of black people Agatha has arranged. This scene is important in two ways. First, it clarifies the role Henry (and even his living space as a sort of micro-community) plays as a source of knowledge for Boysie. Secondly, it illuminates the intersection of race, nationalism, and ethnicity. While examining the wall, Boysie's eyes fall upon a portrait of Malcolm X, to which he responds: "He's a giant. Somebody tell me he is a West Indian, too. A great man!" (276). Malcolm X, though a primary figure in black American nationalism, *was* also of West Indian descent by way of his Grenadian mother (Natambu 6). This acknowledgement of the multiplicity of ethnicities within blackness goes unnoted by Henry. This scene reads as an extremely saddening blindness to the interconnectedness of West Indian and black American identities. Henry's last words in the novel before he commits suicide lend themselves to this reading:

> "I can live through this, because as you know, I am a goddamn Wessindian. But I couldn't live through it if this was the States and I was a black American. But sometimes I can't see no fucking difference between Toronto and Harlem!" (281)

Despite his earlier anti-black American outburst because of the slight to his West Indian identity, Henry still holds on to the possibility of black Canadian and black American alliance. Although his declaration that his West Indian identity somehow enables him to live through the difficulties associated with being black in Canada, Henry's final shocking act of suicide attests to the near-impossibility of survival without such alliances. As it seems, once he loses his admiration for black Americana he also loses his will to live.

The solemn ending of *Storm of Fortune* has the potential to become a galvanizing force to reinitiate the racial tensions that most of the trilogy works to overcome. Yet *The Bigger Light* does not return to the racial tensions so vividly explored in *The Meeting Point*. The trilogy's last novel continues the narrative work of lessening the role of black nationalist rhetoric by having even fewer references to the NOI. The narrative focus is largely on Boysie and Dots, both of whom, unlike Bernice and Henry, rarely demonstrate interest in black America(na). Boysie, the most conservative figure of the novel's narrative, is largely uninterested in black nationalism and even less so in NOI. As the narrator expresses:

> Boysie did not want to be known as a black nationalist either. He was simply a hard-working Barbadian. But he wished he was wealthy and privileged and very conservative. Conservative to him meant a good life and excellent education and being a Canadian. (*The Bigger Light* 17)

Without Henry to act as his bridge between black Americana and a reminder of their West Indian identities, Boysie's conservative leanings freely reveal themselves in his belief in assimilating to Canadian economic ascendency. This conservatism seems incongruous with his identity as a West Indian, which he reveals to be an identity he wishes to shed. He detests nearly everyone who might call attention to his own blackness: new West Indian immigrants, his neighbour Mrs. James who tries to get him involved in "the black community," and his wife Dots. Disassociating himself from "blackness" means distancing himself from those closest to him.

In this novel of the trilogy the particular effect of voluntary immigration is especially evident and adds another dynamic to the varied landscape of Canadian and American racial climates. G.E. Clarke argues that Clarke intimates "it is immigration [...] that creates a negative blackness [...] One is not born 'black'; blackness is a socio-economic hell into which one is plunged"

(241). West Indian immigrants to Canada undergo a racial awakening in which blackness becomes intensified when placed in stark contrast to the dominating whiteness of Canada. This is the kind of awakening Boysie undergoes in *The Bigger Light*. Class undoubtedly plays a role in the shaping of black subjectivity for people from the Caribbean, a place not dominated by whiteness, thus leaving distinctions between people to come by way of class and colourism more so than broad or simplistic binary race categories. Boysie truly sees himself as a member of an economic and therefore racial class separate from new immigrants and others who identify primarily with blackness. Boysie adapts a more ambivalent position in terms of situating himself within a model blackness. He seems to want to give black nationalism a try but only on his own terms. After choosing to give his patronage to the "Black Nationalist barbershop," Boysie soon abandons this space when he finds himself "becoming out of place among those who were more conversant in the new slogans than in the old black ideology" (*The Bigger Light* 23). Instead, he chooses to visit the Italian barbershop, which he envisions as a race-neutral space that does not require him to reveal his racial politics. As he rationalizes: "In the Italian barbershop, he was not forced into becoming a black militant" (23). It is the face-to-face encounter that calls up his anxieties about his racial politics; with the barrier of relative anonymity offered by his letters to the editor of a local newspaper Boysie finds the courage (or desire) to express a racialized solidarity. He ends one of his letters to the editor with the Black Power statement "Power to the People!" He has an unexplainable consciousness about this kind of statement: "He did not know why he had put 'Power to the People' after his name; for he was a man who had long stood outside the paling of that kind of verbal militancy" (93). It is as if the written word holds more persuasive power for him than he is able to understand.

Mrs. James, with whom Boysie develops a relationship, becomes a sort of stand-in for the role left void by Henry. She urges the childless Boysie to act as a father figure for her son and to become an active member of the black community. The trouble is that Boysie does not see himself as a member of this community. He associates blackness with the insulting stereotypes of uncouthness and criminality, characteristics he does not identify with as an entrepreneur concerned with sartorial style. One example of his most egregious stereotyping occurs in an eating establishment frequented by West Indians when he carefully observes a young man in stereotypical black nationalist wear: "He was watching the man, very young and very strong-looking, dressed like black Americans with long hair, and floppy hats pulled threateningly close to one eye, and looking so very strong and masculine and like criminals ... criminals?" (102). The description reads like an observation of an afro-wearing member of the Black Panther Party. Boysie is so caught up in the apparent change in this space that was once familiar to him that he remains rattled until he is safely ensconced in his car. The divide between him and this apparently younger, more knowledgeable and more "dangerous" generation of black men seems to transcend any possibility of racial solidarity or comfort with one another. Boysie's class aspirations make such a racial consciousness incompatible with the kind of class privileged life of which he imagines himself (already) becoming a part.

Boysie briefly considers seeing black American men as role models for himself but finds that their strengths in language and musical expression to be discordant with his Barbadian sensibilities. Boysie draws attention to this discord in his response to a particular song: "The song was not fit, not suitable, the song could not be tied to his past and to his experience. He wondered whether he was wrong in seeing freedom in the singing and in the song as the black American sang it" (240). This conclusion seems to be one for not just Boysie but possibly other characters explored in the trilogy. Here, the experiences of West Indian Canadians and black Americans are not identical and the responding racial politics born out of the American context cannot be mapped onto black Canadian experiences. The trilogy ends with Boysie making his way to the United States, leaving "one kind of space for another one" (288). Although, one must wonder what kind of knowledge the disillusioned Boysie will carry with him from one space to the other. Clarke's decision to open the trilogy with Bernice, a woman concerned with caring for her friends and family, and end with Boysie, who ultimately abandons every tie to his community, paints a very bleak picture for the possibilities of black nationalism and, in Boysie's case, ethnic or racial alliance.

Clarke opened his post-Malcolm X assassination CBC radio broadcast by highlighting the qualities of a typical follower of the doctrine of Elijah Muhammad. He describes the follower as "the hapless black man, the most unskilled, the least educated and—for these two reasons, the most militant" ("Malcolm X" 2). This description of the typical NOI follower draws attention to the often valid basis for discontent with the social status quo among racialized groups. The desire for members of society to live equally among others must be recognized and valued; what radical formations like the NOI and other black nationalist movements often represent is the need for critical engagement. Walcott gestures toward this important understanding when he implores us to, "pay attention to national and other forms of institutional power" when theorizing "diaspora or black Atlantic exchanges, dialogues, conversations and differences" (37). Clarke's Toronto trilogy offers a literary interpretation of this necessity by offering a view of blackness that accounts for the diasporic shifts and connections within a Canadian context.

Endnotes

1. This representation of Jewishness as equal to whiteness runs counter to what Sarah Casteel suggests is a sympathetic portrayal of black/Jewish relations in *The Meeting Point*. For more see Casteel's "Experiences of Arrival: Jewishness and Caribbean-Canadian Identity in Austin Clarke's *The Meeting Point*," reprinted in this volume.

Works Cited

Casteel, Sarah Phillips. "Experiences of Arrival: Jewishness and Caribbean-Canadian Identity in Austin Clarke's The Meeting Point." *Journal of West Indian Literature* 14.1/2 (2005): 113-40. Print.

Chariandy, David. "'That's What You Want, Isn't It?': Austin Clarke and the New Politics of Recognition." *Journal of West Indian Literature* 14.1/2 (2005): 141-65. Print.

Clarke, Austin C. "'Malcolm X'." Vol. Box 58. Comp. McMaster University The William Ready Division of Archives and Research Collections. CBC Radio, March 1965. Print.

———. *Storm of Fortune*. Boston: Little, Brown and Company, 1973. Print.

———. *The Bigger Light*. Boston: Little, Brown and Company, 1975. Print.

———. "The Confessed Bewilderment of Martin Luther King, Jr." *Ebo Voice Pamphlet*. Burlington, Canada: Al Kitab Sudan, February 1968. Print.

———. *The Meeting Point*. 3rd. Toronto: Vintage Canada, 1998. Print.

———. "We Want a Black Poem." *The Walrus*. March 2007. Web. 11 April 2011.

Clarke, George Elliott. *Odysseys Home: Mapping African-Canadian Literature*. Toronto: University of Toronto Press, 2002. Print.

Compton, Wayde. "Black Writers in Search of Place." *The Tyee*. 28 February 2005. Web. 18 November 2012.

Lee, Martha F. *The Nation of Islam: An American Millenarian Movement*. Syracuse: Syracuse University Press, 1996. Print.

Natambu, Kofi. *The Life and Work of Malcolm X*. Indianapolis: Alpha Books, 2002. Print.

Ogbar, Jeffrey O. G. *Black Power: Radical Politics and African American Identity*. Baltimore: The Johns Hopkins University Press, 2005. Print.

Shaw, Robert. "The People's Papers: The Rise and Fall of the Canadian Tabloid." *Broken Pencil*. Winter 2009. Web. 11 April 2011.

Walcott, Rinaldo. *Black Like Who? Writing Black Canada*. 2nd. London: Insomniac Press, 1997. Print.

Afro-Caribbean Immigrant Experiences in the White City: Austin Clarke's Toronto[1]

BATIA BOE STOLAR

Literary representations of the city, like historical photographs, tend by their very nature to capture an aspect of the city and freeze it in a particular moment in time. The literary city mythologizes the city it represents, at times unwittingly, as it eulogizes a bygone era, romanticizes its inhabitants, history, and architecture, and reinforces and sometimes critiques its spatial and political structures. Although literary representations of the city generally paint it in static terms, the city is continuously changing. The arrival of immigrants, for example, has transformed "metropolises" into "cosmopolises" (Isin 231), and the immigrant's space in the city has become a contested cultural and political site. As Edward Soja, emphasizing the "heterogeneity of the postmetropolitan cityspace" (196), explains:

> [C]ityspace is coming more and more to resemble global geographies, incorporating within its encompassing reach a cosmopolitan condensation of all the world's cultures and zones of international tension. The

postmetropolis thus becomes a replicative hub of fusion and diffusion, implosive and explosive growth, a First-Second-Third World city wrapped into one" (153).

The postmetropolitan city is defined by its heterogeneity, by the presence of a diverse range of old and new ethnic groups; in fact, it could be argued that the presence of a large and varied immigrant population is its defining feature. The postmetropolis is the product of immigration. Austin Clarke's literary representations of immigrant life in Toronto investigate the complex relationship between the immigrant and the city, in doing so charting Toronto's difficult transformation into a postmetropolitan city. Clarke's novel, *The Meeting Point* (1967), and collection of short stories, *Nine Men Who Laughed* (1986), reinforce Toronto's revamped image as "the world's most multicultural city" (Doucet), thereby challenging Toronto's traditional image as "the dullest city on earth" (Garreau D1) as well as previous literary representations that depict Toronto as "a white city" (Ball 9). Whereas other literary representations of the Canadian immigrant city, like Michael Ondaatje's *In the Skin of a Lion* (1987), mythologize the historical immigrant labour that literally built Toronto, *Nine Men Who Laughed* and *The Meeting Point* demystify the immigrant city by raising questions about the more recently arrived immigrant's temporal and spatial place in the city. Whereas immigrant labour is retrospectively valorized in Ondaatje's novel to the point of becoming heroic, there is nothing heroic about the labour that Clarke's immigrants perform—when in fact it is available to them. Clarke's texts raise questions not only about the immigrant's gendered place in the city, but about the transformation of the city itself. They call into question whether Toronto really is a harmonious "world within a city," as Tourism Toronto would have us believe (and thus in keeping with the postmetropolitan city Soja describes),[2] or instead a diverse series of cities coexisting (not always harmoniously) within the same geographical boundaries.

Clarke's texts locate the immigrant as being simultaneously inside and outside the city. In Clarke's texts, the immigrant is subjected to discrimination as well as social and economic marginalization, kept outside the city's centralized capital and power. The immigrant's marginalization, and sometimes alienation, within the city produces an "immigrant city," one that exists in the interstitial spaces of the city. The distinction between the immigrant city and the city as constructed in dominant discourse is reinforced by the spatial divisions that demarcate the areas available to the immigrant, and by the tension between the two as the immigrant must negotiate his and her gendered presence within the various contested spaces. Clarke's immigrants, however, must negotiate their presences in different ways as they are faced with different series of sexual and power relations between themselves and the city. Clarke's female West Indian immigrants are absorbed into the domestic spaces of the city, and as such remain inside the city at the same time that they are routinely kept from the public spaces their male counterparts inhabit. In contrast, Clarke's stories privilege those spaces inhabited by immigrants, but the West Indian male immigrants Clarke describes play little, if any, role in constructing those spaces. Clarke's male West Indians are forced to fit themselves into the already constructed spaces of the city. Clarke's male and female immigrants remain outside the city's centre. They remain outside the city's story since they do not form part of the city's making. They are not part of the immigrant labour force that built Toronto, nor are they part of the labour force that continues to build the postmodern glassed structures. Rather, they are relegated to less easily glamorized menial service jobs that maintain the city but do no leave behind visible signs of their presence, or else they are brought into the city specifically to clean and maintain its private, domestic spaces. Toronto in Clarke's texts occupies an elusive and often ambiguous space that is nevertheless central. Its "inner city," unlike that of other cosmopolises, is not a "diasporic space" (Soja 152) but instead a centralized powerhouse that keeps the diasporic subject on its margins. Clarke's Toronto, as we will see, takes the form of a translucently white female character who deters, rejects, consumes, and ejects the male black immigrant who seeks to enter her.

The tension between the immigrant city and the city as constructed in dominant discourse in Clarke's texts reflects a similar tension found in some of the tourist literature that markets Toronto as a multicultural city. In the summer of 1998, for instance, Tourism Toronto promotes the city in a pamphlet as follows:

> When we call ourselves "The World Within a City," we're referring *in part* to Toronto's amazing mosaic of cultures. Within our *many distinct neighbourhoods*, you'll find colourful features representing every part of the globe. However, there's more to this world than the great *ethnic dining and shopping.* The countless things that make world travel fascinating—museums, galleries, major-league sports, prime hotels, natural wonders, history and so many other features—come

> together here in one tremendously accommodating
> city, It's no surprise that more than a million business
> and convention visitors choose to attend functions in
> Toronto each year. (Tourism Toronto; emphasis mine)

Drawing on what Stanley Fish aptly terms "boutique
multiculturalism" as an exotic lure to attract visiting consumers, this promotional material quickly emphasizes
other aspects that make Toronto a great city—aspects
that have nothing at all to do with multiculturalism.
Conversely, the literary representations of the immigrant
city, as we shall see, tend to focus primarily on the "distinct neighbourhoods" rather than on the convention
centres, and present these exotic locations not as tourist
traps but as sites of everyday cultural negotiation.

Tourism Toronto's privileging of boutique multiculturalism points to the continued disregard for the city's
immigrants that is prevalent in Clarke's *Nine Men Who
Laughed* and *The Meeting Point*. As Fish explains, in spite
of their approval, appreciation, and even sympathy for
"the traditions of cultures not their own … boutique
multiculturalists will always stop short of approving
other cultures at a point where some value at their
centre generates an act that offends against the canons
of civilized decency as they have been either declared or
assumed" (378). Hence, the superficial celebration of
diversity maintains cultural difference; the "many distinct neighbourhoods" (or ghettoes) are at once access-
ible to the local or foreign tourist/consumer in search
of the safe exotic experience yet easily circumvented by
those who prefer to keep the "other" at bay but who
nevertheless want to partake of the city. Similarly, the
literary reader as boutique multiculturalist can enter

the "distinct neighbourhoods," both contemporary and historical, without ever having to actually step inside—much less live in—them. Mapped as such, Toronto, as an immigrant city, appears to be made up of peripheral neighbourhoods, which, although an integral part of the city used to attract physical and literary tourism, do not constitute the inner city itself.

Debunking the urban legend that it was the United Nations which externally, thereby authoritatively, crowned Toronto with the coveted title of "the world's most multicultural city," Michael J. Doucet rightly questions how it is even possible to determine such a claim, and asks if such a decision would be "based on a simple count of the number of different ethnic, racial, and linguistic groups living in a given space" (Doucet).[3] Indeed, as a multicultural city, there is nothing unique about Toronto. As Soja observes, "every individual urban centre, from the largest to the smallest, seems increasingly to contain the entire world within it, creating the most culturally heterogeneous cityspaces the world has ever seen" (152). As a postmetropolis, Toronto "can be represented as a product of intensified globalization processes through which the global is becoming localized and the local is becoming globalized at the same time" (152). If the difficulty—if not impossibility—of designating the most multicultural urban centre stems from the problems in defining what a multicultural city is, then it follows that, as Fish suggests, a distinction first needs to be made "between multiculturalism as a philosophical problem and multiculturalism as a demographic fact" (385). It is unclear, however, how such a distinction can be made when the subject in question exemplifies both a demographic reality and the philosophical ideal of a nation. The inextricability of the two is evident in the various ways in which Toronto promotes and writes itself. For example, when "the amalgamated City of Toronto was taking shape late in 1997, the editors of the *Toronto Star* ran a contest to pick a new slogan for the new city. The winning entry was 'Toronto—Home to the World.' When the local politicians came to the task of deciding a motto for the new enlarged City of Toronto, their choice reflected Toronto's post-World War II demographic transformation: 'Diversity—Our Strength'" (Doucet). Similarly, the slogan "Expect the World," used by Toronto's Olympic Council in its unsuccessful bid for the 2008 Summer Olympics, is meant to represent the changing demographics but also the self-consciousness of the city's embracing of its growing diversity:

> People from every part of the world have *chosen* Toronto as their home, and have blended into a new international urban culture. [...] Everyone has a relative in Toronto ... Toronto is a city of the future. Urbane and sophisticated, it is a deliberately multicultural city that rejoices in its diversity. We believe Toronto may well be the most multicultural city on Earth (qtd. in Doucet, emphasis mine).

Yet another possibility in defining the multicultural city is offered by the 1998 "report produced by the Access and Equity Centre of the City of Toronto for Mayor Mel Lastman," entitled *Together We Are One: A Summary Paper on Diversity in Toronto* (Doucet). In this report, an observation is made "that 'no other city in the world has a higher proportion who are foreign-born than Toronto'" (qtd. in Doucet). Laying claim to the validity of the urban legend, this observation effectively renders the "multicultural city" the "immigrant city." While it is unclear what legal status these foreign-born residents have (e.g., landed immigrant, illegal alien, Canadian citizen, non-immigrant, etc.), the marker of multicultural difference is simply located in the resident's birthplace. This gross oversimplification makes synonymous the terms "multi-cultural" and "immigrant," and in doing so marks those who are born in Canada, regardless of race, ethnicity and/or religion, as "Canadian," whereas those who are born outside Canada, regardless of legal or national status, are branded "multicultural." Illogically, this premise suggests that "Canadian" and "multicultural" are two opposing categories, a rather problematic distinction considering the adoption of multiculturalism as official federal government policy. Even if the terms "multicultural" and "immigrant" were interchangeable, what an "immigrant city" is, how it is imagined, constructed, and literarily represented, needs further critical inquiry. Clarke's texts invite such critical analysis because of their often ambiguous or paradoxical representations of Toronto as simultaneously an immigrant, multicultural, global, and white city—or as coexisting cities.

Clarke represents the city by contrasting it with its perceived "other." However, in Clarke's stories the city's "other" is the male Afro-Caribbean immigrant who is living in, but appears to be beyond, the city's limits. By the time that Clarke's male immigrants in *Nine Men Who Laughed* come to inhabit Toronto, as early as two decades after the Macedonian immigrants responsible for constructing the Bloor Street Viaduct, the city has changed considerably. The modernist city of the Macedonian immigrant workers has become a postmodern urban space made of refracting glass. As Engin Isin notes, the "professional ethic" that motivates such projects as glass towers envisions "building a society anew," which although it is a subversion of modernism is nevertheless similar to the modernist impetus of building a new city (262). It is largely because of this professional ethic, Isin argues, that "immigrants, constituted as strangers, are necessary for the functioning, organization, and appropriation of the cosmopolis by the professions" (270). Hence, Clarke's architectural focus shifts from the modernist city water-works to the postmodern glass buildings that house the banks' headquarters, marking the shift in power from the governmental to the corporate.

Another significant shift in Clarke's stories is carto-graphical; unlike the European immigrant areas occupy-ing the east end of the city, Clarke's stories are set in the west end of the city, occupied by Caribbean immigrants. Clarke's stories thus emphasize the peripheral immigrant ghetto has shifted westward. It is worth noting that the east end immigrant ghetto does make an appearance in "A Man." As Joshua Miller-Corbaine rushes west along Bloor Street, he curses "the East end and the young teacher and all the cautious cars slipping into his path, maligning in his native dialect the European immigrants who congregated in this ghetto of the city as they walked across the street. He thought they used the street with a disregard for traffic familiar to those accustomed to inhabiting large fields and farms" (129-30). Because Clarke does not deal with European immigrants, it is not known whether his are newly arrived or whether they are descendants of earlier immigrants. Apparently unaccus-tomed to the movement of urban traffic, the suggestion is that they are new arrivals to Canada and to the city. The German mechanic's thick accent supports this presump-tion. But their arrival date is inconsequential; the east end of the city is still the European ghetto. That Clarke's West Indian immigrants occupy a different section of the city rather than enter the already existing immigrant ghetto calls attention to the segregation between white and black immigrants that is symptomatic of the racial discrimination against West Indian immigrants for housing and employment (Walker 18). Clarke's immigrants are coerced into a ghetto of their own, illuminating a rupture in the universalized multicultural body.

Describing the West Indian ghetto in the west end of the city in "Doing Right," the narrator off-handedly remarks that "Wessindians accustom to parking in the middle o' the road, or on the wrong side, back home. And nobody don't trouble them nor touch their cars. And since they come here, many o' these Wessindians haven't tek-on a change in attitude in regards to who own the public road and who own the motto-cars" (57). The West Indian immigrants claim the street by imposing a rural (equated here, like in "A Man," with native-soil) use of space. In doing so, they enact the very agonistic strategies that outsiders or strangers do; they "*spatialize* their jurisdictions, markets, and spheres of authority, they outcast, exclude, and ban some from those spaces and include, valorize, and enable others in them" (Isin 274). However, fissures within the outcast body are evident and rupture the agonistic authority claimed by those who are disenfranchised. An assimilating and ambitious West Indian "green hornet," looking for financial and career advancement, imposes the Canadian urban order and tickets their illegally parked cars. The West Indians of Clarke's stories attempt to claim the urban landscape by imposing their own landscape. In spite of their attempt to impose a rural order on the urban streets, the urban landscape imposes its own order on them, claiming their presence.

Dissent and disagreement over the rightful use of the urban space is one of the many tensions in Clarke's West Indian ghetto. Multicultural fissures also appear within the black community of the St Clair-Oakwood district. "Doing Right" challenges multiculturalism by questioning what happens when immigrant groups deemed similar by the host country are coerced into sharing the ghetto. In the story, when another West Indian green hornet tickets the expensive-looking car of an African-American man, stereotypically wearing flashy gold chains and rings, the African-American man picks up the green hornet and calls him "nigger." The green hornet replies: "What you call me? I am no damn nigger. I am Indian. Legal immigrant. I just doing my job for the City of Toronto in Metropolitan Toronto. *You* are a blasted American negro!" (62). Watching this altercation, the narrator exclaims:

> Well, multiculturalism gone-out the window now! All the pamphlets and the television commercials that show people of all colours laughing together and saying, "We is Canadians," all them advertisements in *Saturday Night* and *Maclean's*, all them speeches that ministers up in Ottawar make concerning the "different cultures that make up this great unified country of ours," all that lick-up now, and gone through the eddoes. One time. *Bram*! (63)

He waits for the police to arrive and break up the fight, since "the Police does-be up in this St Clair-Oakwood district like flies around a crocus-bag o' sugar at the drop of a cloth-hat" (63). This conspicuous absence points to the inherent racism of Toronto's police department, which has been alluded to when the ambitious green hornet cannot advance and become a "real policeman" in spite of his overzealousness in ticketing illegally parked cars, especially those of West Indians. The narrator calls further attention to the authorities' duplicity when he states that "the big boys in Toronto don't particular notice we unless um is Caribana weekend or when election-time coming and they looking for votes or when the *Star* doing a feature on racism and Wessindians and they want a quotation" (58). In Clarke's stories, the immigrant communities are fragmented from within; immigrants do not unite against an oppressive English-Canadian authority, nor is there someone who speaks and acts from them (however problematic that voice may be). Instead, Clarke's stories identify varying degrees of difficulty within the multicultural system, revealing the inherent hierarchy that is race and class based. Kept outside the multicultural-capitalist pyramid that exploits certain immigrant groups that constitute its working class, Clarke's male immigrants remain outside the pyramid altogether, especially if they are illegal immigrants. Yet, they also have an integral place in the city, as Isin reminds us: "Immigrants, constituted as strangers, are necessary for the functioning, organization, and appropriation of the cosmopolis by the professions" (270).

In spite of the obvious multicultural growth depicted, in part, by the very presence of non-white immigrants in the literary urban landscape, Clarke's stories question whether the city's multicultural growth actually effects change in the otherwise "white city." In "Canadian Experience," for example, Bay Street houses the "business district of banks, brokerages and corporations" where the city centralizes its economic power (32). Surrounded by "tall office buildings" that "look like steel," George, the protagonist who comes to the district to interview at a bank, enters a building that is "built almost entirely out of glass" and "shimmers like gold" (42). For the black immigrant, however, there is no gold to be attained. John Ball argues that "the solid grip that Toronto's white community has historically held over the city's economy, institutions, culture, and self image persists" (9). According to him, although "Toronto's non-white population has swelled from a small fraction to a sizable and visible collection of diversified communities [...] white power has remained well entrenched" (9). In Clarke's story, even the janitorial work is performed by "white" marginalized labour; it is "the Italians and the Greeks and the Portuguese" who clean the office building (49). It should be noted, however, that George does work illegally with the "Italians, Greeks and Portuguese, cleaning the offices of First Canadian Place, a building with at least fifty floors, made of glass, *near* [but significantly not *on*] Bay Street" (37; emphasis mine).

Fragmenting the already dispossessed black immigrant, the buildings' reflecting surfaces keep him from seeing the centre; the reflection of George's body "tears him into stripes and splatters his suit against four panels, and makes him disjointed" (42). Although he is able to enter the building, he is deterred by the word "BANK written on the glass, cheerless and frightening" (43), and by the blue eyes of a woman that "are like ice-water" (44). The imagery of the glass, mirror, and ice-water calls to mind a fairy tale in which the city is made of glass. But there is nothing magical or fragile about Clarke's glass city. It obscures and refracts, casting shadows and doubt.

As his mirror, the city reflects back that it is the black immigrant, not the city, who is fragile. George tells Pam, an aspiring actress and fellow tenant in the rooming house, that the people at the bank "looked on [him] and through [him], right through [him]. [He] was a piece of glass" (44-45). Unlike the city's smoke-and-mirrors multicultural welcome, the black immigrant's glass-like appearance not only reinforces his fragility but also marks him as transparent, invisible. His fragmented image at the beginning of the story, like that in the building, beheads him; he "was cut off at the neck" (31). It is only at the end of the story that he sees himself reflected in another: "his own eyes, and the [subway] driver's makes four" (51). This flicker of recognition suggests that only another black immigrant can actually see George; only another black immigrant can see himself reflected in another black immigrant. Symbolically, such recognition occurs beneath the surface of the city.

Clarke's glass city is a nod to the white North, represented here by an urban rather than a rural landscape. The lonely immigrant is in danger not from a cold, white, sublime wilderness as in, for example, Louis Hémon's *Maria Chapdelaine* (1914), but from an unnatural metallic coldness; a distorting mirror that dislocates and fragments him. The natural world is associated with the homeland, whereas the artificial world, itself a comment on the act of immigration, is associated with the host land. When, for example, George compares Canada and the Caribbean, he does so by contrasting the urban and the rural: "He thinks of the flowers and the glass in that office and of the flowers more violent in colour, growing in wild profusion, untended, round *Edgehill House*, where he was born in a smiling field of comfortable pasture land" (47). The natural disorder of his Barbadian home is seen as warmly human, infused with passion. The unnatural, or urban, order of Toronto, in contrast, is seen as inhuman. The natural/artificial binary also informs the feminization of Clarke's glass city. According to George Elliott Clarke, in

> his short fiction, Clarke agrees, tacitly, with [Jean] Baudrillard [in *Seduction*] that women, whiteness, and hence, white women symbolize attractive, glistening surfaces that can entrap and destroy the unwary, meaning, for Clarke, black male immigrants. Thus, Clarke considers the psychological threat posed to self-conscious blackness by the omnipresence of white-supremacist imagery in North American society. (116)

Toronto is portrayed, rather stereotypically, as an ice queen, unyielding, impenetrable, and unforgiving. Clarke's feminized city is infertile, cold, dispassionate, and, above all, unnatural. Rather conservatively, the story's sexual politics projects the whore/nurturer dichotomy onto a backdrop of white/black racial division, perpetuating "the split between the love of the Mother country—a nearly incestuous desire for that country—versus lust for the stepmother, the new country, a passion expressed in terms of desire for material gain at any price" (G.E. Clarke 120).

The city as stepmother/whore is neither nurturing nor seductive. "She" is also refracted in every white woman with whom George comes into contact. When, for example, George gets ready for his interview, he enters the shared bathroom in the rooming house:

> Mist floated out of the bathroom door, and he
> brushed through it as if he were a man seeking
> passage through a thick, white underbush. And as he
> got inside and could barely see his way to the toilet
> bowl, there she was, with one leg on the cover of the
> bowl, which she had painted black, then red, rough
> dots of bruises on the bottom of her spine, which she
> insisted were cold sores. (38-39)

Enveloped in the suffocating whiteness, George is confronted by Pam's white body. He is not seduced by her; indeed, he is repulsed by her. Her "cold sores" suggest sexual infection and, as orifices, unsatisfied appetite. George's misogyny points to his fear of being devoured by the sexualized white female body. His repulsion is further evident in his reaction to the bank. Riding up the elevator, symbolic of an erection, he cannot penetrate the glass entrance to the bank. Consequently, he loses his erection. He descends below ground, defeated, emasculated as if castrated. The imagery of the ice queen, in contrast, is asexual. "She" simply consumes, digests, and expels the intruder: he travels "through the bowels of that glassed-in building" (50) and is excreted to the underground, where he sees people "coming up out of the subway at greater speed as if they are fleeing the smell of something unwholesome" (40). His function in her body fulfilled, she promptly expels the resultant waste.

The representation of Toronto as ultimately a "white city" suggests that white society may most value multiculturalism as a superficial (or "boutique") front that screens or masks its retention of control over its economic centre. Unlike the unskilled labour available to white immigrants, the already-built city offers little, if any, employment to the newly arrived black immigrant. Although the city continues to grow, the black immigrant is kept from participating in the act of (pro)creation. Arriving "as a non-landed immigrant," George in "Canadian Experience" is forced to live "in and out of low-paying jobs given specifically to non-landed immigrants" while waiting for amnesty (36). Lacking "Canadian Experience," meaning a Canadian education or employment, George can only aspire to low-paying jobs that have been traditionally "black," such as those of "porters, bellhops and maids"—occupations that reinforce the stereotypes of blacks as being limited to service positions (Walker 8). His economic prospects are largely informed by the immigration policies that restrict West Indian immigrants into two main categories: domestics, for single women between the ages of eighteen and thirty-five, who could apply for landed-immigrant status after at least a year of domestic service (Walker 10); and students, who could apply for landed immigrant status upon graduating (Walker 11).

Illegal activity in Clarke's stories is closely connected to immigration, but it is neither romanticized nor offered as a revolutionary tactic. Disillusioned with the Canadian system that inhibits his social and economic advancement, the ambitious green hornet in "Doing Right" dreams up and implements unlawful schemes that victimize illegal West Indian immigrants. Taking advantage of their inability to call on the Canadian authorities for protection, the ambitious green hornet exploits the illegal immigrants, who are already marginalized in the work force. There is nothing honourable or heroic about the ambitious green hornet's schemes, which seek to advance not the West Indian community's standard of living or profile but his own economic gain. Implicit in the story, however, is a revolutionary voice that condemns what George Elliott Clarke calls "a polite, right, *white-iste* caste system" (111) that keeps the black immigrant from economic and social advancement.

Clarke's revolutionary voice is most explicitly unveiled in "Coll. SS. Trins. Ap. Toron.—A Fable," a story that depicts the two paths available to the West Indian male student. Virtually indistinguishable at the outset, Boy Sonny and Sonny Boy arrive "frightened and cold" at Trinity College, University of Toronto, in 1955—"the nearest they could get to a men's college in Oxford and Cambridge" (177). Sonny's assimilation into the white system grants him economic and social power, especially when he acts to maintain white power. His opinion "would percolate up to the leaders in Ottawa, as when he pointed out the need to restrict the number of black immigrants into Canada" (201). Rich but alone, Sonny's success is undermined by Boy's. Finding himself in a hostile environment that disagrees with his "radical black consciousness" (196), Boy's eventual return to the Caribbean allows him to flourish as an activist and succeed in local and international politics. When the successful but nostalgic Sonny calls up Boy in Barbados, he finds that Boy has become the prime minister and is at that moment in Ottawa. Pointedly, the receptionist asks Sonny: "Mr. Boy, do you happen to know if it is possible for you to reach Ottawa from where you are?" (204). Geography aside, this question privileges the black-consciousness activist who refuses to assimilate and buy into the white system, where political and social advancement is relative. Moreover, this question underscores the black immigrant's position in Toronto. Unable to reach Ottawa either as an immigrant or as a naturalized citizen, it is the Barbadian politician who has acquired "Canadian experience" that can make a positive difference.

Nodding to Clarke's own activism, Ball similarly reads into Clarke's stories "[s]omething of the activist's desire to oppose unjust hierarchies, and to rally those whose case he or she advocates into militant self-respect" (10). Clarke writes that he detests "the use of the term 'immigrant' to define the presence of these [nine] men upon the landscape of Toronto" (*Nine Men* 6). Clarke's antagonism questions whether the immigrant city is a deflective image that masks the "real" city of which immigrants are truly not a part. Yet, Clarke also universalizes the immigrant and the immigrant city by writing that the nine men "could also be in London, Paris, New York or Moscow. They happen to be in Toronto" (1), and that they "could be aboriginals, maoris, coloured, native peoples" (2). According to Ball, in spite of his "universalizing gesture" and his "act of translating Toronto into New York or one immigrant's story into a racially different immigrant's story [...] Clarke's critical frame retains a degree of particularity—the minority immigrant in a majority-white city" (11). Clarke's "'immigrant[s]' [are] merely *living*" (Clarke, *Nine* 6).

Clarke's literary representations of the multicultural city portray Toronto from the perspective of the immigrants who are simultaneously inside and outside the city. As outsiders, these literary immigrants are kept from the city's power structures and are thus politically, socially, and economically alienated. Stigmatized by class and/ or by race, they are segregated and isolated. In Clarke's stories, social isolation leads to fragmentation within what is presumed to be a unified multicultural body. Yet, as insiders, these literary male immigrants participate in the complex social structure that makes up the multicultural city—the very structure that necessitates outsiders within.

In his celebrated *Toronto Trilogy*, Clarke further examines the tensions of simultaneous inclusion into and exclusion from the city by focusing more narrowly on the domestic sphere. As Michel Fabre notes, Toronto, in Clarke's novels, "is seldom described in architectural or aesthetic terms" (130). Indeed, for a trilogy about the city, it is curious that the city remains, for the most part, imperceptible. The trilogy depicts the plight of the West Indian domestic, and in doing so relegates most of the action to the interior spaces of the houses of employment or the living quarters of the domestic servants. Amaryll Chanady draws on Arjun Appadurai's term "translocality" and notes "the displacement of individuals on a large scale has contributed to the emergence of many spaces that we could identify as translocalities. Cities such as Toronto, Montreal, and New York [...] are only the most obvious examples of localities in which people from many parts of the hemisphere live together" in harmony, friction, in "porous borders that are constantly traversed by immigrants, migrants, and temporary residents" (335). She reads Clarke's characters as consistent with the "trans-American outcast"; as the "displaced subject [that] differs from the canonical immigrant by remaining on the margins of society with little hope of eventual integration" (336). The response to one's displacement, or exile, is, according to Chanady, best understood by the "literary figuration of displacement within the city and emplacement within a particular building or neighbourhood" (336). Focusing on the domestic space in Caribbean-Canadian fiction, Judith Misrahi-Barak further argues that "[t]he house is the smallest unit in the city but contains some of the problematics of the city at large. The house, or the apartment, [...] often offers a concrete image of what it can be like to have emigrated from the Caribbean to Canada [since] the house is often that of the Canadian employer for whom the West Indian domestic works" (3).

The space of interiority becomes emblematic of the tensions Clarke's characters encounter in the immigrant city. As a space that is simultaneously home and work, private and public, the urban home further obscures the relationship between the immigrant and the city. In the first installment, *The Meeting Point*, Bernice Leach, a Barbadian domestic, is employed by the Burrmanns, a wealthy Jewish family living in Forest Hill. Her position is made possible by the 1955 West Indian Domestic Scheme, which was the federal government's response to the need for childcare to accommodate white women's (re)entry into the work force. Bernice, however, "often wondered why Mrs. Burrmann wanted a servant: she was such a diligent housewife—and this in spite of the novels and the whiskey. [... Bernice was convinced] that Mrs. Burrmann was a better domestic than she" (4). The inception of the West Indian domestic into the city is thus rendered superfluous, an unnecessary excess of the wealthier class that is also characteristic of racist and essentialist stereotyping. Trying to bond with the Afro-Caribbean domestics, Agatha, a Jewish student who is involved with a West Indian man, Henry, tells Bernice, "Henry's always bragging how nice you women can cook your native dishes. You are *born* cooks" (103). Bernice and her sister Estelle are both identified with or as "Aunt Jemima" (24, 56), the stereotype of the black woman as nurturer, cook, and nanny of white children. Bernice "always saw herself as a servant; a sort of twentieth-century slave" (6). Of course, the sexual discrepancies in the immigration policies regulating the arrivals of Caribbean immigrants render the single, female domestic the caregiver and financial provider of the Caribbean males both in the home and host countries. Boysie, Dots' husband, commiserates with Bernice when she receives a letter from her mother asking her to send money. He says: "The moment they see we emigrate, they think we elevate, heh-heh-hee!" (69). Bernice, in addition to sending money to her mother, plans "to send for Terence [her illegitimate son], when he was big enough, and put him through university, if she had to beat the brains into his head. That was her plan for her son" (35).

In the novel, as in the short stories, the male West Indian characters are emasculated. Boysie is financially dependent on his wife, Dots, another Barbadian domestic who works in Rosedale (7), whom he marries as a means of immigrating to Canada: "That is how I come to be here, tonight. [...] But it pains my arse to think o' myself, as a man sponsored, and sponsored, gorblummuh, by a woman at that!" (116). He has "been job-hunting since he come to this country eight months ago" (20), and sometimes borrows money from Bernice to pay for his drinking (70). His attraction to white women is a point of contention between him and Dots, but reminiscent of the Afro-Caribbean male immigrant looking to symbolically enter, and thus succeed within, the ice-cold feminized white city. Even in his sexual fantasies about a German anti-Semitic domestic, Brigitte, who he learns makes more than double the wages Dots makes, he finds himself denied entry: he stops thinking about her "because Brigitte had shut up her lap tight tight tight, like Hiddy-Biddy" (114). Like Boysie, Henry is also unemployed, having come to Canada to work as a railroad porter (113), and like Boysie, is also attracted to white women. His eventual marriage to Agatha in *Storm of Fortune* (1973), the second volume, tests the limits of racial integration when Henry, the victim of racial violence in *The Meeting Point*, commits suicide.

The West Indian domestics thus occupy a curious space within the city that further grants them a different perspective than their male counterparts. As a private space, Bernice thinks of her apartment in her employer's home as "her home away from home. This apartment contained more facilities than she had ever known back in Barbados. It was clean; she kept it clean. It was large, for her; [...] But it was lonely" (28-29). Isolated in her employers' home, she looks out the window from the Burrmanns' kitchen, telling Dots: "Child, it is at this window, looking out almost every night, that I think I could see the meaning of the whole world" (40). Her statement resonates of Toronto's self-image as the world-within-a-city, but Bernice's musings are undermined by the fact that she can only see the meaning of the whole world from her subordinate position as a domestic worker in someone else's house. Outside the house, in the public spaces of the city, Bernice is routinely reminded of her subservient position. When she grows too comfortable living in Forest Hill, "it was pointed out to her that *on this street* she was to remember she wasn't a housewife. A head would lean out of a passing car; or would draw back a window blind, to wonder and to consider the possibility that the two healthy-looking children belonged by blood to the woman into whose hands they had entrusted their hands" (7, emphasis mine). Subjected to civilian surveillance, Henry, like Bernice, is accosted by the police when he, a West Indian man, is found walking on the Forest Hill street en route to Bernice's apartment in the Burrmanns' home (107).

It is within the microcosm that is the interior space that post-war Toronto is represented in Clarke's trilogy most explicitly as a multicultural site of racial, cultural, religious, and sexual negotiations. In *The Meeting Point*, Dots tells Bernice: "It happens every damn day, black woman and white man. […] But have you never pass through Yorkville, Yorkville Village? Near by Bloor and Avenue Road. Or the Little Trinidad Club? Toronto integrated now, gal. It is a technicolour city, now" (48). The black/white relations in *The Meeting Point* are, like technicolour, already exaggerated within the domestic space, and thus appear to be ironically reduced to a didactic binary opposition. As Sarah Phillips Casteel notes: "In the first two volumes of the trilogy, virtually all of the non-Caribbean characters are Jewish, [and,] in the course of juxtaposing the Jewish and Caribbean experiences of arrival, Clarke devotes considerable attention to his Jewish characters' anxieties surrounding their racial and social status" (117-18). Clarke's subtle examination of these anxieties is undermined by the critical trend of "conflat[ing] Jewishness with whiteness" (118), whereas Clarke's "treatment of Jewishness calls into question static, binary constructions of black and white" (119). Indeed, much is made in the novel about the racial tensions that exist between the Jewish employers, Mr. and Mrs. Burrmann, their children, their neighbours, and the Afro-Caribbean domestic workers and relatives, Bernice, Dots, Estelle, who inhabit the same domestic spaces. Confronted with the racist upbringing of their neighbours (Mrs. Gasstein's children), Selene and Ruthie, Mrs. Burrmann's daughters, educate their friends that Bernice, their "maid [...] is a *person*" (24). In the aftermath of being the object of the boy's racist curiosity, Bernice sees the four "Jewish children" who she identifies as "little spoilt brats" (24) as "four white children" (25). The novel, however, suggests the racial negotiations are more complex. Mrs. Burrmann has brought up her children to see Bernice as "a person," and her social gatherings usually end with the white guests singing Negro Spirituals (12) and civil rights songs like *We Shall Overcome* (12, 119). However, her response to the broadcast news of Reverend Dr. Martin Luther King leading African-Americans in protest in the U.S. capital leads her to exclaim: "Praise God, it doesn't happen here" (16). The West Indian characters see themselves as slaves: "We were not born here. We in captivity here" (83); they have been brought "here" to work, and their employers' casual exchange of their "sweat" (8) is a reminder of the master-slave colonial relations. Early in the novel, for instance, Mrs. Burrmann offers Mrs. Gasstein Bernice's labour, telling her, "you don't even have to bother paying her anything" (8); "Bernice is my maid[.] That's what I pay her to do" (9).

Mrs. Burrmann is "the boss in the household" (5). She comes "from a very rich and respectable Jewish home" (5), grew up "in a more respectably rich and sub-urban area of the city" (147), listens to classical music, Beethoven's Sixth Symphony (19), is "domineering and distant; sophisticated and arrogant, giving the guests the impression that she was the artistic one in the family; the cultured one" (5). She is, therefore, more closely related to the ice-queen city in Clarke's short stories, Mrs. Burrmann (*brr*—man) symbolizes, for Bernice, "the snow; she symbolized also, the uneasiness and inconvenience of the snow" (9). The snow is, throughout the novel, overwhelming and ambiguous. The thought of "facing a Canadian winter without a job" was terrifying for Bernice (28). For Dots, the outside view of the window yields "[s]now, and more snow. Snow climbing up outta the sidewalk, and up on the houses like thief climbing through a window" (40). For Boysie, "[t]hat damn snow real pretty" (71), "the prettiest thing [he] ha[s] ever see in [his] whole kiss-me-arse life" (72). Dots is described as wearing powder "that was like snow" and her tears, after Bernice's sister, Estelle, finally arrives, "slid down the white powder on her face, leaving a black mark across the whiteness of the powder" (80). As Fabre notes, "[t]he metropolis is only evoked in winter, […] and the cold seems to act as an anaesthetic [sic] to prevent communication. Snow is everywhere" (130). Cold, pretty, criminal, and masking, the snow—the ice-queen and Mrs. Burrmann by extension—is all-encompassing, regulating the behaviour of the newcomers.

In contrast to his wife's whiteness, and coldness, Sam Burrmann is described in more ambivalent terms. Physically, he "did not have what Bernice came to know as 'the typical Jewish features'; and she felt that had he so wished, he could pass as an Italian, in summer; a very clear-skin washed-out Negro in winter. But she knew he was a Jew—in more ways than one" (210). He, not unlike Clarke's male West Indian characters, "really never felt at home, at home" (147). Although he lives in Forest Hill, he grows up "on Palmerston Boulevard *in the guts* of old downtown Toronto, in the days when Jews inhabited and ruled that entire section bounded by College, north to Bloor Street, east to Spadina Avenue and as far west as Bathurst Street" (147, emphasis mine). His memories "recall a time when Jewish and Caribbean immigrants had lived in much closer contact in Toronto's downtown" (Fabre 132). He associated with "the 'gangsters' [who] were young 'coloured boys,' sons of West Indians who had come to Canada to work as porters on the railroads, and as domestics in white, rich kitchens and homes" (Clarke, *Meeting* 147). As a child, a Jewish man "did not see any difference between Sammy [Burrmann] and Jeffrey, who was black" (149). His socio-economic rise is hinged on his marriage and, more importantly, on allowing his friend, Jeffrey, to be incarcerated for stealing the apple he steals as a child. His cowardice breaks up the inter-racial "gang," symbolic of the disintegration of interracial relationships in the novels. His "ability to capitalize on his lighter skin and to secure his future at the cost of his friend's incarceration [further] anticipates the post-war economic rise of Canadian Jews and their incorporation into a newly expanding category of whiteness that opens its doors to Jews while continuing to firmly exclude blacks" (Fabre 133). Sam Burrmann's preference for jazz music and clubs, his sexual relationship with A-Train, and his eventual relationship with Estelle, in which he takes on the position of the white master with a black female slave, inform his ambivalent relationship to his own racial identity. Like the domestic women who financially and legally support the men in their lives, Sam Burrmann serves a similar function. Estelle, Dots tells Bernice, is "in this country looking for a man" (154). When Estelle confronts Sam about her pregnancy, his response is "to change the conversation" and offer "to help her take out landed immigrant's papers. 'That's what you want, isn't it?'" (303). His question, or assumption, shifts the balance of power between them as he assumes a position of serving her, at the same time that he eschews taking paternal responsibility in a conventional patriarchal way.

Unlike the promotional materials that celebrate Toronto's diversity, *The Meeting Point* does not offer an uncomplicated view of the translocal city. It resists buying into the narrative that oppressed groups will work together to overcome discrimination and exploitation. Although it appears to reduce the conflict to a black-white common denominator, it nevertheless reminds us that these are not homogeneous and uncomplicated categories. As former marginalized groups ascend the social strata, in part because new more visibly different groups arrive, and shift their occupation of urban territories, they serve to obfuscate the city, its centralized power, obscuring it from view. In Clarke's trilogy, Boysie and Dot's ascension in socio-economic status serves to parallel the West Indian immigrants with former European ones, as they become, like Sam Burrmann, more distanced from their more humble beginnings. Their material success, however, does not imply that *all* West Indian immigrants eventually reach the comforts of the suburban middle-class, especially when considering Clarke's trilogy and short stories in tandem. The attainment of material success denotes the ways in which the Afro-Caribbean immigrants participate in their own alienation from the Caribbean community. The inclusion of Clarke's West Indian characters into the domestic suburban spaces, moreover, reinforces their systematic exclusion from the city's centralized power and calls attention to the contradictory space they occupy within the city. Public spaces, like city streets, become contested territories; in the West Indian ghetto, a West Indian sensibility can be imposed, whereas in predominantly white neighbourhoods, the

West Indian immigrant becomes more visible and as such the target of racial violence. Entry into the white spaces of the city, like assimilation into white society, allows for some urban boundaries to become more fluid, but, as Clarke's characters in *Nine Men Who Laughed* and the Toronto trilogy illustrate, such entries and racial assimilation become inclusive methods of legitimately eliminating blackness from the white city.

Endnotes

1. The introduction and section on Clarke's *Nine Men Who Laughed* in this article were previously published in my article "Building and Living the Immigrant City: Michael Ondaatje's and Austin Clarke's Toronto." *Downtown Canada: Writing Canadian Cities.* Ed. Justin D. Edwards and Douglas Ivison. Toronto: U of Toronto P, 2005. 122-141. Print.

2. "The World Within a City" is a slogan launched by Tourism Toronto in the summer of 1998.

3. Doucet does not contest the fact that "Toronto has become *one of the most* multicultural centres in the world, a place recently described as a 'City of Nations'" (Doucet). His article merely follows the trajectory of the urban myth as it has appeared in the mainstream media, political speeches, Canadian and American travel guides, and so forth.

Works Cited

Ball, John Clement. "White City, Black Ancestry: The Immigrant's Toronto in the Stories of Austin Clarke and Dionne Brand." *Open Letter* Series 8, no. 8 (1994): 9-19. Print.

Casteel, Sarah Phillips. "Experiences of Arrival: Jewishness and Caribbean-Canadian Identity in Austin Clarke's *The Meeting Point*." *Journal of West Indian Literature* 14.1&2 (2005): 113-40. Print.

Chanady, Amaryll. "The Trans-American Outcast and Figurations of Displacement." *Comparative Literature* 61.3 (2009): 335-45. Print.

Clarke, Austin. *The Meeting Point*. 1967. Toronto: Vintage, 1998. Print.

-----. *Nine Men Who Laughed*. Markham, ON: Penguin, 1986. Print.

Clarke, George Elliott. "Clarke vs. Clarke: Tory Elitism in Austin Clarke's Short Fiction." *West Coast Line* 22(31/1) (1997): 110-28. Print.

Doucet, Michael J. "The Anatomy of an Urban Legend: Toronto's Multicultural Reputation." 2001. Web. 20 July 2002. <http://ceris.metropolis.net/Virtual%20Library/other/doucet3.html>.

Fabre, Michel. "Changing the Metropolis or Being Changed By It? Toronto West Indians in Austin Clarke's Trilogy." *Recherches Anglaises et Nord-Americaines* 24(1991): 129-35. Print.

Fish, Stanley. "Boutique Multiculturalism, or Why Liberals Are Incapable of Thinking about Hate Speech." *Critical Inquiry* 23.2 (1997): 378-95. Print.

Garreau, Joel. "Manifest Destiny Lives! We Want the Blue Jays and Niagara Falls ... Mounties, Maybe ...

But Not Quebec." *Washington Post* 17 June 1990: D1. Print.

Isin, Engin F. *Being Political: Genealogies of Citizenship.* Minneapolis: U of Minnesota P, 2002. Print.

Judith Misrahi-Barak, "The Cityscape in a Few Caribbean-Canadian Short Stories." *Journal of the Short Story in English* 31(1998): 9-22. Web. 3 February 2013. <http://jsse.revues.org/index154.html>.

Ondaatje, Michael. *In the Skin of a Lion.* 1987. Toronto: Vintage Canada, 1996. Print.

Soja, Edward W. *Postmetropolis: Critical Studies of Cities and Regions.* Oxford: Blackwell, 2000. Print.

Tourism Toronto. *Toronto: The World within a City.* Toronto: Tourism Toronto, n.d. Print.

Walker, James W. St. G. *The West Indians in Canada.* Ottawa: Canadian historical Association, 1984. Print.

"Playin' 'Mas," Hustling Respect: Multicultural Masculinities in Two Stories by Austin Clarke*

DANIEL COLEMAN

Austin Clarke has published fifteen volumes of fiction and autobiography since 1964, making him one of the most prolific writers living in Canada today. Yet, despite the Barbadian-born writer's considerable Canadian success, most of the responses to Clarke's work to date have come from critics who share his Caribbean background. Lloyd W. Brown's *El Dorado and Paradise: Canada and the Caribbean in Austin Clarke's Fiction* (1989), the 1994 biography by Stella Algoo-Baksh, and articles by Victor Ramraj, Horace Goddard, Frank Birbalsingh, Anthony Boxill, and Keith S. Henry all make use of that background to delineate the complex genealogy of Caribbean migration in Clarke's works. Their analyses focus on the important issues of immigrant dislocation, the residual effects of colonial history, West Indian family structures, the migrant character's ambivalent relations to places of origin and destination, and conflicts in Canada over employment or racial prejudice.

I wish to focus, in the following reading of two short stories from Clarke's Penguin Short Fiction collection *Nine*

Men Who Laughed (1986), on the ways in which the male West Indian migrant's experience of cross-cultural refraction produces disruptive parody when he takes on certain urban Canadian norms for masculinity. Such a focus involves a reading strategy that is "inappropriate": first, where Clarke and his critics in general emphasize issues of race over those of gender, I have tipped the balance in the other direction; and second, I have linked three discussions of gendered performativity that were formulated in completely different disciplinary paradigms. The first is Judith Butler's influential theory, articulated in philosophical and post-structuralist terms, of gender as a socially prescribed performance; the second is the folklorist Roger Abraham's description, based on ethnographic research and methodology, of the performative tradition of what he calls the "man-of-words" in Caribbean Creole culture; and the third is the identification by sociologists such as Julius Hudson of a common African-American urban form of masculine performance called the "hustler." Hopefully, this inappropriate linkage will produce a mutually informative dialogue among these diverse methods of analysis.

Clarke's two stories about Joshua Miller-Corbaine, "A Man" and "How He Does It," are excellent sites for an analysis of masculinity in multicultural transition. At the same time that the two stories demonstrate how gender is in fact something we "do," how masculinities are practiced or performed, they also show how these performances can become troubled and troubling when they negotiate the displacements of cross-cultural refraction. The two stories about a Caribbean man in Toronto address not only the social codes for masculinity that he encounters in the Canadian metropolis, but also the ways the masculine codes he brings from the island and from contact with African-American urban culture displace and challenge these metropolitan ones.

Every morning, when all the men on his street are leaving for work, Joshua Miller-Corbaine, this "tall and black and majestic" man (123), emerges from his three-storied suburban Toronto house dressed in a dark, pin-striped suit spanned by the gold chain of his pocket watch, a snow-white shirt with a soft silk tie, and black Bally shoes. He carries a black leather attaché case engraved with his initials. The case is stuffed with law books and sheaves of jurisprudence. He eases himself carefully onto the leather seat of his silver-grey Cadillac Eldorado, and, having loaded in his wife and son, slides the car noiselessly out of the circular driveway in the direction of Yonge and York Mills, where he will drop off his son Winchester at Upper Canada College and his wife Mary at the high school where she teaches. He then wheels the automobile around and heads towards the part of the city called the Annex where he spends part of his working day.

Joshua has carefully gathered around himself all the accessories of the man of taste, the man of wealth. He is very conscious of his image—of the way clothing, possessions, diction, gestures, posture, even gait, "make the man." "He hunched his shoulders when he walked," we are told in "A Man":

> He felt it gave him a determined, academic and serious look. He felt it was the look of someone burdened by intellectual problems, the look of someone who spent most of the day and most of the night poring over academic and legalistic matters which ordinary men could not grasp. (123-24)

He has cultivated a nervous tic which he soothes regularly by shrugging his shoulders to adjust the fit of his jacket and the straightness of his tie. This mannerism, the narrator informs us, "was born of his admiration for an Englishman who taught literature in private school back in Barbados" (124). This comment suggests that one of the major influences on Joshua's performance comes from the class-structure of the colonial West Indies; there he learned to admire the cut of suits made in London, which, we are told, was where "his heart, his standards of fast living and his first love remained" (119).

With some adaptation to the social protocols of Toronto, Joshua's upper-class performance has garnered him the success he dreamed about back in Bridgetown. He has married the wealth of a mining company president's daughter; his son attends Canada's most prestigious private school; he has three mistresses, two of whom are also extremely wealthy; he lives in luxury and is the envy of his male West Indian friends. His house, his clothes, and his money, like his car, constitute the Eldorado of the immigrant's dream.[1]

But it is all a masquerade. In Creole terms, Joshua is "playin' 'mas" to good effect in Toronto. For, despite appearances, he is not a Bay Street corporate lawyer. He is not a bachelor. He is not the independent man of means he has claimed to be for the past thirty years. Instead, he is a kept man. He spends his days visiting the women who sponsor his front. His house, his car, his attaché case and gold watch, even his suits—all the accoutrements of his impressive image—are gifts from his wife and lovers. Completely dependent upon the white women to whom he is a refined gigolo, Joshua must carefully craft every action to contribute to the masquerade upon which, not only he but also his various audiences—the women, his neighbours, and his West Indian male friends—depend. And the performance is taking its toll. He has a stomach ulcer, and his temper is getting short. One wonders how long he can keep it up.

Joshua is a prime example of the kind of heightened performativity that is a striking feature of so many of the male characters not just of Austin Clarke's fifteen published volumes, but also of other male Caribbean authors such as Earl Lovelace, Dany Laferrière, Samuel Selvon, Harold Sonny Ladoo, and George Lamming. These characters are very conscientious about *acting male*, about using all the techniques of drama from gestures to costumes to props and sets, even to dialogue from a script. While we can usefully examine this striking performativity with reference to Butler's gender theory, her formulations need to be balanced by the specific cultural analysis of Abrahams' research in African-Caribbean traditions of male performativity. For her abstract theory assumes a more universal, coherent social order than the folklorist would allow.

Butler writes that "gender is always a doing" (*Gender* 25). Gender is the product, she insists, of a person's enactment of socially imposed scripts for sexed behaviour. The impeccably attired Joshua illustrates nicely her assertion that "Gender is the repeated stylization of the body, a set of repeated acts within a highly rigid regulatory frame that congeal over time to produce the appearance of substance, of a natural sort of being" (33). Joshua's posture, the practiced shrug of his shoulders, the cut of his suits, the upper-middle-class Trinidadian-mixed-with-English accent[2] constitute this "repeated stylization" of his body that produces him as man of wealth and influence. Each of these elements of his performance plays to specific social scripts not just of gender, but also of ethnicity, race, and class.

Now, it would be easy at this point to misunderstand Butler's performance theory by concluding that a person puts on a gender in the morning like choosing which suit or dress to wear today. "Performativity," Butler cautions in her second book, *Bodies That Matter*, is "not a singular 'act,'" (12). A human being becomes gendered, she insists, by a repeated process of citation, by re-citation, where the "norm" of sex is cited in each person's daily practices. Connell makes much the same point when he suggests that a person's physical sense of gender "grows through a personal history of social practice, a life-history-in-society" (84). Gender, therefore, is not a matter of spontaneous deciding; rather, it is more the accumulation of performances or recitations of the social scripts by which we live. Society imposes and enforces such scripts, but Butler's troubling (and potentially liberating) point is that *people play them out*. And, in the inevitable uniqueness of each performer's own history, experience, and aptitude, there exists the potential for various interpretations, diverse recitations, even modifications of the socially regulated script.

This potential excites a gender-troubler like Butler, because it leads her to speculate about how to produce intentionally these variations on the social script. It leads her to the central question of *Gender Trouble*: "If repetition is bound to persist as the mechanism of the cultural reproduction of identities, then ... [w]hat kind of subversive repetition might call into question the regulatory practice of identity itself?" (32). We need to look, she suggests, for "self-consciously denaturalized position[s]" (110)—de Lauretis calls them "eccentric" subject positions—from which we can observe how the naturalness of gender is constituted. Given the metropolitan, "First World" purview of her work, Butler turns to drag parodies, and to gay and lesbian adaptations of heterosexual gender codes for this denaturalization, believing that the potential for gender transformation is to be found in the "possibility of a failure to repeat, a de-formity, or a parodic repetition" (141). But there are many places to look for denaturalized or eccentric positions—some of them completely unselfconscious.

Joshua's performance of the man of means is flawless in its rendering of the social codes of class and gender, but it is "denaturalized" by the inflections he brings to that performance from African-Caribbean culture. In *The Man-of-Words in the West Indies: Performance and the Emergence of Creole Culture* (1983), Roger Abrahams uses research he carried out on the islands of Nevis, St. Vincent, Tobago, and Trinidad in the 1960s to describe the complex codes that inform men's social performances in the Caribbean.[3] After some years observing the patterns of verbal performance that distinguish African male behaviours in American cities—playing the dozens, jiving, rapping, etc., Abrahams went to the Caribbean to see what relations he could find between American and Caribbean African cultural performances. While he found remarkable continuities between the two (e.g. "rhyming" is the Creole equivalent of "playing the dozens"), he found in the West Indies a remarkably defined tradition of verbal and social performances, a tradition that was consciously and deliberately taught to young people as they were growing up.

Two distinct but related sets of values shape the performative tradition of what Abrahams calls the "man-of-words." On the one hand, there is the tradition of "sweet talk" whose arena is the private, orderly world of house, yard, and church. The sweet talker operates in the mode of the preacher or speech-maker whose polished and sophisticated rhetoric is called for at serious community events such as weddings, funerals, political gatherings, or "thanksgivings" after a sickness or some other adversity. Sweet talk emphasizes being sensible, Abrahams notes; it has as its primary aim the achievement of respectability. The tradition of "broad talk," on the other hand, is the mode of the "'mas" player or carnival performer whose arena occupies the public, male-dominated rum-shops and cross-roads. The broad or "bad" talker delights in nonsense and rudeness couched in colloquial diction and biting invective. He aggressively competes with other men-of-words by "makin' mock" and "givin' fatigue," distinguishing his position in the group through wit and notoriety. Whereas sweet talk values respectability above all else, broad talk values reputation (151-52).

The two values of respectability and reputation reflect the hybrid inheritances of Creole culture, for respectability is often formulated in reference to the "high" culture of colonial Britain whereas reputation is formulated in terms of the African tradition of the Anansi or trickster figure whose rebellious disregard of the very idea of high culture itself affirms the "low" and disempowered. Thus, for instance, the sweet talker demonstrates his sophistication through allusions to Shakespeare and the Bible and employs as many Latinate phrases as possible, while the broad talker uses Creole invective, elaborate curses and mockery, and delights in non-sequiturs and puns. Sweet talk affirms the social order and its traditions; broad talk ridicules them. The sweet talker wishes to solidify his status in a superior class, while the broad talker wants to deflate the pretentious and (paradoxically) distinguish himself as the champion of lower-class solidarity.

We must keep in mind, however, that despite this distinction between sweet talk and broad talk, the truly effective man-of-words is the one who can adopt either expressive mode to a given situation. As Abrahams insists:

> A man-of-words is worth nothing unless he can, on the one hand, stitch together a startling piece of oratorical rhetoric, and, on the other, capture the attention, the allegiance, and the admiration of the audience through his fluency, his strength of voice, and his social maneuverability and psychological resilience ... West Indian creativity, and indeed, Afro-American creativity are built upon this competitive and highly contrastive superimposition of voices, ones that speak in different codes and cadences. (xxx)

The ability to improvise, then, is key to the success of the man-of-words. Out of the repertoire of performances that stretch between the two poles of the "sweet" and the "broad," he must produce one appropriate to the occasion before him. What happens then, in Joshua's case? What happens when the man-of-words moves to another culture? How does the performative tradition he imbibed in his West Indian childhood shape his masculine practices in metropolitan Toronto?

Austin Clarke's two stories about Joshua describe a man who innovates; he brings the twin goals of respectability and reputation to the metropolitan context and tries to find ways to achieve them in his new situation. The division of values symbolized by the domestic yard and the public cross-roads in island culture, however, needs re-orientation in Toronto. Here respectability finds its primary expressions in public symbols such as high-status employment, an expensive car, a home in a wealthy neighbourhood, and other material possessions. A reputation for dramatic flair continues to need validation from a homosocial network of male relationships, but immigration means that Joshua's network is now limited to the circle of other West Indian men who can appreciate the performance, so it occurs in a much more circumscribed arena than it did back in the islands. Rather than establishing respectability in the yard at home, Joshua must seek it in the public arenas of corporate business and conspicuous consumption, and instead of establishing a reputation for wit and notoriety at the cross-roads, he works on that reputation in the living rooms and bachelor suites of his West Indian friends. So Toronto requires him to improvise his performances for a new symbolic landscape.

One sign of respectability does appear to transfer directly from the island to the Canadian city and that is the deference commanded by the man in fine clothes. Throughout the two stories, the reader's attention is repeatedly drawn to the upper-middle-class elegance of Joshua's clothes. (A similar concern with the class-register of clothing preoccupies the characters of Boysie Cumberbatch, Henry White, and John Moore from Clarke's novels, as well as many of the male protagonists in his five collections of short stories.) This concern with fine suits and tailored shirts constitutes a kind of cross-dressing on the level of class. In *Vested Interests*, a far-ranging study of how cross-dressing produces cultural anxiety, Marjorie Garbor asserts that "class, gender, sexuality, and even race and ethnicity ... are themselves brought to crisis in dress codes and sumptuary regulation" (28). Joshua's clothes enable him to improvise a role for himself within the exclusive circles of upper-middle-class masculinity in Toronto. Along with his other accoutrements, they are meant to gain him respect. Why? Because Canadian corporate culture says you wear a business suit, glance at a gold watch, drive a Cadillac, carry an attaché case, have a son in Upper Canada College, regularly prove your virility in several women's beds, and practice corporate law to show you are a real successful man. With enough industry, talent, and capital, anybody can do it. But it assumes all along that you are white, too.

This quietly maintained racial barrier highlights the reason why, in migrating to a North American metropolis, Joshua encounters another performative tradition, a second set of codes for African men's behaviour. Where the tradition in the West Indies incorporated a contest between the African trickster and British "high" culture, the North American one juxtaposes that trickster with American-style capitalism. Whereas the plantation paradigm in the islands maintained the inferiority of Africans by blocking their access to education and thus to the civility of the "gentleman," capitalist metropolitan culture maintains their oppression by blocking their access to upper-echelon employment. The figure of the inner-city hustler represents an African American performative tradition that has evolved in response to this consistent discrimination against African Americans in capitalist culture.

As long ago as the 1952 publication of *Black Skin, White Masks*, Frantz Fanon pointed out that economic exclusion was the primary cause of black men's feelings of inferiority (13). Robert Staples applies Fanon's analysis to the American urban scene: "[B]lack male sexuality ... is a secondary symbol of manhood in a society that denies him the primary signs of masculinity, such as high status jobs" (14). Caught between expectations that a man prove his worth by achieving socioeconomic success and the racism that disqualifies him from the marketplace, black masculinity, according to black British critics Kobena Mercer and Isaac Julien, "is a highly contradictory formation as it is a *subordinated* masculinity" (112). In the Canadian context, Clarke's biographer Stella Algoo-Baksh claims that "Canada often perpetuates the emasculation of the black male by denying him the resources he needs to discharge his conventional manly duties to his family" (101). She quotes Clarke himself who declares, on the basis of his own early experiences trying to find work in Toronto, "that the 'invisible but solid hand of prejudice' would always confront the black man with barriers to respectable employment in Canada" (47-48). Just as the tradition of the West Indian man-of-words combined the aspiration for British-style respectability with a carnivalesque mockery of high-culture proprieties, so also the tradition of the metropolitan hustler combines an aspiration for capitalist success with a licentious disregard for the social protocols for attaining that success. In both traditions, the performer ascribes to and rebels against the codes and practices of the status quo.

Thus, Joshua's masquerade as lawyer-about-town is inflected by both island and metropolitan traditions, and like them it conveys both espousal of and dissatisfaction with metropolitan codes for masculine success. This duality allows Clarke to produce simultaneously a pathetic portrait of the man who ascribes to codes that are hostile to him and a critique of the racist logic that operates within those codes. It lets Clarke show both how males benefit in the short-term by perpetrating a phallocentric system[4] and how they suffer from that very participation. For, to the extent that Joshua's charade succeeds, it shows how thin the "proofs" of mainstream masculine "authenticity" really are, while to the extent that it fails, it reveals the violence these codes inflict on their actors.

Basically, Joshua fuses the performative flair of the West Indian man-of-words with the metropolitan figure of the street hustler. The hustler emerged in the African-American ghettos of the early half of this century in response to the American Dream. This figure aspires to the *goals* of that dream, but because of his race and class he is disqualified from the *means* to achieve them. So he innovates. Hustling, as African American sociologist Julius Hudson describes it, is "a way of 'making it' without killing oneself on whitey's jobs" (413). The hustler short-circuits his way to masculine success—that is, in socioeconomic terms. The members of this subculture are conspicuous consumers, and the symbols they acquire are the clothes, jewellery, and automobiles that together compose an image of sexual and economic male potency:

> The attire of the hustler represents one of the most significant aspects of his "front" or *modus operandi* ... [O]ne's wardrobe is a factor in the determination of the hustler's peer-established prestige ranking ... [T]he Cadillac ... is the most popular car in this subculture ... Moreover, a special model Eldorado, renamed El Cavalaro ... is currently the ultimate in hustlers' automobile selection ... In addition to clothes and automobiles, hustlers spend a great deal of money on jewellery. They usually adorn themselves with gold-diamond rings and watches. (Hudson 413-14)

Their motto is: dress for success. You will attract money if you look like you already have some. Jingle the keys to the Eldorado in your pants pocket.

Of the many kinds of "hustles" or "games" that Hudson describes—which include pool hall speculating, drug-dealing, and petty larceny, the one that fits Joshua's scheme best is a kind of pimping game, not the kind that derives an income from prostitution or from professional female shoplifters, but one in which the hustler gets rich from functioning as a gigolo to women who already have money:

> The pimp in this case is usually a good-looking, well-dressed, and well-built guy, but the most important characteristic in this type of pimping is the ability to sexually satisfy a female. Thus this pimp is the gigolo type. Once he establishes his superiority in this area, he encounters virtually no obstacles to the attainment of the female's money ... Often such pimps get their broads to buy them expensive automobiles and other desired goods. (420)

What I find fascinating about this figure is the way he simultaneously affirms and undermines the dominant culture's socioeconomic codes of masculine success. What I find disturbing is the way he confirms the racist stereotype of the black stud in the process.

Capitalist phallocentrism avers that a real man is rich and controls women. Joshua proves his authenticity on both counts, by controlling his women and making himself rich. But in doing so he undermines those codes by revealing how his hard-won masculinity—in both economic and sexual terms—*depends* upon the women it seeks to control. Here is a great paradox of phallocentric masculinity: that the supposedly autonomous male depends upon "his" women. On the one hand, Joshua seems the paragon of male independence. He needs nothing outside himself—not his family, not his West Indian friends, not a university degree, not even the social system of employment or a position in the institution of the law—to succeed. But on the other hand, he is absolutely a kept man. His wife has provided the house and car; his mistresses, the money for his expensive suits and jewellery. Collectively, they give him what he *does* each day. In this sense, his masculinity is something these women have made. They sponsor his performance.

But the conflict between the social script which urges him to assert independence and Joshua's real dependence chafes him until it erupts in hatred of the very women on whom he depends. He hates his wife (128); he hates the rich woman who lives in the Annex and buys his suits (131); and he is beginning to hate Rachel, the young mistress he likes most (145). He feels trapped by them, by the life they have made for him, and he lashes out in violent response. "He had been beating her off and on for ten years," says the narrator of Joshua's connection with the woman in the Annex. "Whenever she cornered him about his work ... or about his wife ... he beat her" (131). But the entrapment is a mutual one. For, when she confronts him about his philandering, we are told that her strange love for him is based on her acknowledgement of what she calls his "independence" (131). So she endures his beatings, even admires him, for the very fiction of his independence that she herself has created. Brown writes:

> [I]n his sexual and social themes, Clarke emphasizes the reciprocal nature of roles and perceptions.

> Joshua succeeds in his schemes ... because in their own way the women need his illusions as much as he does ... Their female dependency complements his dependency on them for economic support and as props for his overweening ego. In fact, Joshua's women really duplicate his blend of dependency and manipulative power. (*El Dorado* 143-44)

Both trapped in the performance of their respective roles, Joshua and his mistress feed off of each other's need, perpetuating the recitation of their co-dependency.

By successfully hustling upper-middle-class status, and by maintaining the surface illusion of his self-sufficiency, Clarke's character demonstrates how metropolitan masculinity *is* in fact that surface, that performance. Joshua fakes the lawyer's life—mimics the law, as it were—to grab the golden apple of social prestige. He reaches the capitalist ideal's *ends* by short-cutting the *means*, and in the process, reveals that the presumed codes of propriety (the Protestant work ethic,[5] the I'm-a-contributing-member-of-society ethic) are really in pursuit of that same golden apple with just as ruthless and "lawless" a heart. His performance exposes one of the capitalist social script's most essential features—the hustle for respectability.

Joshua's cross-cultural refraction triggers this exposure. His performance of the corporate script for socio-economically based male success is inflected by the complex combination of West Indian and urban black performative traditions he has inherited through cultural and racial history. That inflection causes his performance to veer into a parody that exposes the corporate code's own superficiality. The two stories about Joshua are striking examples of the way the cultural disruption of the migrant narrative can bring to light repressed contradictions within what Kaja Silverman, in *Male Subjectivity at the Margins*, has called masculinity's "dominant fiction" (15ff.). Joshua's story reveals much about how the masculinities conscripted in Bridgetown or Port-au-Prince or Bombay or Colombo are troubled by and bring trouble to the conscriptions of maleness in Toronto or Vancouver or Montreal. Joshua's refracted performance is unsettling, not because it constitutes a direct challenge to Canadian masculine ideologies, but because it elaborates a discomfort rarely acknowledged but widely felt by urban Canadian men: that Western capitalism is structured by men's aggressive over-compensation for inner self-doubt.

To assess the unsettling effects of Joshua's story, I am going to focus, in the following paragraphs, on the very different narrative voices of the two stories "A Man" and "How He Does It." My aim here is to attend to something Judith Butler says little about, and that is the question of audience. Who watches the identity performances she describes? She says "society" invigilates gender performances, but who constitutes that society? Who interprets the performer's self-styling drama? How does the audience's gaze influence the performance? What roles do pre-existing performative traditions assign the audience? And what effect does the interaction between performance and audience have on the social script itself?

Abrahams, in contrast to Butler, emphasizes the determining presence of the audience in West Indian performative tradition. Not only does the man-of-words compete with other performers for the attention and approval of the audience, he says, but also the audience themselves often become competitors to the performer as they take on the broad talker's role of hecklers who make some "mock" and "boderation" of their own. By placing the two versions of Joshua's story in two very different narrative voices, Clarke highlights the importance of audience to an understanding of the performative paradigm.

A couple of scenes in "A Man" indicate the concerns of one section of Joshua's audience, the "respectable" people up high, left and right of the stage, in the private boxes. In the first scene, Joshua is in his car, fleeing from his rich lover's accusations about his philandering. He is also fleeing his own violent response to her accusation, his slugging her in the eye. "He had never driven so fast in the city," the narrator tells us:

> He had just gone through the second red light when he pressed the brakes. The Cadillac came to a standstill beside a yellow police cruiser. The officer looked at him. He glared at the policeman, his glare turned to terror and he lowered his eyes ... The police officer ignored him. The fear rose and he continued at a slower rate, limp as a dishrag. (134)

The policeman pairs logically with another watcher. In this second scene, Joshua is not alone in the car. Knowing that his wife will be away for the weekend, he has invited his mistress, Rachel, over to his place for a "dirty weekend." They pull up, and Rachel gets out, exclaiming loudly her delight at his lovely home. Joshua "flashed his eyes across the lawn," reports the narrator. "Standing erect and sombre as a judge, which he was, was his neighbour ... [Joshua's] stomach dropped. He had no stomach now. And he was weak" (146). The policeman and the judge are watching. The law.

But it is not Joshua who tells us about them. Nor do they offer any comments themselves. It is the narrator who draws our attention to their silent, threatening presence. And it makes sense that he should do so, because that is where he himself belongs—in the box reserved for judges and policemen, arbiters of the law. The narrator of "A Man"—with his third-person omniscience, his privileged access to Joshua's thoughts, his dignified prose and supposed objectivity, his security in the voyeur's unreflexive gaze—aligns himself with the law that judges. He intrudes, comments, analyzes, and in so doing, he appeals to, defines, a readership of social regulators and moral commentators. His concern for order and propriety connects him with that current in West Indian performative tradition whose prime concern is respectability, but since the story takes place in Toronto, he is linked with institutions which arbiter respectability in Canada: the courts and the police. It is no coincidence that these institutions are the ones that most often express public disapproval of the newly arrived immigrant.

Right from the opening sentence, this narrator condemns Joshua's masquerade. Throughout the story, he reminds us of Joshua's stomach ulcer, the bodily sign of his hypocrisy. He tells us both about Joshua's abusive violence and about his consequent guilt. It is the narrator who breaks from the usual focalization upon Joshua to inform us that the rich mistress is not taken in by Joshua's performance: "[S]he thought he looked like a man who did not have schedules and appointments; seeing also beneath his handsome build the tension in his walk, which his well-tailored clothes, that she admired and had bought, could not conceal" (125). Repeatedly, the narrator reveals Joshua as nothing more than a chimera created by Hugo Boss and Giorgio Armani. This is the message the narrator conveys when Joshua careens desperately around his house trying to convert the family home into a bachelor pad in preparation for Rachel's visit. After grabbing pictures off the walls, dresses from closets, sanitary pads from the bathroom, nylons from the bedroom floor, he collapses exhausted in a chair. As the narrator informs us:

> He noted with some disappointment, that nothing in this house in which he had spent so much time had his stamp on it. No one could guess that he lived here.
>
> Here he was, for the last two hours, trying to remove all trace of his wife's presence in the house, and what did he discover? He had come face to face with the cold fact that no smell, no idiosyncrasy, no photograph, no snap-shot, no cigarette box used even for paper clips and for discarded calling cards, nothing of his stamp was on his own home. (140)

He has left nothing of his own stamp upon the house, the narrator implies, because he does not have a stamp of his own in the first place. Underneath the finery, there is only hot air. Through his assumption of moral superiority over Joshua, the narrator invites readers to enter into an ironic contract, a conspiracy of superiors between readers and narrator that Wayne Booth would call the "Snotty Sublime" (211). Joshua thinks he is succeeding in his masquerade, but we know better. He has no idea how easily we can see through him. It is the irony of drama which lets characters make fools of themselves on stage, while we the audience chuckle knowingly, smug in the (authorized) perspicacity of our private booth.

In the ironic contract that operates between us and the narrator in "A Man," Clarke plays upon a pleasurable anxiety that structures many a masculine psyche: the male compulsion to prove over and over again—with *prima facie* evidence, as Joshua puts it—that "I really am a man." Really. Our anxious pleasure focuses on whether or not Joshua's performance will be exposed as a sham. How will he get past this challenge? And the next one? And the next? The titillating anxiety, though, is false suspense. And we know it is false. The narrator has told us all along that Joshua is a fake. But the suspense still operates through a kind of dramatic irony: when will the character learn about himself what we already know? He has been exposed to us right from the start; it is just a matter of time until he realizes it himself.

Here Clarke leads us to a fundamental critique of upwardly ambitious masculinity: a subjectivity that remains ignorant of what it knows, that refuses to know what it knows. That knows the artificiality of its performance and yet believes in that performance. This is a subjectivity structured by multiple layers of irony: the dramatic irony of the performer who does not know what his audience knows about him; the self-protecting irony that acts as if it did not know what it knows; the situational irony of the compulsion to enact an ideal that is itself bogus. The dominant fiction insists that "male" is the standard, the substantial plenitude against which "otherness" is measured; but the male performer (and often his audience too) is plagued by the nagging feeling that the masquerade is wearing thin. He has too much invested, though, in the act to throw it all off. At the same time that he exposes to our censure the vacuum at Joshua's core, Clarke's narrator entices us onwards through the story with the prospect of an ultimate exposure—with which he duly gratifies us at the end. Joshua's wife comes home unexpectedly and finds Joshua with Rachel naked in the living room. The conclusion is a strange mixture of anticlimax and satisfaction: anticlimactic because the exposure does not tell us anything we did not already know; satisfying because the tension of whether or not the act will "pass" is relieved—we are assured that it will not.

But the question remains: what does the irony accomplish? Presumably, ironic writing operates what Freud called a "tendentious" project upon its reader. It wants to have a critical impact (*Jokes* 90-116). So what effect does the ironic contract in the story have on the gender performances of the audience? Does the pact of the "Snotty Sublime" between us and the narrator invite any kind of self-knowledge? Or does it assure us that we are all immensely superior to such obvious foibles and therefore blind us to our own performative incoherencies? Certainly, it critiques the object of ridicule, but does this critique trouble or does it placate the audience? Does it do both?

By deploying a very different narrator in the second version of the story, "How He Does It," Clarke gives us an alternate perspective on these questions. He ushers us to seats in a very different part of the theatre. In contrast to the disapproving narrator of "A Man"—whose formal, "standardized" Queen's English aligns him with the whole long line of "respectable" narrators inherited by the colonies from Britain—this new narrator is not omniscient, not objective, not given access to Joshua's or anybody else's thoughts. He does not speak Oxonian or even U-of-Torontonian English, nor does he enjoy the voyeur's privilege of detachment. He does not know about—or, at least, fails to mention—the beating or the policeman or the stomach ulcer. A member of the group of Joshua's "Wessindian" male friends, this narrator invites us to join the "in" group who have blown their week's savings on the front seats in the house, right down on the main floor, centre stage. This new group is still very much involved in evaluating Joshua's performance, but they judge him by the codes of a very different tradition.

In place of the moralizing respectability of the earlier official-sounding narrator, this narrator is a member of the homosocial brotherhood who have a keen taste for Joshua's saga of male prowess. These men admire and envy their lawyer-friend's reputation-enhancing performance. Rather than ending his story with Joshua's final humiliation, he delightedly shows us how Joshua invents a way to survive a confrontation between his wife and his mistress: how he beats the system. In his story, Joshua "play 'mas" so convincingly that Rachel more readily believes his improvised explanation ("She's my maid") than the wife's true story. But even in this much more convivial atmosphere, there still roves the watchful eye. Our new narrator explains:

> He came from Trinidad in 1952 to go to University and this is now the year 1986, and all the boys who went to university with him, who know him, who come and gone and some who stay, and see him around the place, none o' these boys, not one, don't know yet if really and truly this fellow have a job, and what the job is. Or if, in all them years, he ever had a job!

> Arguments have rage from 1952 till the present day, and still nobody can't come to a conclusion, stating that the fellow is a lawyer, a semi-lawyer, a community lawyer or no lawyer at all. And not one of his colleagues have the nerve or the gall to tell him to his face, 'Man, you only *playing* you is a lawyer!'
>
> But behind his back they does-laugh and say, 'He *playing* he's a lawyer!' And some does-say after they laugh, 'But if he was a lawyer, he would be the best goddamn lawyer outta all the boys!', meaning all the Wessindian boys. (208)

Even in this friendlier narrative context, then, there remains an atmosphere of distrust, or at least of ironic distance. "The boys" set a series of tests to try Joshua's credibility, and he passes them all. One of them follows him downtown and sees him emerge from the High Courts on Queen Street in the company of men dressed in lawyers' black robes (211). Another asks for a $500 loan, to see if he carries around the kind of money they expect of his status, and he pulls out a monogrammed wallet and skins off five brand new hundred dollar notes. "After that ... we decide the boy is a hero. He got to be good! And he have class" (214). He passes the wine test, bringing to their next party not some cheap hooch, but six bottles of Dom Perignon (215). He passes the virility test by possessing an expensive mistress. Upon meeting Rachel, the narrator reveals in his outburst of admiration how inseparably connected are the sexual and the commercial in his concept of respectable masculinity. This woman, "full in the breasts, full in the hips, *solid as the best securities in the stock market down Bay Street*," fits exactly his idea of the successful male's companion. "This was woman. A lawyer's woman!" (217, my emphasis).

Lastly, Joshua passes the language test that the narrator sets for him on one of the days when he drops by to get the narrator to fill out some of the blanks in a legal form: "I was so intrigue by the legalistic document and still trying to trap-he and see if he know these terms only by learning them by heart or from hearing a real lawyer use them, that I type-in "*Plainclothes*" instead o' *Plaintiff*. He spot it quick quick. And I decide that he is a real brilliant lawyer" (210). What interests me most here is not so much what we learn about Joshua, but what we learn about one audience he plays to, what we learn about the currency in which "the boys" measure successful masculinity: high social circles, money, expensive tastes in wine and women, and sophisticated language.

It is particularly in the realm of language, though, that the irony I traced in the earlier story emerges again in this very different narrative structure. Where the first narrator claimed superiority over Joshua, this second one professes inferiority. And he does it on the level of language. On one of the afternoons when Joshua drops by with a form that needs filling out, the narrator says:

> [T]he big big document ... begin with "*Whereas*", and have in "*aforemention*" and "*In the Metropolitan Court of the County of York, in the Judicial District of.*" I see these important-looking legalistical terms, and my brain stop working ... I try reading the thing, but it didn't mek no sense to me, 'cause my brain can't take "*Whereases*" and "*Wherefores.*" (209, emphasis in original)

He claims to be convinced of Joshua's verity by his own inability to comprehend the lawyer's polysyllabic sophistication, but then he goes on to pepper his speech with accurate and witty uses of the very terminology his brain supposedly cannot take:

> So we stop worrying ourselves concerning the *status quo* of the fellow aforemention, and conclude that it was a *prima facie* case that nobody, from 1952 till 1986, could walk-'bout Toronto dress like a lawyer, walk like a lawyer, talk like a lawyer, married to a woman, have a child from the woman and for fifteen years living with the same woman, having parties, living in a' exclusive street, as a matter o' fact *next door to a judge* ... unless the judge wasn't no *real* judge! ... and be brave enough to pretend that he was a more *bona fides* honourable gentleman than the honourable gentleman next door! And that his own *bona fides* could be questioned and that it was not a case o' *quid pro quo*. (211, emphasis and ellipses in original)

In mixing the Latin legal phrases with the contractions and enjambments of rhythmic patois, the Wessindian narrator combines sweet and broad talk to great effect. He demonstrates a casual mastery of Joshua's supposedly exclusive discourse and, by doing so, questions the respectability of the discourse itself. The judgmental irony that had been neatly channelled toward Joshua alone in the first story shoots now in a number of directions. If anybody can manipulate the highfalutin legalese, then might not the judge be a fake too? What is the "good faith"—the *bona fides*—of being an "honourable gentleman"? If social subjectivities are a series of performances, is any good faith possible? What about the narrator himself who plays naïve, but isn't?

The multidirectional irony (Hutcheon, *Splitting* 60-1; Ball) takes in not only the governing system represented by the judge, but also the homosocial system represented by the "boys" who are so eagerly hoodwinked by Joshua's act and the educational system one product of which is a woman who has two Ph.D.s in Social Studies and Ethnic Cultures and is absolutely in the dark about her own marriage. Does this general eruption of ironies produce anything except negative ground, a hermeneutic crater? How can the reader sort through the multi-directionality of this irony?

Risking the intentional fallacies of a by-gone era of critical theory, and leaping over the many deaths of the author in a more recent one, I will appeal to the producer of Joshua's two performances for help. What are Clarke's purposes in these stories—at least as much as we can infer about them from the stories themselves and from their publication along with the other seven in the collection *Nine Men*? "These stories were written," writes Clarke in his bitter Introduction to the collection, "to destroy the definitions that *others* have used to portray so-called immigrants, black people" (6). Rather than letting others define this cultural community, he wants to discover a "black aesthetic" (6). But, he hastens to add: "I eschew my own term 'black aesthetic' if it suggests that *Nine Men Who Laughed* is a literature about black men" (6-7). Well, we have seen how Joshua's performance disorients definitions, not only undermining white stereotypes of under-class immigrant men, but also exposing the contradictions in capitalist culture's own self-definitions. And we have seen how this parodic subversion and exposure is produced when an immigrant man's per-formances of metropolitan masculinity are inflected by two pre-existent African traditions of male performativ-ity—the West Indian tradition of the man-of-words and the American tradition of the inner-city hustler. Thus, as

Clarke claims, the stories "A Man" and "How He Does It" do indeed constitute more than a literature about black men. Among other things, they constitute a literature about how the multicultural genealogy of a black man in white-dominated capitalist culture can bring trouble to that culture's founding values even as that man tries to adapt himself to them.

As I pointed out earlier, the two traditions of the man-of-words and the hustler each incorporate a tension between complicity with and rebellion against the status quo. Accordingly, Clarke does not claim heroic resistance for the African-descended characters in *Nine Men*. Instead, his attitude toward them comprises a tension between censure and sympathy that produces the "finely balanced ironies" that Brown says characterize the whole of Clarke's writings (*El Dorado* 7). On the one hand, Clarke provides this critique:

> When a character says, 'This fucking system' or 'This system makes me laugh' (out of frustration or, more realistically, because he has become lazy, too lazy to think clearly), he is not trying to reduce either the seriousness of the hurt inflicted upon him by the system or to make the system's racism less abrasive: he is confessing to his own inadequacy to take a strict moral position and destroy the system. All nine men laugh because they are, perhaps, already morally dead. (5)

This is heavy censure indeed, blaming the disenfranchised for not having the inner resources to rise up in protest, for not having the power to defeat the system that marginalizes them. On the other hand, Clarke speaks admiringly about his characters' abilities to develop performances that resist the dominant system. He writes:

> Improvisation is the single most essential quality [these West Indian men] would have used in the islands to ensure victory over a formerly oppressive system or to prevent their lives from being shortened by that system. Improvisation made sure that they did not accede to complete human degradation. (7)

The ability to improvise, he suggests, will enable them to resist degradation in Canada too. In the end, Clarke's attitude towards his characters remains a mixture of criticism and muted hope.

Clarke's assertion in this second passage returns us to Judith Butler's speculations about the value of performative subversions. In the ability to *improvise*, to "read" a new scene and produce a performance, the actor demonstrates the ability to exert a kind of agency *within* the set of social circumstances, the cultural scripts, that he or she is given. For, as Butler reminds us, we do not choose whether or not to repeat the gender roles our circumstances assign us. "The task," she asserts, "is not whether to repeat, but how to repeat or, indeed, to repeat and, through a radical proliferation of gender, *to displace* the very gender norms that enable the repetition itself" (*Gender*, 148). Clarke's two stories about Joshua demonstrate how the narrative of cross-cultural migration, which involves refraction between diverse codes and traditions for gendered behaviour, can produce the proliferation and displacement Butler proposes. For when Joshua "does" his version of metropolitan capitalist masculinity in Toronto, he brings elements of West Indian male performativity alloyed with elements of African American urban male performativity into his new performance and these "imported" elements cause his improvisation of metropolitan codes to bend into parody that exposes the incoherent partialities and provisionalities within those codes. This exposure occurs whatever Joshua's—and perhaps even Clarke's—intentions might have been, for it is the result of the way the migrant narrative's mixture of diverse cultural genealogies and traditions pits ideological elements within these codes against each other.

Joshua does not function as a guide to a new masculinity. Simultaneously a producer and a product of capitalist phallocentrism, he perpetuates the system of misogyny that founds his very livelihood. Austin Clarke's achievement, however, is to have shown, through Joshua's multiculturally refracted performance, through these two stories of cultural disruption in a migrant male's narrative, how seamed with contradictions the category of manhood is in the first place.

Endnotes

* This essay was originally published as Chapter One of *Masculine Migrations: Reading the Postcolonial Male in "New Canadian" Narratives* (University of Toronto Press, 1998).

1. In *El Dorado and Paradise,* Lloyd Brown organizes his study of Clarke's oeuvre around two myths that impinge upon the lives of Clarke's Barbadian characters: Caribbean as Paradise and Canada as El Dorado.

2. The scenario is identical in both stories, and so is the name—at least the "J.M.G.M.-C." of "A Man" matches the "Joshua Miller-Corbaine" of "How He Does It"—but other details do not match exactly. In the first story, Joshua is from Barbados, and, in the second, he's rumoured to be from Trinidad. And, in

the first, Trudeau is the Canadian prime minister, while, in the second, the present date is 1986, during the term of Prime Minister Brian Mulroney. Perhaps the time difference is an indication of how long Joshua manages to maintain his performance. And one could also speculate that the different places of origin indicate the indeterminacy of the gossip that surrounds Joshua, particularly in the second story.

3. For a comparison to Abrahams' study of performance folklore, see Graham Dann's sociological research on masculine behaviour in *The Barbadian Male: Sexual Attitudes and Practice*.

4. bell hooks distinguishes between 'patriarchy' and 'phallocentrism' by suggesting that the former refers to the system which assumes a man's masculinity resides in his ability to provide for and protect his family, while the latter refers to the system that believes his masculinity resides in the phallus, a belief that she argues was produced by a capitalism that needed workmen who could be separated easily from family relationships (*Black Looks* 89ff.).

5. Many commentators on the hustler express an ambivalence about his relation to the mainstream Protestant ethic. Richard Majors and Janet Mancini Billson put the following words in the hustler's mouth: "I hustle, white man, because it is something you hate, and it therefore defies the principles you are most proud of ... the Protestant work ethic" (88). But they also acknowledge Hudson's suggestion that, "[a]lthough the hustling ethic appears to be diametrically opposed to the Protestant ethic, it is really an outgrowth of it ... [I]n the final analysis this behaviour could be appropriately classified as

adaptive behaviour" (Hudson 424). Valentine, in her brilliantly titled *Hustling and Other Hard Work*, sees hustling as a black alternative route towards the American success dream (120). West Indian British critics Kobena Mercer and Isaac Julien maintain no such ambivalence: "The figure of the 'hustler' is often romantically depicted as a social outsider, whereas in fact this life-style involves an essential investment in the idea that a 'real' man must be an active and independent economic agent, an idea which forms the cornerstone of patriarchal capitalism and its ethic of 'success'" (114).

Works Cited

Abrahams, Roger. *The Man-of-Words in the West Indies: Performance and the Emergence of Creole Culture*. Baltimore: Johns Hopkins University Press, 1983.

Algoo-Baksh, Stella. *Austin C. Clarke: A Biography*. Toronto: ECW Press/Press of the University of the West Indies, 1994.

Ball, John C. "Postcolonialism and the Discourse of Satire." Paper delivered at the Canadian Association for Commonwealth Literature and Language Studies Conference. Carlton University, Ottawa, 31 May 1993.

Birbalsingh, Frank. "West Indians in Canada: The Toronto Novels of Austin Clarke." *Journal of Caribbean Studies* 5.1&2 (Fall 1985/Spring 1986): 71-77. Rptd. in Birbalsingh's *Passion and Exile: Essays in Caribbean Literature*. London: Hansib, 1988. 137-41.

Booth, Wayne. *A Rhetoric of Irony*. Chicago: University of Chicago Press, 1974.

Boxill, Anthony. "Austin C. Clarke." *Dictionary of Literary Biography* vol. 53. *Canadian Writers Since 1960*. 1st series. Ed. W.H. New. Detroit: Gale, 1986. 124-29.

Brown, Lloyd W. "Austin Clarke in Canadian Reviews." *Canadian Literature* 38 (Autumn 1968): 101-104.

____. *El Dorado and Paradise: Canada and the Caribbean in Austin Clarke's Fiction*. London, ON: Centre for Social and Humanistic Studies, University of Western Ontario/ Parkersburg, Iowa: Caribbean Books, 1989.

Butler, Judith. *Bodies That Matter: On the Discursive Limits of "Sex."* New York and London: Routledge, 1993.

____. *Gender Trouble: Feminism and the Subversion of Identity*. New York and London: Routledge, 1990.

Clarke, Austin. *Nine Men Who Laughed*. Markham: Penguin, 1986.

Connell, Robert W. *Gender and Power: Society, the Person and Sexual Politics*. Stanford: Stanford University Press, 1987.

Dann, Graham. *The Barbadian Male: Sexual Attitudes and Practice*. London and Basingstoke: Macmillan Caribbean, 1987.

De Lauretis, Teresa. "Eccentric Subjects: Feminist Theory and Historical Consciousness." *Feminist Studies* 16.1 (Spring 1990): 115-50.

Fanon, Frantz. *Black Skin, White Masks*. Trans. Charles Lam Markmann. 1967. London: Pluto Press, 1986. Translation of *Peau Noire, Masques Blancs*. Paris: Editions de Seuil, 1952.

Freud, Sigmund. *Jokes and Their Relation to the Unconscious*. Trans. James Strachey. New York: W.W. Norton, 1960.

Garber, Marjorie. *Vested Interests: Cross-Dressing and Cultural Anxiety*. New York: HarperPerennial, 1993.

Goddard, Horace. "The Immigrants' Pain: The Socio-Literary Context of Austin Clarke's Trilogy." *ACLALS Bulletin* 8 (1989): 39-57.

Henry, Keith S. "An Assessment of Austin Clarke, West Indian-Canadian Novelist." *College Language Association Journal* 29.1 (Sept 1985): 9-32.

hooks, bell. *Black Looks: Race and Representation*. Toronto: Between the Lines, 1992.

Hudson, Julius. "The Hustling Ethic." In *Rappin' and Stylin' Out*. Ed. T. Kochman. Urbana: University of Illinois Press, 1972. 410-24.

Hutcheon, Linda. *Splitting Images: Contemporary Canadian Ironies*. Toronto: Oxford University Press, 1991.

Majors, Richard, and Janet Mancini Billson. *Cool Pose: The Dilemmas of Black Manhood in America*. New York: Lexington Books, 1992.

Mercer, Kobena and Isaac Julien. "Race, Sexual Politics and Black Masculinity: A Dossier." In *Male Order: Unwrapping Masculinity*. Eds. Rowena Chapman and Jonathan Rutherford. London: Lawrence and Wishart, 1988. 97-164.

Ramraj, Victor. "Temporizing Laughter: The Later Stories of Austin Clarke." In *Short Fiction in the New Literatures in English*. Ed. Jacqueline Bardolph. Nice: Faculté des lettres et sciences humaines de Nice, 1989. 127-31.

Sanders, Leslie. "Austin Clarke." In *Profiles in Canadian Literature*. Ed. Jeffrey M. Heath. 4th ed. Toronto and Charlottetown: Dundurn Press, 1982. 93-100.

Silverman, Kaja. *Male Subjectivity at the Margins*. New York and London: Routledge, 1992.

Staples, Robert. *Black Masculinity: The Black Male's Role in American Society*. San Francisco: Black Scholar Press, 1982.

Valentine, Bettylou. *Hustling and Other Hard Work: Life Styles in the Ghetto*. New York: The Free Press, 1978.

"Voices Under the Window" of Representation: Austin Clarke's Poetics of (Body)-Memory in *The Meeting Point*[1]

MICHAEL A. BUCKNOR

Austin Clarke's reputation as the first major Caribbean/Canadian writer is well established.[2] For almost forty years of his publishing career, he produced over 20 publications (sixteen works of fiction, three memoirs, a collection of selected writings and one essay publication). His first novel, *The Survivors of the Crossing*, was published in 1964 and his latest work, *The Polished Hoe*, was published in 2002. Clarke has gained some recognition: one published book length study, one biography, an *Austin Clarke Reader*, several articles and numerous reviews. However, the history of early Clarke criticism exposes a critical enterprise limited to representationalist assumptions of mimeticism and aestheticism. A review of the critical reception of his 1967 *The Meeting Point* (hereafter referred to as *Meeting*), for example, shows that, generally, Clarke's work has been limited to readings addressing the authenticity of representation in it.[3] The novel is consistently commended for Clarke's use of language and generally criticized for its weak plot, while there is disagreement among critics regarding the success of his realism. *Meeting* is a useful focus in this paper because it is one of the earliest Caribbean/Canadian attempts to figure Canada as a point of cross-cultural contact and also because it demonstrates the tendency in early Clarke criticism to treat Caribbean/Canadian writing primarily in terms of represented content. These readings are often legitimized by assumptions of mimeticism or organicism. In this regard, *Meeting* is viewed as a novel of excess in which distortions of the real or disruptions of order are dismissed as aesthetic flaws. Consequently, very little attention has been given to Clarke's semiological refractions or to the fact that "represented content" that is treated as history is a function of memory. My intention in this paper, then, is to propose a reading strategy centred on a poetics of (body)-memory[4] as an alternative to early Clarke criticism predicated on either representations of the real or of harmonious design.

In my reading, Clarke's self-conscious attention to memory as filter of experience in *Meeting* allows us to investigate the significance of memory to diasporic writings. The novel presents the experiences of a Barbadian immigrant, Bernice, who comes to Canada as a domestic helper to work for the Jewish-Canadian Burrmann family. The story develops around the complications that arise when her sister joins her for a visit. In short, the usual diasporic themes of cultural displacement, adjustments to a new culture and the presence of hegemonies of race, class and culture are evident. Although the story is ostensibly told by an omniscient narrator, Bernice's voice and memories dominate, thereby displacing the authoritative narrative perspective. Both temporality and linearity are disrupted and a cycle of repetition is initiated by the characters' constant reveries. By performing the past, Clarke upsets the easy equation of narrative writing with historical reality, and commands a reading that accentuates what I call a body-memory poetics. As I will show, reading body-memory as a determinant of Clarke's composition explains certain aporias that compromise realist representational readings. Instead of reading through the "window" of mimetic representation or through the lens of organicism, I offer the "broken glass" of memory which highlights memory as trace: incomplete, translative and provisional (Rushdie 15, 12).

Because of the dominance of mimeticism, memory in diasporic writings has often been dismissed as mere nostalgia. In his discussion of Caribbean/British writing in *Writers in Exile: The Identity of Home in Modern Fiction*, Andrew Gurr, for example, comes to the conclusion that "[t]he creation of a human identity through the re-creation of home is anything but a sentimental act" (26). He weaves his way to this conclusion via some very convoluted manoeuvres. First, by positioning the British metropolis as the centre and places like the "static," "small," and "confined" communities of Caribbean countries as the margin, he establishes a one-way flow of influences in the cross-cultural expression of exiled writers (7-8). Second, working from his first assumption, he claims that writers from the margins, seduced by the "artistic freedom" of the centre, need to "compensate for [their] sense of cultural subservience" (7-8). Third, he argues that, following their desire to win a superior foreign audience, exiled writers tend to privilege mimetic representation as a way of reproducing "exact descriptions" of their past (14-15). Thus, the writers' "minutiae" of description or "explicitness of prose" is a sentimental act of compensation for lost "home" or a means of locating themselves (15, 19).

This realist representational reading is necessary for Gurr's hegemonic ideology that seeks to promote the British metropolis as centre of creative expression and home to modern writing. If these writers are ashamed of their past, as Gurr claims, why would they want to foreground that past in writing after finding "artistic freedom" in the metropolis? And why would the re-creation of a "backward," "inferior," culture satisfy the literary tastes of a superior culture? Made anxious by "third world" infiltration of "first world" literary camps, Gurr can only accept the success of these exiled writers by claiming an international/cosmopolitan identity that marginalizes the home cultures of diasporic writers. Unable to deal with the celebration of the "margin" by "exiled" writers, Gurr discounts memory by his patronizing and patriarchal label—"sentimental."[5] By valorizing mimetic readings and by impeaching memory as mere nostalgia, Gurr promotes his hegemonic ideals of British superiority.

Similarly, from reviewers of Clarke's *Meeting* to Lloyd Brown, in his pioneering work, *El Dorado and Paradise: Canada and the Caribbean in Austin Clarke's Fiction*, most critics were committed to mimeticist or organicist readings in service of varying hidden ideologies. Consequently, disagreement over the text's realism was inevitable given people's differing value systems/ideological preferences. In one breath, for example, Ulric Rice commends Clarke's realism when he states that the "the book is readable and the story does reflect aspects of life with which an immigrant domestic might have to cope in a big foreign country" (8). However, in the next (breath), he points out gaps in Clarke's representation of certain scenes and objects to the detailed attention to excrement and swearing. So while Rice values the text for its representational success, he is uncomfortable when it becomes too realistic in the presentation of the abject. This matter of excess in representation surfaces also in Keith S. Henry's article, "An Assessment of Austin Clarke, West Indian-Canadian Novelist," when he argues that: "*The Meeting Point*, although by no means a failure, is not Austin Clarke in the fullness of his powers. It is perhaps **too** unrelievedly distressing, **too much** a social document, **too much** in harness to political and social fact" (my emphasis, 23). His personal and/or his ideological taste is masked under the critical rhetoric of a representational reading. Without questioning the matter of representation in itself, Lloyd Brown has pointed to the critical mask of some reviewers such as Miriam Waddington who hold views similar to those of Henry and Rice ("Austin Clarke in Canadian Reviews"). Ironically, the detailed representation of the abject would be quite normal for one branch of realist portrayal known as naturalism.[6] It is surprising then that Rice characterizes this kind of representation of Clarke's work as "heavy-handed muck raking"(8). From Rice's evaluation it is clear that moral concerns are surfacing within his carefully promoted aesthetic criteria.

Stan Fefferman, by contrast, praises Clarke's "tough moral stand," but dismisses the protagonist's vision as necessarily "distorted" because Bernice views Canada from the perspective of "her character and background" (22). Clarke's realism is therefore compromised by "stereotypical" perceptions of white society that produce flat characters. Miriam Waddington has a similar view of Bernice. In her review, she claims that "Bernice's character remains static throughout the story. [...] She remains, to the end, a fragmented personality, emotionally shallow, volcanic and childish in all her relationships" ("No Meeting Points" 77). Although Lloyd Brown is critical of the lack of "solidity" in Bernice's character, he posits an opposite view to Fefferman's and Waddington's when he acknowledges that Bernice changes constantly throughout the story. For him, Bernice "remains Protean to the end, constantly changing and wavering, discarding and assuming one posture or judgement after another" (*El Dorado* 71). All three critics, however, are frustrated by the disjunction between Clarke's portrayal of Bernice and their expectations of realistic representation. These critiques, using "representation" as the cornerstone of aesthetic judgement, unwittingly expose mimeticism as a façade for ideology and raise the problems of epistemological certainty, verbal transparency and language adequacy.[7]

These reviewers, in their specific ideological readings of Clarke's "representation," reveal that neither Clarke's narrative nor their critical responses issue from "unmediated" reality. Edward Said and Homi Bhabha in the late 1970s and early 1980s, respectively, draw attention to the way in which literary criticism via certain privileged readings (including representationalist ones) ignore the "constructedness" of literary discourse. Discussing the dispute over representation between colonialist and post-colonialist critics, Bhabha identifies the non-recognition of "writing as a signifying system" as the crucial problem ("Representation and the Colonial Text" 98). This "process which conceives of meaning as a system of production within determinate institutions and systems of representation—ideological, historical, aesthetic, political" is elided so that the critics' own ideological and historical production of meaning is masked (Bhabha 98-99). It is important that, as Edward Said argues, "the critic of texts [...] investigat[e] the system of discourse by which the 'world' is divided, administered, plundered, by which humanity is thrust into pigeonholes" ("Interview" 41). A more self-conscious approach on the part of the two critics might reveal their own historically produced readings of Clarke, mired in moralism (Rice) and scepticism regarding the alien, black, Caribbean woman's ability to judge the "white world" (Fefferman).[8]

The self-consciousness these reviewers lack is the very attribute that weakens Clarke's realistic representation, according to Andrew Salkey (Clarke's friend and fellow Caribbean writer). In Salkey's vision of naturalism (another word for realism), Clarke's *Meeting* is compromised by self-reflexive political observations:

> Some of the political insertions, although extremely telling, seem too awarely introduced and may have been made valid in fictional terms had they been the root and rhythm of the natural design of the novel. (3)

The problematic of representation for Salkey is connected to his ideology of art-in-service-of-nationalism. His nationalist frame privileges realistic art that re-presents "authentic images" in an aesthetically harmonious structure. Clarke's self-reflexivity, which calls attention to his own role in the construction of reality, helps to dismantle Salkey's "natural design." Therefore, Clarke reveals that the represented world is not "independent of the means of its representation" (Bhabha, "Representation" 104).[9] Salkey's desire for aesthetic harmony in the representation of a "pre-given reality" exposes representationalist criticism as that which "represses the ideological and discursive construction" in literary production (Bhabha, "Representation" 105). Moreover, Salkey's reading, limited to mimeticism and New Critical organicism,[10] ignores the possibility that meta-discourse might be part of Clarke's artistry.

As much as Lloyd Brown's seminal work, *El Dorado and Paradise*, represents an important shift in the criticism, Brown also remains committed to aestheticism primarily defined through organicism. Instead of restricting Clarke's works to "sociological tracts" as other critics have done, Brown echoes the "well-wrought urn" school, proposing that one should spend more time examining the works as "expressive design, as experience molded by the artist's shaping" (*El Dorado* xiv).[11] However, Brown reduces Clarke's oeuvre to an overarching design of binaries in which discrepancies, paradoxes and tensions are re-negotiated into ironic reversals and dualities. He locates narrative centres, identifies constancy and progression of plot and establishes a balanced structure in Clarke's works (*El Dorado* 69). Offering a kind of formalist reading, Brown views textual surfaces (characters, images, plot situations) as symbolic of deep-structure ambiguities. With this assumption of a "structurality of structure," according to Jacques Derrida, "one cannot in fact conceive of an unorganized structure" ("Structure" 278).[12] Brown's expectation of smooth plot lines, detailed characterization and thematic symmetry is foiled by Clarke's uneven narrative.

Like other critics before him,[13] Brown is unable to make any critical response to an interruptive practice and so he dismisses what does not fit his expectations as examples of failed artistry and poor representation. He replaces the transparent window of mimetic representation with the reflective mirror of expressive and symbolic representation.[14] In Brown's symbolic critique, Clarke's design is a mirror image of Brown's thematic focus—ambiguity. By limiting himself to assumptions of representation and harmony, Brown avoids confronting both the theme of the inadequacy of language to represent life and the shattering shards of Clarke's aesthetics of disruption. Therefore, that which escapes language is unaccounted for, the materiality of language beyond semantic meaning is lost and the many textual gaps create critical blind spots for him. With expectations of language sufficiency and aesthetic harmony, such readings of representation run the risk of ignoring significant aspects of Caribbean/Canadian writing and marking such texts like *Meeting* as novels of excess.

To make more critical gains of Clarke's interruptive, disorderly text of excess, I am proposing a reading based on what I have been calling body-memory poetics as outlined in an essay on (Jamaican-Canadian) Lillian Allen's dub poetry.[15] A summary of those critical assumptions will help to point out how this kind of reading might be performed on Clarke's text. In taking off from Pamela Banting's translation poetics as outlined in her book *Body, Inc*, body-memory poetics attempts to re-conceive representation not in terms of equivalence or parallelism but in terms of transformation. Since language (as both a linguistic and literary code) is the primary form in which these literary representations take place, emphasis is shifted from represented content to compositional process. Clarke's content is always being mediated by the expressive resources available to him, by his memory and by his imagination. The work by feminists, in particular, has helped to spotlight attention on the human body as a material and discursive site for understanding how cultural history is recorded. Rather than discounting Clarke's memories and versions of history by way of the mirrors of mimeticism, body-memory poetics recuperates memories in their distorted and disharmonious manifestations as significant to our understanding of writing in the diaspora.

My understanding of how the body remembers seems instructive about processes of recording the past. If culture needs material embodiment to locate itself, then the human body is one useful site to understand the process of historical encoding. Furthermore, since human bodies, as neuro-scientists, ethnographers and sociologists have posited, can record their own histories, attention might fruitfully be given to the meta-dimension of material sites. What does the body record and reveal about its own history? How might a focus on material (textual) self-reflexivity provide insights about writing in the diaspora? Could our understanding of the processes of memory recordings and retrieval in the body illuminate our understanding of memory recordings in other material sites like texts? These are the questions that led me to use the model of body-memory operations to examine literary texts as sites of cultural deposits, (even as I recognized that these are very different material sites). A poetics of memory, in my view, is one that attends to the way in which the body processes memory. According to a variety of theorists, the body is an overdetermined field that "stores" histories, merges a complex system of signs and retrieves deposits of cultural memory. And it is the body's ability to store, process and retrieve historical information that alerts us to the body's extra-translative dimension. More than a mere site for the translation of other matter (like language, discourse) into bodily matter, the body has the capacity to reorganize itself to accommodate alien matter. That process of re-composition involves unexpected interruptive re-call, disruptive code-switching and repetitive retrieval. On each level of Clarke's narrative, linguistic and social coding, his aesthetic form exposes the re-compositional process of body-memory. Body-memory, which by nature is dynamic, translative, repetitive and random in its occurrences, provides a way of accounting for Austin Clarke's disruptive and performative creative composition.

My proposal of an alternative reading strategy rooted in theories of body-memory is supported by Clarke's own admissions about incorporating his memories in his work and by the subtle interweave of biography and fiction in his corpus. In responding to Marion Richmond's questions about his bi-national identity, Clarke makes this confession: "[Although] I am a Canadian citizen ... the best of me is Barbadian; the best of my memories are Barbadian" (*Other Solitudes* 69).[16] While Clarke is quite uneasy about the conflation of his life with his art,[17] he admits that his boyhood memories have been used in his stories: "But you see I feel that a writer has very little material that is not primarily in its source, that is to say in his own life" (Craig 116). Clarke's thinly veiled autobiographies—*Growing Up Stupid Under the Union Jack*, called a memoir and the political thriller, *The Prime Minister*, his fictional account of his actual return to Barbados—would seem to validate his admission. Beyond these two life-based accounts, most of Clarke's fiction seems to re-circulate incidents, scenes and even conversations (most of which are found in his memoir) from one fictional text to another. Clarke's "auto-intertextuality,"[18] especially between memoir and fiction, establishes him as a writer who often crosses the border between autobiography and artifice, history and fiction. My interest in Clarke's use of memory is not concerned with the content analysis of representational criticism in order to match character and author, creative construct and life; instead, I am interested in the ways in which Clarke's cultural memory becomes a resource for his creative expression.

On the most basic level, Clarke's own memories help to construct the fictional memories of his Barbadian and other characters and to explore the nature of memory itself. Many of Clarke's characters are constantly remembering the past; their memories are triggered by a "shell of referents" (Rose 34). In one such recall, Sam experiences nausea produced by something like a "badly digested apple"; the memory of vomiting on the day he participated in his friend's wrongful apprehension is registered in his stomach (107). In another recall, Bernice "experience[s] a sensation similar to strangulation" when she sees the reflection of light on the snow, a warning that snow is about to fall (37). The twinkling light not only evokes a body-memory but it reminds her of the song "Twinkle, twinkle, little star" learnt as a child (37). Later, her sister remembers this song on a starry night (185). Whether, it is the sound of bells (222-23) or a flash of images (14), memory is presented as sensory recall. Clarke also indicates the nature of memory through imagery. The images of fingers, kisses or smells (37, 216) reinforce the visceral nature of some memories while a flash of pictures (14) represents memory as incomplete and random in its occurrences. Clarke reinforces the idea that the body is a record of history and memory when Bernice tries to cosmetically erase signs of her racial history from her skin by using complexion-lighteners (33). Clarke's story is not just about what people remember nor just about the nature of memory itself; it is about the process of preserving memory in the re-composition of the past.

Clarke's thematization of memory invites us to peer beyond the plane glass of mimetic representation. The significance of body-memory as theme is highlighted by the narrative arrangement; *Meeting* is interrupted by memory sequences (dreams and reveries included) framed by brackets, italics, ellipses and quotation marks. Punctuation and typographical idiosyncrasies are perhaps as significant to a full reading as words on the page. According to Clarke, in an interview with Terrence Craig, "sometimes [...] content is less important than the way the words are put together" (121). He recognizes, like bell hooks, that "we may learn from the spaces of silence as well as spaces of speech" (hooks 300) and so shifts our attention from firm semantic terrain to strategies of punctuation at the textual margins. Bracketed, italicized, quote-designated asides draw attention to the inner speech of body-memory and Clarke's attempt to translate the bodily encoded into a scribal code. By making body-memory the dominant screen of experience, Clarke acknowledges the validity of material existence that resists representation. Furthermore, by way of his non-verbal marks, Clarke tries to translate the body of experience stored in memory and recovers voices usually excluded from official discourse.

The bracketed sections of this novel often contain musings, day-dreams, memories, thoughts which remain

buried in the body, a realm of private language, normally
excluded in public discourse. By Clarke's inclusions, we
are encouraged to take note of these gaps in our reading
and to notice the slippages in language. Both Bernice's
"real" opinion of Mrs. Burrmann's "'priceless, absolutely
priceless' candelabra" and Mrs. Burrmann's actual valua-
tion of the art object are enclosed in brackets: "(Those
thieving bastards down there in Yorkville Village, selling
a lot o' junk for art! But she had bought it for seventy-five
dollars; and insisted in company that it was a bargain)"
(8). The way in which these asides are inserted into
the narrator's description of Mrs. Burrmann's round
table display, alerts us to the untrustworthiness of the
picture-perfect scenario. Similarly, the ability of Dots
and Bernice to enter into the consumer economy does
not bring their wider social acceptance; they could purchase swim-wear but they did not feel welcome at the
"community pool," as Dots' bracketed reflection reveals:
"('Where I would wear this thing, eh, gal? In the backyard in the summer? 'Cause I have never seen one Negro
person in any o' these swimming pools they have all over
this city!')" (21). Much like Henry's bank book with the
large number of unofficial zeros, the official document
can be very misleading.[19] We are warned by the narrator
of this unreliability in authoritative stories when Agatha's
account of her relationship with Henry is qualified by the
aside: "That was Agatha's story, as she told it (in parts,
and in part)" (190). The partial (pun intended) nature
of all stories is highlighted here and throughout the text.
The exclusive focus on words by critics committed to
analysis of mimetic or expressive representation denies
any appreciation of the disruptions by which Clarke
de-constructs his narrative and linguistic edifices. Cracks

created in the story by his bracketed insertions expose the inadequacy of his "official narrative" and call attention to meaning beyond words. By bracketing body-memories, Clarke bares the inadequacy of the verbal enterprise and points to the possibility that the body contains an alternative account of history.

Like parentheses, italics announce an alternative code for translating silence. Bernice's transgressive thoughts about "whitemailing" Mrs. Burrmann are only publicly expressed through her body signs, her hand-clapping and her laughter. Privately, her devices of deceit are marked by the italics; she plans to use her knowledge of Mrs. Burrmann's illicit behaviour to extort money from her employer:

> An idle word *would make Mr. Burrmann's tear loose in this woman's backside, if he is a man in truth. Lord, a idle word on my behalf could do a lot o' harm in this household! and look how I have the balance of power in my hand!* Her power cascaded into laughter. (7)

Bernice's ability to withhold her words gives her power. To wield this power, however, she would have to enter the commercial economy and force Mrs. Burrmann to buy her silence. Power resides not only in the use of language but also in its withholding. When Clarke translates Bernice's "speechlessness" on another occasion, he marks the translation with italics and indicates that silence does not mean assent. In this case, Bernice's silence is an alternative interpretation of the lighting of black candles. When Mrs. Burrmann, in preparing for a special dinner party, sets up four lighted red candles and a black one, two possibilities surface in Bernice's mind—that the "black candle" is a subliminal reference to her or that, as viewed in her culture, it indicates involvement in obeah (8). Her race and history influence her reading of the candles. For Bernice, a black candle is not normally associated with decoration. In this case, it is a sign of Bernice's cultural (mis)reading and her disagreement with accepted interpretations. Similarly, Mrs. Burrmann reads Bernice's smiles as compliance, while, "behind the smiling face, Bernice was abusing her in her mind" (13). Transgressive intentions, strong disagreement and abusive anger are contained in her body and the italics register the memory of those bodily encodings. Clarke demonstrates through his alternative coding of experience by way of the italics that some realities escape public language and, with the slippages with language, we need to read in between the gaps. Nevertheless, Clarke is also exploiting language as a sign system via the typographical possibilities in order to represent the limits of representation.

A history of deep-seated hurts or feelings tends to remain buried in the flesh and these emotions may not be easily transferred into public expression as Clarke indicates with respect to Mr. Burrmann. Typographical disruptions in the form of italics force one to notice the disjunction between public show as recorded in the normal script of the narrator and the italicized private thought:

> As he embraced, and kissed her, he thought: *goddamn, look what I picked up off the street! look at me, Sam Burrmann, screwing about with this big black nig— Negro woman, goddammit, but baby, you 're barking up the wrong tree.* (187)

None of Burrmann's public acts, neither the kiss, the embrace, nor the public declaration of love express the full story. Furthermore, his strange linguistic eruptions indicate the difficulty of putting the deep, body-sensations into words. His respectable language becomes irreverent and racy and even a little Afro-American jive (presumably picked up from his former Black-Canadian friends) seeps into his unsaid-speech. Spiced with "god-damn" and "baby," his memory recaptures his submerged feelings of ambivalence towards blacks that now inform his present. Later, as his body remembers his sexual excitement, those remembered pleasures translate into a more compassionate discourse. The language disruptions announced through the type face draw attention to the traces of body-memory translated in words, even as it marks a site of excess—the realm of material existence which remains outside the narrator's discourse.

Italics also mark memories of conversations, past experiences in Barbados and occasions of remembering. As well, they locate the private world of Bernice's past that is bracketed and made marginal by her present circum-stances. However, by their constant intrusions into her daily life, the marginal world of body-memory is recovered. The present, it seems, is always invested with fragments of the past. As the narrator describes Bernice's action in the present the narration merges with her memory and the break between time sequences is signalled by italics and the narrator's cue that "all these things come back to her" (22). The writer publishes her private conversations and letters that are composed, revised and erased all in the mind. Clarke's attention to multiple texts, various versions, and the processes of composition underlines how history as a function of memory is a matter of reconstructing traces. By showing how memory filters experience, Clarke indi-cates that like the past that is encoded partially in memory, our material experiences are never fully reported. Clarke's attempt to recover "submerged histories" is embroiled in the question of language-inadequacy. As Pamela Banting argues, because of the body's materiality, it is never fully co-opted in language (*Body, Inc* 202). Body-memory is in excess of all its translations. Bernice's memories, though triggered by Lonnie's letter, remain sometimes in her body's imaginative hold and we are forced to recognize the italicized sections as translations of her mind/body recall.

Not only does Clarke use brackets and italics to trace the zone of the unsaid, ellipses also expose the gaps within the text not as failed representations but as translations. Thus, a lack of success in attaining full equivalence, total containment, and faithful rendition of experience in language is laid bare in the empty spaces. Memory as narrative frame in this novel exposes the fractures of infidelity in verbal representation and this is reinforced when the memory is lodged in a dream sequence. Dreams by their very nature are already made available through variant memory codes: colours, outlines, shades, sounds, images, flashes of insight. For a person to narrate her/his dreams, s/he has to transcribe them into signification, enter them into speech or written language. Since written language is radically different from the dream code, it cannot fully capture the shades, flashes and flushes of sensation that the dream body produces. Something is always lost in the translation. As Mrs. Burrmann tries to retrieve that bodily experience, only traces are available:

> "Now, let's see ... this little boy, now that I think of it ... I can't for anything remember who he looked like ... but this little boy, with a big head ... I remember

> that ... and big eyes ... you know that little boy across
> the street ... Mrs Gasstein's ... what's his name ... ?
> anyways, that little bastard wanted to make love to
> me ...! ha-hah ..." (26)

The gaps and the repetition of the sign of "the little
boy" help to compensate for the loss of full recall. Apart
from the purpose of narrative foreshadowing and its
psychoanalytic implications, this dream in its narrative
form underscores the elliptical nature of language. Read
as a poetics of body-memory, which emphasises trace and
translation, these episodes undermine notions of faithful representation. Attempts to finalize meaning easily,
without acknowledging that language is not only refer-
ential but also a material presence, are frustrated. This
frustration is also Mrs. Burrmann's who fails not just to
recall the dream but also to register experiences which are
bodily encoded. Her need to translate reinforces that the
reading of the dream has to be provisional, uncertain and
open to revision.

Another example of the inadequate containment
within sign-systems is shown through the ellipses associated with Bernice's intuitions about her sister getting
pregnant: "'The more I think 'bout it, the more I feel
sure that my sister may get herself in the family-way,
sometime ....'" (191). These fractures in the body of
the text draw attention to the ellipses themselves as
invested with meaning. As Bhabha argues, a reading of
liminal spaces is implicated in "hybrid," diasporic or,
international literatures. Notice how Mrs. Burrmann
communicates with Estelle through the space of pause
and suspension:

> Mrs. Burrmann was watching her closely, peering at her through the crystal glass. "You see, my husband works very hard, many times late at night ..."
>
> "Yes, ma'am." "... and that is why I spend so much time by myself, alone." She paused. Estelle could see she was staring at her, through her glass. It was the pause that got Estelle completely mixed up. (204)

While on the surface, Mrs Burrmann's attitude and language seem quite friendly, she is able to communicate subliminally through silence and pause something sinister and disturbing. Without mentioning a word about the affair between Estelle and her husband she discloses her suspicions. Meanings are not only coded in words, but also in the spaces (ellipses) between words.

Clarke's elliptical structure undercuts the pure, undefiled, self-sufficient narrative of "truth" and "realism." By showing gaps in memory, he calls attention to representation as a system of codes and discourses in the production of meaning.[20] The gaps invite each reader to be sensitive to code switching and to engage in the provisional process of translation. Ellipses act as signals of his narrative shifts, movements from past to present, from narrative perspective to character viewpoint, from private to public space and from one sign system to another. As both narrative break and narrative bridge, ellipses hold the story in suspension, marking hesitance, pause and reflection. In effect, they are signals of interruption into a smooth narrative flow as indicated when Bernice's reverie about the music breaks off into a comment to Mrs. Burrmann: "Man, this is music to make you want to dance and jump up and throw your dress over your head ... 'That is a very nice tune you playing, ma'am'" (24).

By creating linguistic bridges that break, these paginal gaps expose the variety of codes at work in the story and encourage us not to rely on any one sign system.

Beyond demonstrating memory as interruption and interference (translation), Austin Clarke presents memory as re-articulation by his persistent staging of performances. By using the Caribbean cultural tradition of performance, Clarke foregrounds the context of each re-telling of the past, each narrator's history in that re-telling and the need for each reader to read within and beyond the codes that articulate the past. Memory is not the retrieval of a "fixed" past but a revision of history cuddled in language, what Steven Rose calls "transmuted re-creations" (307). Lloyd Brown correctly identifies the performative element in Clarke's work, but his emphasis on adequate representation rather than partial translation compromises his insight. Brown acknowledges that, "Clarke's facility with his dialect forms is rooted in a strong self-consciousness about language and style" (*El Dorado* 152). As such, Clarke's self-conscious (he)artistry stages both life in performance and performance in life. Doubly-inscribed, the meta-fictional element stages the "distinctively self-conscious sense of artistry that is so intrinsic to a Caribbean sense of style" (*El Dorado* 156). However, in his book, Brown limits this strategy to **representations** of Caribbean "showiness" or **expressions** of ambiguity, instead of reading this double-emphasis on self-reflexivity as evidence of the "rhythm of memory and imagination" typical of Caribbean works, as Brown does in a previous article (my emphasis "Making Style" 138).[21] As a surplus element over and above mimetic representation or aesthetic harmony, Clarke's performative poetics, already seen by Brown as "clues to [...]

individual perception and cultural traditions," is now viewed as artistic "lapses" (*El Dorado* 154, 157). Thus, when Brown criticizes Clarke's language as "too aware of itself" and condemns Clarke's style as melodramatic, he fails to credit "verbal straining" and "lack of control" as evidences of bodies-in-translation and a poetics of cultural memory (*El Dorado* 152-185).

From rum-talk to church-testimony, gossip to storytelling, from occasions of exhibition to scenes of reading, Clarke uses the Caribbean performance tradition to present memory as a re-coding of the distant and recent past. He therefore alerts us to the various discourses invested in the contexts that produce memories and to the meta-discursive nature of memory itself. At the end of Part 2, Clarke begins a new section with what resembles stage directions, giving the positions of characters, describing the setting and indicating lighting; the framing for dialogue then follows. Through this notation, he initiates us into the realm of the dramatic and convenes an important occasion for remembering. By the additional overlay of a frieze-like, photographic framing, Clarke engages with generic "bungling" and multiplies the variety of codes at work in this novel. By marking this episode as drama, Clarke exposes performance as always contextual and cautions against seeing a one-to-one relationship between representation and reality. When the episode is read as a dramatic text or photographic montage, one recognizes how much has been lost in the translation of "reality". Moreover, read in the light of the tradition of the Caribbean performative, this episode reveals that the occasion may be more important for the exhibition of verbal dexterity than for offering faithful representation.

The transplanted Caribbean wake held in Bernice's upstairs apartment in honour of her mother's passing is a good example of the Caribbean performance tradition. According to Roger D. Abrahams, in *The Man of Words in the West Indies: Performance and the Emergence of Creole Culture*, the traditional wake is a perfect occasion for "impromptu" performances (xvi), story-telling which includes "Nansi 'tory, nas'y 'tory and nonsen 'tory" (157),[22] "competitive speechmaking," "occasional arguments" (xvi) and for discussions of "the interpenetration of life and death" (180). However, this wake is redefined by the Canadian context. In Canada, the collection of a few friends in an upstairs apartment of a house replaces the usually large community gathering in the yard. The only music comes from strains of the "Fourth Movement from Beethoven's Sixth Symphony" (171) and all the stories about life and death are overshadowed by the discourses of economics and race. Performance of the wake ritual reveals how cultural codes are partially retained and revised by a new environment and context.

Part of the Caribbean performance culture that is retained is the verbal exuberance of story-telling and competitive debates at wakes. Dots' accounts are rich in verbal virtuosity; her tales of warnings and exhortations are spiced with the rhetorical tools of exaggeration, repetition, invective, metaphoric language, onomatopoeia, dramatic expression, and biblical allusion. On such occasions, Abrahams observes, the "[person]-of-words [...] is capable of turning any conversation into a show" (xvi). The story of Lottie's sudden death is suitable for Dots' verbal display:

> You remember when the news 'o Lottie's death hit us, as we was relaxing in Dr. Hunter' basement, drinking two beers? You remember when the news 'o Lottie's death came, it came in such a manner and fashion, that I had to open my mouth wide and say, "Jesus Christ! It isn't, couldn't be true. Lottie not dead." (171)

She continues:

> I couldn't believe it was the same Lottie who I had rested my eyes on that morning, walking 'cross Sherbourne Street going up Bloor Street, Jesus God, not the same Lottie, flourishing at ten o'clock and cut down at ten-past-ten, the same day. Not the same Lottie? But death came, and bram! it take Lottie with it. That is death, Boysie. If you have ears to hear, and if that brandy hasn't start doing something to your hearing and vision, that is what I want you to know concerning death. (171)

Here, Dots begins with repetition as the dominant code-repetition of phrases, words (redundancy) and tense forms that end with a dramatic disclaimer couched in a curse. The full text then builds on the biblical allusions that carry the heavy weight of funeral readings shadowed finally by the book of "Revelation." The past is retrieved for a present day lesson to her husband about being careful on the road. For Clarke, these kinds of performances allow him to participate in the ritual of rehearsing his Caribbean verbal patterns.

Body-memory as re-articulation is reinforced by other examples of storytelling. Bernice's account of Mrs. Burrmann's unfair demands on the day of the airport pick-up reveals the way in which the past can be manipulated as a way of impressing her friends. Described as a "psych-iatry of lies" (49), her story, when compared with the previously reported version (13), exposes Bernice's distortions. By embellishing the story, she presents herself as a no-nonsense helper. Boysie's recognition of Bernice's exaggeration prompts him to tell a story of people who use their marginal-immigrant status to their advantage:

> "[A] German friend 'o mine tell me that the Europeans is bigger liars than anybody else when they come over here. He says everyone 'o them does say they was counts or kings back in Europe. Nobody don't be no plain, simple immigrant, no more." (49)

The time of tall-tales leads to a jostling among the audience for even more stories that prove the teller's verbal skill. Much like Dots' verbal display, at the wake that engages Boysie in debate, these speech competitions alert us to the codes of Caribbean performance rituals. This "text" is not reduced to its content; the rhythm of emotion in its ability to stir the audience is equally important. The dramatic code of performances can be witnessed in other stories like Clotelle's financial misfortunes (126-27), the deportation of the pregnant Jamaican domestic helper (149) and the humorous tale of the children's search for Bernice's tail beneath her underclothes (61). All stories are imbued not only with the performance codes, but with the discourses of race, gender, money and power as well. Clotelle's economic vulnerability eases her into the stranglehold of commercial conspiracy, the Jamaican woman's limited power facilitates her punishment for the crime of the privileged white male employer, and Bernice suffers indignity at the hands of innocent children corrupted by racism. The emphasis on story-telling as performance reminds us how the performance of body-memory is also about re-contextualization.

The conventional wake-setting, like most performative spaces for the display of "verbal dexterity" (Abrahams xv), is also a theatre in which subversive ideology can surface. In Dots' memories, the discourses of economics and race that affect the Caribbean/Canadian are exposed. Dots is doubly depressed by the death because of economic factors: "It hit me hard hard because I know Bernice here, poor soul, now packing and spending money 'pon plane ticket, when she should be banking that same money 'gainst a rainy day" (171). Similarly, Bernice is initially concerned with money when she is relieved by the news that her Mammy is still alive: "Christalmighty! and I would have gone down there by plane, and would have had to pay back every cent of that money for the plane ticket ..." (178). Also, as Dots reflects on death, the stories she remembers (Lottie's death, the accident between a black and a white driver) are about the vulnerability of the black Caribbean immigrant. Lottie's accident, with the apparent lack of concern shown by passersby, becomes the occasion for recalling the racist response of the police who, with the complicity of the onlookers and white motorist, wrongfully accuse a black driver. Dots uses these stories as a warning to her husband: "Careful, Boysie, this country ain't your country. And the police, the white people and the papers reminds you it is not your place of birth nor belonging, neither" (173).

We recognise that the context of wake-stories is over-determined by grief, performance, ideological discourses all held in body-memory. Thus, Dots' accounts are not mimetic "representations" of reality but translations burdened by her body-memories. Nonetheless, this re-articulation does not exclude the political implications of her story nor its validity. Her versions circulate with other accounts of the selective treatment of black immigrants by the police and their supportive nationalist discourse of belonging and non-belonging trumpeted by the media and official policy. By calling attention to performance codes, Clarke acknowledges that the racist/economic situation can only be viewed from specific contexts, and, in this case these discourses are filtered through Caribbean/Canadian bodies. Other Caribbean modes that allow for the revival of a body-memory as performance are cross-roads gossip, rum-shop gab and church testimony. Gossip provides another opportunity for exhibiting one's performance skills through the dramatic recall of life-stories and the re-tailing/telling of other people's business. Re-convened in the basement of a church, the "carry-go-bring-come" exchange of information and sharing of suffering creates a comfort zone for Caribbean/Canadian domestics to express themselves freely. It also facilitates an open forum for women's protest and support. Through the tangle of tongues, a Caribbean community is invoked, investing the Canadian context with new social codes.

Similarly, rum-bar talk erects a space of irreverence and exaggeration for the performance of Caribbean macho-masculinities. Boysie views his dependence on his wife for finances and for his immigration to Canada as evidence of his emasculation. He therefore uses the bar-counter as a platform for berating his wife and for lamenting his loss of manhood in "a kind of mad poetic articulateness" (84). In the Paramount, Henry, too waxes eloquent in his "Harlem American slang" ("dig?"), offering a thesis on interracial sex which presents the black stud as a judge/hero who exacts a sexual price from white women for the history of racial injustice. Readers who focus on content exclusive of code often view this passage as evidence of "sensationalism" and, consequently, authorial irresponsibility (Birbalsingh *Frontiers* 90). In my reading, "sensationalism" is not attributable to authorial excess, instead it flows from the "over proof rum" of Caribbean performance in perfect distillation. Both Boysie's and Henry's bar-room performative over-spill express their strong emotional responses to issues of race and gender. Such responses issue from their body-memory, as well, since they have had a history of facing up to racism which continues to surface in their new context. Even in church-testimony, the overtones of race are present. When Grenadian Gertrude, in her usual Caribbean call-and-response style testimony, invokes the customary reference to being "washed whiter than snow" "in the precious blood of the lamb," she confuses the "tongue-tied congregation" (23-24). Her glaring black-ness, in a Canadian religious context where skin-colour is a specific cultural code, makes the traditional religious allusion problematic for her race-sensitive congregation.

Clarke's revitalization of the Caribbean performance tradition is evident not only in characters' language but also in their action. Scenes of exhibition like the impromptu fashion show by Dots and Bernice, Estelle's cigarette smoking exhibition and Boysie's dramatic demonstration of parking a car are examples. One of the values of living in Canada for Bernice is the economic support that her job provides. Therefore, "in a pit of depression," she is able to visit Eaton's department store and purchase "two hundred dollars in dresses" "plus a ninety-dollar swim suit" (21). However, "there was nowhere to go. And so she called her friend, Dots, and the two of them alternately dressed themselves in the dresses, and modelled the swim suit" (21). Finding themselves without the social occasions for wearing these outfits, the women amuse themselves by playing the masquerade or "dress-up". The private nature of their exhibition is a reminder that this tendency to "dress-to-kill" so typical of the Caribbean dramatic style is not fully possible in Canada. Estelle, recently arrived from Barbados, does not forget these social codes when she introduces the Barbadian/Canadians to her new habit with the flair of an exhibitionist: "Estelle took out a package of cigarettes, and made a big stage-show in lighting one" (61). Boysie, too, is described as one with the tendency toward "overstatement":

> [I]t was his way with other things too. Like the way he parked the car now: spinning the steering wheel, when he knew it couldn't turn anymore; and then allowing the wheel to unwind itself through his hands. He always wanted to impress whoever was present. (129)

These characters' desire for and tendency to participate in dramatic exhibition of clothes, smoking or parking a car allow Clarke to re-enact the Caribbean performance rituals. Clarke's thematization of performances in this narrative facilitates his recomposition of his body-memory as much as his body-memory merges with his composition.

Rather than a reading primarily invested in assessing the represented content, a reading by way of a poetics of body-memory might make fruitful critical gains from examining the meta-fictional aspects of Clarke's text.

What might Clarke's own text say about the codes of representation or even representation itself? What might it suggest about the process of writing (in the) diaspora or the relationship between history and fictional composition? While a poetics of body-memory might not take us away from the issue of representation itself, it forces us to consider the material context of writing and the textual critique of the limits of representation. Those critics like Miriam Waddington who read these episodes through the clear panes of representation rather than through the fractured glass of body-memory ignore the importance of context in their reading. Unlike Miriam Waddington, Anthony Boxill and Stan Fefferman who claim that Clarke's point in the novel is that there is "no meeting point for white and black, rich and poor,"[23] I believe that Clarke directs attention to both meeting-points and barriers at cross-cultural intersections (Boxill 72). Cross-cultural contact cannot be de-historicized and Clarke's attention to body-memory is his attempt to demonstrate how the present is influenced by the past. Waddington's liberal-humanist logic that desires a more positive view of white-black relations marks her history as much as Austin Clarke's emphasis on the issues of race and class as barriers to cross-cultural exchanges marks his. I agree with Rinaldo Walcott that "Clarke does not propose in his works a liberal humanist project, with a desire to jettison all difference in the name of some universal criteria for belonging" ("'Tom Say ...': A Preface" 12). These critics' avoidance of context precludes any attention to the issues of race and class that inhibit the equal acceptance of new members in Canadian society. Exposing the fractures in the edifices of Canadian myths of nationhood, Clarke suggests that Canada's international society will have to negotiate difference.

Toronto, in Clarke's view, is a meeting point for different cultures, a postcolonial cross-road that brings together multiple histories and memories. By recovering body-memories, Clarke suggests that the official story of cross-cultural tranquility may hide the deep hurts of race and class division that retard cross-cultural exchanges. The ability of some characters to have brief meaningful moments of solidarity (Bernice and Mrs. Burrmann through grief (167), Caribbean domestics through exile (101), Sam and Jeffrey through community youth rebellion (107)) indicates that there are meeting points. However, bridges between cultures in Canada are often burdened by hegemonic ideologies based on race and class. As Clarke biographer, Stella Algoo-Baksh, suggests, "both blacks and whites may fail to maintain a satisfying union because of a variety of potential influences that emanate from their backgrounds and the conditions of their existence" (103). The postcolonial crosses of Canada's international context demands that people's differences are acknowledged as a first step towards coming together. The one-dimensional, black-and-white vision of Canada can be enhanced by making space for the technicolour spectrum of Canada's multi-racial, multi-ethnic and multi-cultural dimensions. Clarke's insistence on tracing difference via a compositional process that erupts with his memory through the aesthetic and social codes alerts us to alternative narratives of nationhood. Moreover, Clarke's meta-fictional attention to his own compositional process might help us to begin to recognize the value of memories to diasporic poetics.

Endnotes

1. This paper in its second incarnation won the McIntosh Dissertation Award in 1997 at the University of Western Ontario. I am indebted to Prof. Maureen Warner-Lewis, Prof. Barbara Lalla (University of the West Indies, Mona and St. Augustine respectively), Prof. Stan Dragland and Prof. Pamela Banting (then of the University of Western Ontario) for their invaluable help on this paper.

2. See Stella Algoo-Baksh's *Austin C. Clarke: A Biography* in which she claims Clarke as "Canada's first major black writer" (9). Also see Monika Kaup's survey of West Indian Canadian Writing in which she observes that: "Austin Clarke, who came, as a student, to Toronto in 1955, the same year that the first female domestic workers were brought from the West Indies under the new Domestic Worker Scheme, laid the groundwork for West Indian writing in Canada with his novels and short stories." ("West Indian" 172)

3. Much of the criticism of this novel is contained in the 1960s reviews and a smattering of articles (only a few in the 1990s) most of which privilege a mimeticist reading. A few critics are exceptions to the many that reduce Clarke's works to the documentary diary or selective symbolic reflections prevalent in various kinds of traditional representational readings. As early as 1980, Edward Baugh signals a shift in the criticism; he explores *Meeting* and the other books in the trilogy in terms of the Caribbean writer's play with the elastic "linguistic possibilities" of his heritage. Instead of focussing only on content, Baugh encourages an examination of the linguistic codes in

which these works are produced. Although neither Daniel Coleman nor Robert D. Hammer looks at *Meeting*, they are among the other exceptions that consider Clarke's work outside of the grid of realist representation. Coleman, for example, explores the production of masculinities through a variety of codes including the Caribbean performative as an index of "cross-cultural refraction" in his book *Masculine Migrations: Reading the Postcolonial Male in "New Canadian" Narratives* (3). Rather than taking the representation of gender as given, he investigates the systems of representation that produce gendered positions. Similarly, Hamner, in his article "Overseas Male: Austin Clarke's *Growing Up Stupid Under the Union Jack*," questions the efficacy of mimetic representational readings and suggests that both writer and critic mediate experience.

4. The term (body)-memory is almost a redundancy since memories are primarily of and produced in the body. Although memories may be triggered by a "shell of referents" (pictures, artifacts, diaries), actual remembering is a bodily function (Rose 34). The term (body)-memory is one way of distinguishing between encodings of the past external to the body and actual memories produced in and by the body and to reinforce the notion that memory usually conceived as a purely mental activity is centrally connected to the body. Initially, I use brackets to draw attention to fact that memories are mostly bodily contained, however, I will omit the brackets from subsequent references.

5. In *The Senses Still: Perceptions and Memory as Material Culture in Modernity*, C. Nadia Seremetakis discusses

the "impeachment of nostalgia" in terms of Gurr's "sentimental" label. According to Seremetakis, "In English the word nostalgia [...] implies trivializing romantic sentimentality" (4). She argues that, "this reduction of the term confines the past and removes it from any transactional and material relation to the present ...[;] nostalgia ... freezes the past in such a manner as to preclude it from any capacity for social transformation in the present ..." (4). Gurr's impeachment of memory, by way of his patronizing label "sentimental," allows him to discount the importance of exiled memories and, thereby, to disavow any transformation of the "centre" by the "margin." One should not miss his patriarchal manoeuvre as well; he uses the well-worn masculinist strategy of appropriating discourse associated with women to condemn other phenomena.

6. Naturalism, according to M.H. Abrams, "is sometimes claimed to be an even more accurate picture of life than realism" and it usually has "a special selection of subject matter (*Glossary of Literary Terms* 153). Such portrayals "sometimes includ[e] an almost medical frankness about activities and bodily functions usually unmentioned in earlier literature" (154).

7. According to M.H. Abrams:

"Mimetic criticism views literary works as an imitation, or reflection, or representation of the world and human life, and the primary criterion applied to a work is that of the 'truth' of its representation to the objects it represents, or should represent. This mode of criticism, which first appeared in Plato and (in a qualified way) in Aristotle, is characteristic of modern theories of literary realism." (*Glossary* 39).

The assumption of a known reality external to the codes that represent that reality exposes the dilemma of establishing ontological certainty without first settling epistemological concerns. The idea that language is transparent of reality and adequate to experience is a part of the problem created by such assumptions. The naturalness or immediacy expected of linguistic signification is easily challenged. A statement of Raymond Tallis quoted in Gerald Vizenor's article, "The Ruins of Representation: Shadow Survivance and the Literature of Dominance," expresses that challenge to representationalism: "We never touch presence unmediated by signs—immediate presence, presence itself. Mediation is primary; immediacy but an impossible elusive dream" (Vizenor 143).

8. Homi Bhabha explains how the attempts by representationalist critics to pretend that extra-literary discourses are not part of aesthetic judgements can be seen as a perfect example of the innocent mask of ideology:

"[T]his conscious separation of the literary from other discourses, this act of exclusion is in itself ideological in its claims to neutrality and innocence, and prepares the way for the appropriation of the text as object of a moral discourse that claims universality for its imperatives." (*Representation* 101)

9. In an interview with Terrence Craig, Clarke is careful to note that while the fictional characters and their situations should not be confused with his own life, he becomes the filter of all his fictional material. As such, he acknowledges how his own life frames the material:

"I regard myself as a sponge. Now that has a very insidious connotation, but I regard myself as a sponge in the sense that I soak in all that I see happening around me, to be re-ordered, organized, and then put back on to the readers." (119)

10. Salkey's representational reading not only relies on some kind of "truth" correspondence with a pre-given reality but it also presumes a kind of transparency through an unobtrusive, imaginative recreation of that reality. Much of his clarity of vision is helped by the almost natural design expected of organic structures. For Salkey, his New Critical approach which privileges a kind of objective criticism that views a "literary product as a self-sufficient and autonomous object, or else as a world-in-itself, [...] to be analyzed and judged by 'intrinsic' criteria" (Abrams 40), bolsters his representational reading. However, as Gerald Vizenor quotes Will Wright as saying, "Coherent knowledge 'must begin to articulate its inherent reference to language as a formal structure, rather than to some particular form of language as magical access'" (Vizenor 141).

11. The irony in Brown's analysis is that while he wants to acknowledge Clarke's shaping role, his symbolic paradigm renders the body of the writer redundant. According to Pamela Banting in *Body, Inc.*, representational poetics "elides the bodily in favour of maintaining a distance between materiality and its mental reproductions" (xv). This distance cannot account for the presence of the writer in his works. I am not positing a regressive move towards authorial intention, merely suggesting that ignoring the writer's bodily imprint on his own work fails to account for

the writer's shaping influence which is in excess of organic design.

12. Derrida further points out how structural analysis is "constituted on the basis of a fundamental immobility and a reassuring certitude, which itself is beyond the reach of play" ("Structure" 279). In this regard, anything that disrupts the balance of the "structure" is dismissed. For Derrida, such a reading is the function of a specific critical orientation; one that resists the "confusion of opposites" (287).

13. Brown, for example, argues that:

"There is an overall incompleteness about the plot that smacks of a soap opera: apart from Henry White's death the sub-plots lack the sense of completeness which allows a sequel to be both self-contained and a part of a continuous whole. The stories of the various protagonists seem abruptly suspended at the end, too obviously to be continued." (73)

Similarly, Keith S. Henry believes that Clarke's "desire for unexpected, unpredictable plot lines is becoming a destructive obsession" (24). Also, Ruth Blake comments on Clarke's "slender plot," which Stan Fefferman labels "faulty" and "awkward" (Blake 4, Fefferman 22). Such comments attest to critics' obedience to an aesthetics of harmony. Thus, Clarke's disruption is constructed as "weak artistry" or "bad representation". Daniel Coleman, who focuses on the performance of masculinities in two short-story collections, is one of the few exceptions among critics to take any notice of Clarke's disruptive poetics. For Coleman, Clarke's performative framing of masculinity helps to trouble "urban norms for masculine behaviour" ("Hustling Status" 74). Clarke himself has defended his unconventional plots by suggesting that his view of life as "circular" cannot be straight-jacketed into the conventional notions of plot structure (Craig 126). Furthermore, he tries "to have the story go forward not on one plane but on several planes, and the injection into the narrative of the thinking of the man" (Craig 122). For me, it is this attention to memory—"the thinking of the man"—that helps to account for his disruptive plot structures. Although, Clarke expresses memory in terms of a mental activity (stream of consciousness/ modernist construct), he recognizes memory as a disruptive force in his writing. As I have argued, considering the body as a mediation of memory might more usefully account for those disruptions.

14. Unlike mimeticists who often do not acknowledge language as a symbolic code through which reality is constructed, expressive representationalists do. Brown in his kind of representational reading situates himself within "expressive criticism [that] treats a literary work primarily in relation to its author. It defines poetry as an expression, or overflow, or utterance of feelings, or as **the product of the poet's imagination**" (my emphasis, Abrams 40). However, Brown inevitably limits the literary production to the writer's imaginative design. As a consequence, Brown's critique is highly selective and reductionist. Moreover, he de-contextualizes literary production by eclipsing the critics' role in the production of meaning and views the literary expression as an object rather than a process.

15. See my article, "Body-vibes: (S)pacing the Performance in Lillian Allen's Dub Poetry."

16. Clarke has even disclosed that he has "retained voices and sounds from all those years, and even now [...] could repeat snatches of conversations" (Birbalsingh *Frontiers* 99).

17. In an interview with Terrence Craig, Clarke emphatically declares, "I have always insisted that Austin Clarke should be separated from the novels of Austin Clarke" (Craig 119). In an interview, Clarke also takes issue with his biographer Stella Algoo-Baksh whose view that "Clarke's life is also important as a record of the raw experience that has provided him with basic material for his writing" was taken too far (*Austin C. Clarke: A Biography* 8).

18. In an article entitled, "'Paradoxical and Outrageous Discrepancy': Transgression, Auto-Intertextuality, and Faulkner's Yoknapatawpha," Martin Kreiswirth uses the term "auto-intertextuality" to describe Faulkner's "cross-referencing between texts" (163). Clarke engages in a similar kind of narrative overlap for which Faulkner (whom Clarke acknowledges as an influence) is known. Like Faulkner, some of Clarke's narrative repetitions can be understood as a way of satisfying his financial needs by recirculating material. As Clarke explains: "I would be writing a novel and I would select a part and rework it as a short story, but use it in its original form in the novel. It was purely a matter of making money" (Birbalsingh *Frontiers* 93). But as Kreiswirth argues, this practical solution to a financial problem is inadequate to explain auto-intertextuality. For Clarke, however, I think that his narrative echoes are not just a consequence of the nature of fiction (as Kreiswirth argues for Faulkner). I think the

conflation of history and fiction is also a function of memory.

19. While Henry has only $15.14 in all his five bankbooks and the book from the Trust company, one of his bankbooks has a recorded balance of $140,000. The narrator explains this discrepancy thus: "Studying the wine coloured book again, he smiled. Fourteen thousand dollars twenty-three cents was the balance. He smiled again, took out his ball point pen, and as smoothly as butter, wrote in another naught, making the total one hundred and forty thousand dollars. And twenty-three cents. "Damn! one little naught, and I multiply this balance ten times!" ... His last legitimate deposit in this bank account had been posted months before, in August. It was fifteen dollars." (206)

20. By this acknowledgement, Clarke seems to illustrate Linda Hutcheon's idea in *The Politics of Representation in Canadian Art and Literature* that, "narrative fiction is not the representation of any material reality but the representation of language. Our access through narrative to the world of experience—past or present—is always mediated by the powers and limits of our verbal representations of it" (22). Hutcheon's comment echoes a similar argument about translation by Jacques Derrida. In *The Ear of the Other*, he states that: "A translation puts us not in the presence of what 'pure language' is, that is, the fact that there is language, that language is language. This is what we learn from a translation, rather than meaning contained in the translated text." (124) Both Hutcheon and Derrida warn against

the representational assumption that language is adequate to experience.

21. In a very insightful article, "'Making Style': The West Indian Writer and the Carnival Tradition," Lloyd Brown, in examining the references to Carnival in works by Caribbean writers, argues that "the writer's interest in traditions like the Carnival has the effect of integrating his literary form with the materials and structures of folk art" (135). Brown aptly defines the Caribbean performative as "making style" or "popping style;" "the very essence of a social tradition which finds its most faithful expression in the exuberance, the strutting and the flamboyant play-acting of the carnival" (131).

22. These terms—"'Nansy 'tory," "nas'y 'tory," and "non-sen 'tory"—are roughly translated as Anancy story, (nasty) risqué stories and nonsense tales, respectively (Abrahams 157).

23. Miriam Waddington declares that "there are no meeting points in Austin Clarke's novel" ("No Meeting Points" 78). So does Stan Fefferman who claims that "the view that finally emerges from *The Meeting Point* is that there is no real meeting point between people" (22). Anthony Boxill echoes the same sentiments in his review (72). Using Waddington as his main example, Lloyd Brown rejects such evaluations in his article "Austin Clarke in Canadian Reviews." To a large extent, I agree with Brown's assessment in *El Dorado and Paradise* that Clarke shows that, "as a multicultural society of immigrants, Canada is a meeting point, the intersection of diverse cultures and ethnic groups" (64).

Works Cited

Abrahams, Roger D. *The Man-of-Words in the West Indies Performance and the Emergence of Creole Culture.* Baltimore: Johns Hopkins UP, 1983.

Abrams, M. H. *A Glossary of Literary Terms.* 4th ed. New York: Holt, 1981.

Algoo-Baksh, Stella. *Austin C. Clarke: A Biography.* Toronto: ECWP, 1994.

Banting, Pamela. *Body, Inc.: A Theory of Translation Poetics.* Winnipeg: Turnstone, 1995.

Baugh, Edward. "Friday in Crusoe's City: The Question of Language in Two West Indian Novels of Exile." *Adah Bulletin* 5.3 (1980): 1-12.

Bhabha, Homi. "Representation and the Colonial Text: A Critical Exploration of Some Forms of Mimeticism." *Gloversmith.* 93-122.

Birbalsingh, Frank. *Frontiers of Caribbean Literature in English.* London: Macmillan, 1996.

Blake, Ruth. "For Summer Reading." *Workers Vanguard* Mid-July, 1967. 4.

Boxill, Anthony. "'The Novels of Austin C. Clarke.' Rev. of *The Survivors of the Crossing, Among Thistles and Thorns, The Meeting Point,* by Austin C. Clarke." *Fiddlehead* 75 (1968): 69-72.

Brown, Lloyd W. "Austin Clarke in Canadian Reviews." *Canadian Literature* 38 (1968): 101-104.

_____. *El Dorado and Paradise.* London, ON: U of Western Ontario and Caribbean Books, 1989.

_____. "'Making Style': The West Indian Writer and the Carnival Tradition." *Caribbean Studies.* 18.3-4 (1978-79): 131-38.

Bucknor, Michael Andrew. "Body-Vibes: (S)pacing the Performance in Lillian Allen's Dub Poetry." *Thamyris* 5.8 (1998): 301-320.

Callaghan, Barry, ed. *The Austin Clarke Reader*. Toronto: Exile Editions, 1996.

Clarke, Austin. "Austin Clarke: Caribbean-Canadians." In Birbalsingh.

_____. *Growing Up Stupid Under the Union Jack*. Toronto: McClelland and Stewart, 1980.

_____. *The Meeting Point*. Toronto: Macmillan, 1967.

_____.*The Polished Hoe*. Toronto: Thomas Allen P, 2002.

_____. *Survivors of the Crossing*. London: Heinemann, 1964.

_____. *The Prime Minister*. Don Mills, ON: General, 1977.

Coleman, Daniel. "Hustling Status, Scamming Manhood: Race, Performance, and Masculinity in Austin Clarke's Fiction." *Masculinities* 3(Spring 1995): 74-88.

_____. *Masculine Migrations: Reading the Postcolonial Male in 'New Canadian' Narratives*. Toronto: U of Toronto P, 1998.

Craig, Terrence. "Interview with Austin Clarke". *WLWE* 26.1 (Spring 1986): 115-27.

Derrida, Jacques. "Sending: On Representation." ["Envoi"]. Trans. Peter Caws And Mary Ann Caws. *Social Research* 49.2 (1982): 294-326.

_____. "Structure, Sign and Play in the Discourse of the Human Sciences." *Writing and Difference*. Trans. Alan Bass. London: Routledge, 1978.

_____. *The Ear of The Other: Otobiography, Transference, Translation: Texts and Discussions with Jacques*

Derrida. Ed. Christie V. McDonald. Trans. Peggy Kamuf. New York: Schocken, 1985.

Fefferman, Stan. "Mismating at *The Meeting Point*." *Toronto Telegram* 21 May 1967: 22.

Gloversmith, Frank. *The Theory of Reading*. Brighton: Harvester, 1984.

Gurr, Andrew. *Writers In Exile: The Identity of Home in Modern Fiction*. Atlantic Highlands, New Jersey: Humanities, 1981.

Hamner, Robert D. "Overseas Male: Austin Clarke's *Growing up Stupid Under the Union Jack*." *CLA Journal* 36.2 (1992): 123-33.

Henry, Keith S. "An Assessment of Austin Clarke, West Indian-Canadian Novelist." *CLA Journal* 29.1 (1985): 9-32.

Hutcheon, Linda. *The Politics of Representation in Canadian Art and Literature*. North York, Ontario: York University, 1988.

Hutcheon, Linda and Marion Richmond, eds. *Other Solitudes: Canadian Multicultural Fictions*. Toronto: Oxford UP, 1990.

Kaup, Monika. "West Indian Canadian Writing: Crossing the Border from Exile to Immigration." *ECW* 57 (Winter 1995): 171-93.

Kreiswirth, Martin. "'Paradoxical and Outrageous Discrepancy': Transgression, Auto-Intertextuality, and Faulkner's Yoknapatawpha." Donald M. Kartiganer and Anne J. Abadie, Eds. Faulkner and the Artist: Faulkner Jackson: UP of Mississippi, 1996.

Rice, Ulric. "Lot of the Domestics in Canada." *Advocate Magazine* March 26, 1967. 8.

Rose, Steven. *The Making of Memory: From Molecules to Mind*. New York: Doubleday, 1992.

Rushdie, Salman. *Imaginary Homelands*. London: Granta, 1991.

Said, Edward. "Interview." *Diacritics* (Fall 1976): 30-47.

Salkey, Andrew. "Review of *The Meeting Point*." *Caribbean Magazine* 89. ts., Austin Clarke Papers, McMaster University. 1-3.

Seremetakis, C. Nadia, ed. *The Senses Still: Perception and Memory as Material Culture in Modernity*. Boulder: Westview, 1994.

Vizenor, Gerald. "The Ruins of Representation: Shadow Survivance and the Literature of Dominance." *An Other Tongue: Nation and Ethnicity in the Linguistic Borderlands*. Ed. Alfred Artega. Durham: Duke University, 1994. 139-67.

Waddington, Miriam. "No Meeting Points." Rev. of *The Meeting Point* by Austin Clarke. *Canadian Literature* 35 (1968): 74-78.

Walcott, Rinaldo. "'Tom Say ...': A Preface." Callaghan.

Signifying Contamination: On Austin Clarke's *Nine Men Who Laughed*

SMARO KAMBOURELI

For a writer to "wrestle with his shadows," he must be certain of casting one ...

Françoise Lionnet (322)

I

It has become almost typical for writers of postcolonial and multicultural critical discourses to begin by rehearsing the polarities of centre and margin, of us and them, and of other configurations that bear similar eventualities. More often than not, this is accompanied by the writers' self-proclamation, an enunciation that defines them in unequivocal (that is, "real") terms of race and ethnicity. This metacritical instance of self-location speaks of the perceived need to identify the position from which writers speak in terms that, blending as they do the personal with the collective, assign the writing a certain kind of credible valence and political authenticity. Thus, the self-consciousness employed in this strategy becomes the double means of, first, warding off the hegemonic elements that have produced the polarities I have cited and, second, avoiding any critical misguidedness or cultural appropriation, especially when the racial and cultural traditions of writers and their subjects of study do not coincide. This kind of self-reflexivity produces a cultural autobiography, an autobiography that declares collective and individual specificities as they are determined by historical contingencies. It thus articulates the inescapable double bind of all such cultural endeavours, namely that of complicity.

For white critics of minority discourse, this strategy might often take the form of veiled apologia—a rhetorical gesture that at once acknowledges and appeases guilt by association. By displacing their guilt and anxiety, white critics find a discourse that eases their complicity. To borrow Cornel West's words, "theirs is a gesture that is simultaneously progressive and co-opted" (12). While the intent of this metacriticism is to prepare the ground for their criticism's reception, it also pays homage to a different kind of authenticity, one that has been subjugated and contaminated by the critics' own tradition, an authenticity whose retrieval from its colonized history is the valorized point of departure of all such criticism. Yet, even when cultural determinism is not only avoided but also becomes, itself, the object of critique, there is a tendency to fetishize origins.

Despite the fact that it is fraught with ambivalence, the us-and-them paradigm attains a certain naturalness that belies the mobility and permeability of power relations in which postcolonial and multicultural discourse engages. This strategy of self-location testifies, on the one hand, to the cultural gap separating these critics from their critical subjects, and, on the other, seeks to diminish the ideological distance between them. Since this critical stance endorses from the start the desire of minority subjects to define themselves in their own terms as well as analyse and change their disenfranchised histories, the two groups' insularity is dispersed but is, at the same time, redefined as a space that might still be occupied by the dominant position of what Gayatri Spivak calls "the West as Subject." In her critique of contemporary theorists such as Michel Foucault, Gilles Deleuze, and Felix Guattari, Spivak wonders whether they actually move beyond the politics of "an interested desire to conserve the subject of the West, or the West as Subject" (66). The self-reflexive articulation of a politics of identity is a concentrated attempt, an authentic desire, to question radically narratives of domination, but it does not necessarily avoid the pitfalls of reinstalling traces of those narratives in its own discourse. As Homi Bhabha puts it:

> The enunciation of cultural difference problematizes the binary division of past and present, tradition and modernity, at the level of cultural representation and its authoritative address. It is the problem of how, in signifying the present, something comes to be repeated, relocated and translated in the name of tradition, in the guise of a pastness that is not necessarily a faithful sign of historical memory but a strategy of representing authority in terms of the artifice of the archaic. (35)

This problem of repetition, of rehearsing the very paradigms one sets out to dismantle, assumes a different form and takes on a different political direction when the strategy of self-location is practised by postcolonial and multicultural critics who are persons of colour or of ethnic-minority background. Their critical self-reflexivity becomes an instance of what Trinh Minh-ha calls "planned authenticity," an authenticity that she sees "as a product of hegemony and a remarkable counterpart of universal standardization. ... We no longer wish to erase your difference. We demand, on the contrary, that you remember and assert it" (89). This strategic assertion of one's identity seems to affix critical discourse on minority issues to the very tradition that has largely induced marginality. There is a certain positivity to this self-naming act in that it exposes the appropriating tactics of the dominant tradition and reclaims the subjectivity apprehended from the minority subject, but also a negativism in that this instance of self-appellation is structurally related to its minority position. There is the implied risk, then, of remaining unnameable if one insists on not residing on the borderline that at once separates and links the binary structure of us and them.

Yet, writers who do not employ this strategy also run the risk of being aligned with the dominant tradition. For example, in her essay "South Asian Poetry in Canada: In Search of a Place," Arun Mukherjee devotes only a note to Michael Ondaatje because "[i]nsofar as Michael Ondaatje's work does not speak of his otherness and visibility, he is excluded from this paper" (96n6). This note is not just an example of the critic establishing the parameters of her argument. The effect of Mukherjee's strategy here is both disciplinary and ironic. The fact that, instead of not mentioning Ondaatje at all, she relegates her references to him to a note is an instance of disciplinary action, and a public one at that. What informs Mukherjee's strategy is her implicit assumption that Ondaatje, despite the postmodern space most of his texts occupy and the many cameo appearances he makes in his writing, has not, at least so far, identified his position in terms that speak of a marginalized otherness. The implicit imperative here is that a subject cannot—should not, in fact—divorce itself from its colonial history. As Mukherjee says in a more recent essay, "Ironies of Colour in the Great White North," "self-identification by race is an important piece of contextual knowledge for understanding the work of the non-white writers" (162). Furthermore, otherness, Mukherjee suggests, ought to bear signs of a certain inscription—signs Ondaatje's work lacks, at least according to her reading. Hence the need to discipline him by marginalizing him in her essay.

The normative element that seems to underlie Mukherjee's strategy in both essays is how the experience of colonization has the dynamic effect of prompting the colonized to identify with others in a similar position, an effect that depends on the authenticity of a "common experience of racism" ("Ironies" 168). The result is a discourse that, as described by Mukherjee herself, "is obsessively centred on exploring the racial difference, attacking the racism of Eurocentric discourse and forging a positive racial identity that is grounded in the memory of the historical struggle of the community" ("Ironies" 170). The perception, here, of a social ensemble that suspends particularities in the name of a common cause is not meant to evoke hybridization. This is precisely what is ironic in her position. It invokes a singularity of collective identity that is threatened as much by mainstream society as by such "apostate" figures as Ondaatje and Neil Bissoondath.[1] There is the possibility, then, as articulated

by Diana Brydon, that this "view of cultural authenticity" might "condemn" the postcolonial subject "to a
continued marginality" (196). Or, to cite Ali Behdad,
"[a]uthenticity ... entails positioning the investigating
subject in a compartmentalized category that assumes
final determinacy" (47). Thus, to write from a position
marked, however minimally, from a racial and/or ethnic
perspective involves the tendency to literalize origins and
race, as well as to homogenize the experience attributed
to them, even though this literalization might be at odds
with the particular methodologies practised by critics.

That Mukherjee's proposal to critique the universalizing tactics of the Western tradition[2] is not, predictably,
entirely free of similar methods of homogenizing is not
so much a signal of flaws inherent in her argument as
it is an indication of the impossibility of identifying a
space of authenticity as long as the critical act departs
from, and arrives at, interstices of cultural and political
consequences that can be analysed only dialogically. The
alternative to this homogenizing might lie in what Trinh
calls a "critical difference from myself," as opposed to a
"difference reduced to identity—authenticity" (89). "A
critical difference from myself," she says, "means that I
am not i, am within and without i. I/i can be I or i, you
and me both involved" (90). Trinh's dis/identification
trope illustrates not only the complexity of the strategy
of self-location, but also the problems of relying on
such categories as centre, margin, and origins without
addressing the epistemological grounding that gives rise
to them. Far from delivering the clarity the strategy of
self-location promises, it transgresses the very authentic
position it states, thus confronting the reader with a collusion of critical knowledges.

It might very well be that this critical topos of self-location derives from the same imperative that drives Foucault to talk about the "urgent need" that arises "at a given historical moment" to develop a "strategic function" (195), one that necessitates the use of what he calls "apparatus":

> [T]he apparatus is essentially of a strategic nature, which means assuming that it is a matter of a certain manipulation of relations of forces, either developing them in a particular direction, blocking them, stabilising them, utilising them, etc. The apparatus is thus always inscribed in a play of power, but it is also always linked to certain coordinates of knowledge which issue from it but, to an equal degree, condition it (196).

The strategic function of the apparatus, then, is that it operates as a "site of a double process" whereby "heterogeneous elements" are linked (195, 194). What such a strategy reveals is, on the one hand, a certain fetishization of the very constructs that induce anxiety in the critical act and, on the other, the impossibility of establishing, or proceeding from, an unalloyed ground of singular difference.

II

It is within this critical context of self-location, and the directionality it promises to the reader, that I wish to examine Austin Clarke's *Nine Men Who Laughed*. Despite its many formal elements that position it within the realist tradition of most Canadian ethnic writing, this collection of short stories is characterized by a self-reflexivity that allows it to look critically at itself as well as at the cultural tradition within which it is located. Its self-reflexiveness is mediated by the introduction and, as its title suggests, by laughter. Both the introduction and laughter install in the text a network of discourses that are produced by, and themselves produce, a great sense of complicity that deconstructs the binary structure of us and them. I will discuss the diffusion of this paradigm by focusing on the introduction, and reading some of the stories only by way of illuminating Clarke's own reading of his stories in his introductory remarks.

What us and them have come to designate in the terrain of postcolonial discourse—the dominant and marginal groups of society respectively—is reversed here. "[A]ll of them [nine men] exist on the periphery of rewards, and suffer from unfair chastisements" (1), we read early in the introduction. Yet the conventional referentiality of the paradigm us and them is changed three pages into the text. "In Barbados, at Harrison College, where I was schooled and trained in the British system of values—a public school education—we were taught that only fools laughed" (3). Clarke's strategy of self-location, his identification with his characters' condition, breaks down the authorial distance that separates him from them, thus translating them into us. If, to quote Gordon Collier, the model "Us/Them summarizes cultural epistemology reductively, setting up a fateful and often fatal dynamic of encounter and confrontation" (xiii), then Clarke's reversal changes the terms of this dynamic and initiates, as I hope to show, a chain of signifying events and aporias that continue what his strategy of self-location has begun: the contamination of those markers that authenticate the space identity inhabits, the dissolution of boundary lines.

Clarke's strategy operates through the trope of irony as described by Mukherjee: "The relationship of a non-white author to her or his audience is an ironic one. ... [T]he writer uses 'we' to stand for a particular racial/ethnic group, whereas 'you' or 'they' very often stands for a white person or persons" ("Ironies" 168). Yet, although Mukherjee argues that "the target audience" of this discourse is that "of the non-white Canadian writers," those "who share the writers' world view and experience and, hence, 'get' their ironies" (168), I would like to propose that, at least in Clarke's case, the author does not discriminate among his readers but, instead, targets a mixed audience. His apostrophe to a deliberately (and unavoidably so, I should add) heterogeneous audience is a political strategy that becomes the self-reflexive figure of its own eventuality. That Clarke's address and his stories are intended to draw white readers is obvious, because in them he undertakes to explain inside knowledge about the immigrant experience of blacks. His immigrants "are made to forget" their "status ... at home" (1); laughter is their "only available weapon against resentment" (2); their answer "I just here, living" to the question "How are things, man?" contains "all the criticism ... all the truth of being in a foreign place" (6): this is evidence of Clarke negotiating the positions of insiders and outsiders. If Clarke is concerned about whether his white readers will "get" the meaning of his characters' lives, he compensates by writing his introduction. His prefatory comments, then, restitute the paradigm of us and them at the same time that they show the residual conflicts that make it difficult, if not impossible, to solidify the differences it delineates.

AUSTIN CLARKE: ESSAYS ON HIS WORKS

Far from claiming that I am able to get all the nuances—ironic or not—in Clarke's text, I will proceed from the double contention that my reading of the text, to appropriate Henry Louis Gates' words, will address only what I can see and that some texts (or certain parts of them) often refuse to speak.[3] I see Clarke's introductory remarks as constituting an instance of critical contamination, a discourse about displacement that also itself displaces the source of its enunciation. As such, his discourse is in keeping with Homi Bhabha's articulation of contingency: "The contingent," Bhabha says, "is contiguity, metonymy, the touching of spatial boundaries at a tangent, and, at the same time, the contingent is the temporality of the indeterminate and the undecidable" (186). It is within this hybrid figure of space and time that Clarke's preface is located—as are his readers.

If the introduction offers readers a preview of the stories, then perhaps it is to the stories that we should first go in order to determine why contamination figures so prominently in this text. As Clarke says in the introduction, "[a]ll these [nine] men have forgotten, at that most critical point in their lives, the moment of their contact with hostility" (2). Contact of them with us constructs the site, and experience, of contamination. Indeed, contamination bears its own distinct marks, an olfactory presence that permeates virtually all nine narratives. It is a smell to which only the most stuffed-up reader could remain immune. Yet, understanding where it comes from, or what its consequences might be, is a different matter altogether.

Here is an example from the story "The Smell," in which, as the title suggests, everything smells—everything signifies:[4]

> But the smell in his voice, which I could taste, but
> which I could not decode or call by name and essence,
> sent me back to the tone in his daughter's voice. There
> was the same smell, the same unspoken explanation.
> Greater insight or more deliberate maliciousness and
> malevolence would have convinced me of the name,
> the highness of the smell. ... But I allowed the smell
> of detection to elude me because of the age of our
> friendship. (161-62)

Here, smell is an agent of discovery as it teases the speaker with the promise of insight. It disseminates knowledge but, paradoxically, it does so with an elaborate array of detours and deferrals. For it keeps the speaker, who detects with his nose, guessing at best, disbelieving at worst. The tactile sense of smell can be traced, but what it emanates from can be opaque or transparent, depending on our ability to discern and our cultural histories. "Did he mean that this man and the daughter who likes him so much and defends him were engaged in some kind of carnal ...? No! ... But I tried to go over in my mind the certainty of the two smells, one of wood burning, the other of roast-corn as I waited. ... I still had a faint touch of the smell, but I was certain that what I was hearing was a mistake of seeing" (167). The speaker calls himself "a fool" (168), for he realizes that he should have sniffed at the truth earlier. Nevertheless, his social and psychological conditioning prevents him from "seeing" that his best friend has a consensual incestuous relationship with his daughter. Smell, then, does not simply suggest a point of aberrant contact, the touching space of the incest taboo that defines the contingent in this story; smell has a bilateral function here, for it also announces the speaker's complicity.

What he smells and sees at any given moment is determined as much by his cultural background as by the "tricks of [his] imagination" (156), which inaugurate the psychoanalytic language of desire and need. Having declared himself a "fool," having "found the source of the smell" (170), this first-person narrator engages in an elaborate attempt to understand how he could have misread all the clues available to him. His reasoning is at once a feeble effort to exonerate himself and a register of the different needs and desires that he and the father in the story express:

> [The father] did not know I was looking. For he was convinced that he had convinced me that there was no further need to follow smells. He passed his left hand over the middle of the photograph. The middle of the photograph was where the breasts of the subject were. And the subject is his daughter. But it was filial love. Nothing more. I saw nothing unusual in this gesture, even though I had just told him ... that his zipper was still undone. Then, before zipping-up his zipper, he passed his hand over his penis. It is a gesture that makes even a man turn his eyes aside. And I turned mine while he was doing it. But it is his daughter, after all; for chrissakes! It was merely a manifestation of his love and passion for a daughter he was now prevented from seeing because of the Restraining Order. (171)

Although the entire story could be seen as being about the narrator's attempt to read the causality of his own misreading, he remains a reader who relies on his faltering memory (which he acknowledges) and on the logic that states that such social codes as filial love are inviolable.

Nevertheless, his misreading, even when unveiled, continues to circulate as evidence of the social and psychological contingencies he represents. It is not only his friend's environment that smells, a sign "that something was wrong" (160), but also "the smell of detection" the narrator "allowed ... to elude" him that registers the extent of contamination in this story (162). In the introduction, Clarke says that his stories "are intended to rip away the film, the cataract of perception, in order to provide clear vision, even if what is seen is crueller, less palatable than the picture exhibited previously" (6). The force of his surgical metaphor is meant to be corrective. The "cataract of perception" is just one example in this book of the metaphors and images of "pathologies" articulating the symptoms as well as the effects of contamination (3). Yet, it seems that it is not only the configured us that could benefit from Clarke's "clear vision." In the world that Clarke constructs—a world that includes author, readers, and all the characters that people his stories—nothing, no one, is immune to the forces that taint what is taken to be authentic: the genuine article is contaminated before it is even discovered. The epistemological foundations of perception itself are shaken. Clarke's intention, then, to offer the reader a clear vision is deconstructed by those of his strategies that suggest the impossibility of reaching clarity.

Thus, as an idiom of social codes, and by extension an agent of historical memory, smell becomes a metaphor for reading *Nine Men Who Laughed*. The interpretive results of this reading might be occluded by the readers' own (often unperceived) need to confirm what they already know, but they are certainly also inscribed in the text's formal and rhetorical strategies. In this sense, smell, together with all the other images of contamination in these stories, functions as an enactive site in that it takes the measure of various displacements, triggers differentiation, and, finally, alerts the reader to what matters.

Contamination, both as a physical state and as a sign of overlapping but conflicting constituencies, suggests dislocation and interpenetration, and therefore constructs a site of epistemic violence that almost invariably results in transgression. This I see as being not only the index to these narratives' composition, but also the method Clarke employs as the writer of the introduction to his own stories. Contamination invokes an appropriate reading but, since its referents are characterized by fragility because of their shifting identities and strategies of power, it converts the body of the text and the bodies represented by it into undecidable figures. Contamination is not the prerogative of one kind of subject alone, nor is it a register exclusively of negative conditions; the contact that initiates it affects all those partaking in it. The ensuing undecidability does not imply a lack of moral responsibility on the writer's part; on the contrary, it speaks of a disbelief in stable categories, of the intractability of meanings that are generated within the borderline space of contaminated bodies. This is precisely what lies behind the disturbing but strong image of suicide with which Clarke concludes his introduction:

> I eschew my own term "black aesthetic" if it suggests that *Nine Men Who Laughed* is a literature about black men. It would be suicidal to permit that categorization of these stories. The men are black only because they live in Toronto, in a society which has officially branded them "immigrants" from the West Indies. ... But I doubt very much whether

these nine men, restricted though they are by their status of "immigrant," would define themselves or describe their lives in these negative terms. For to consider themselves "immigrants," to accept this as the paramount definition of their presence here, to consider themselves slaves, would be to commit the unlaughable and mortal sin of suicide. (6-7)

III

Clarke writes his introduction both as author and reader, but avoids situating himself securely in either position. The introduction as a text that is at once outside and inside the text proper becomes the borderline space he occupies. When he writes that "[h]ardships exist in spite of the potentialities and known abilities of the nine men" (1), he speaks as both author and reader, a double figure whose hybrid identity does not articulate a dialectical contradiction but rather the surplus economy of the nine short stories. When he says that the nine men "have all lived as students of some kind, in an established and nationally recognized Canadian institution of learning. But they have lived under a cloud of confusion. Under a smear of self-doubt. They have been educated in a system which holds no regard for their intelligence" (1), he relaunches his stories by tacitly communicating his desire to investigate further his characters' interiority and historicity. In this respect, the introduction locates and frames the stories, announces their thematic and linguistic paradoxes.

Interestingly, the introduction is not enunciated in the Barbadian dialect of four of the stories, which is also the language of most of the dialogue in the book: "the language these men would use when they are by themselves, when they are with friends, when they are apart from strangers. It is more suitable and more appropriate than formal English, which is incapable, in this context, of translating the essence of the 'black aesthetic'" (6). Yet, it is in this "formal," "incapable" language that Clarke writes the introduction. His choice demonstrates his deliberate strategy of self-location. Not only does he avoid having his Barbadian dialect misunderstood by readers who are they to the we of the community he writes about, but he also reinforces the irony of his use of "formal English." Castigating the "system" by using its own discourse, Clarke shifts the system's control and exemplifies the contaminating effects of contact on the dominant system as well as the immigrants. Clarke's forked tongue turns the system's insular power upon itself. His is a strategy of ambivalence as it undermines his author/ity while, at the same time, articulating the politics of his positionality.

Writing the introduction as the reader of a text that he has written, Clarke enjoys the privileged status of an insider, a status, however, that is suspended when he ventures to "other" himself as author. By placing his authorial voice outside the text proper, Clarke marginalizes formally that which conventionally occupies the centre, a strategy that reflects the impurity of literary forms. The incipient position of the introduction makes it at once centre and margin, thus illustrating its borderline status. But if the centre is marginalized, where does this situate the margin?[5] The answer to this question can be found, I think, by examining the identity of the ninth man to whom the title of the collection alludes, and by understanding how Clarke reconstructs "the prepossessiveness of the new culture," Canada (2). Thematically and formally, the ambivalent identity of the ninth man and the feminization of Canada in Clarke's introduction help to demonstrate the liminality of origins.

IV

Clarke's repeated remark in his introduction that *Nine Men Who Laughed* is about nine men would seem to be a very obvious, if not redundant, one. Furthermore, although the nine stories of the collection suggest a correspondence to these nine men, and despite the persistent emphasis on their number, it is not always apparent who the men are.

In six of the stories—"A Funeral," "Canadian Experience," "Doing Right," "If Only: Only If ...," "A Man," and "How He Does It"—there is no doubt as to which of the characters belong to the group of the nine men.[6] In the remaining stories, however, the identification of central characters with the group of nine men remains ambivalent at best. In "The Smell," the man in question could be the narrator, who, as we have seen, calls himself a "fool," thus aligning himself with the nine men in the introduction who "were taught," as Clarke says, "that only fools laughed" (3). But he could also be the incestuous father, a "fool" of a sinister sort whose behaviour is, putting it mildly, a poignant example of one of the things Clarke means when he says that "[a]ll nine men laugh because they are, perhaps, already morally dead" (5). A similar ambivalence, or interchangeability of central male characters, also occurs in "Coll. ss. Trins. Ap. Toron.—A

Fable," a story about two friends who arrive in Canada from Barbados to study at Trinity College. For the first three pages of the story, the third-person narrator does not distinguish between them. "They," thinking of themselves as "black Englishmen," as "British and Russian. Half and half," are pitted against a "Canada [that] was faceless" (178). They are products of a colonial education system, and they are identical to each other, as their names—Boy Sonny and Sonny Boy—reflect. Their identities are contaminated upon their arrival in Canada; their identification with one another is upset when Boy takes a moral and political stance, the consequences of which make him painfully aware that Sonny "was not his twin, not even his brother, so he knew he would have to make his own life" (193). Either (or both) of them could be one of the nine men.

The result of these characters' hybridity as well as a sign of how problematical the construction of cultural identity is, this ambivalence shows that the ostensible certainty with which Clarke refers to the nine male protagonists of the nine stories is misleading. It might very well be that his authorial intentionality is at odds with the intentionality of his reading performance. This could be the case with "A Short Acquaintance," the fourth story in *Nine Men Who Laughed* that remains to be considered. Contrary to what Clarke's persistent focus on the nine men would lead us to believe, this story is about women, about the "misunderstanding [that] defines all of" them (75; see Brown 142). With the exception of such figures as "the black-Canadian security guard who made suggestive faces and pressed his right hand over his fly" (89), the supercilious police officers who stare at the thighs of the female bank tellers (90), and the man in the female narrator's fantasies who might bring "thrills and orgasms" to the plastic sterility of her apartment (84, 83), there are no male characters in this story. It is, then, troubling that Clarke does not acknowledge this in his introduction in a way that might elucidate the narrator's moral anxiety and complicity in the fate of a fellow female bank teller who is jilted by her fiancé, and eventually found murdered. Nor does he account at all for the seeming discrepancy in the number of his male protagonists.

Perhaps the reader is expected to assume that the missing man is the runaway fiancé of the bank teller, or the man who fatally assaulted her. "Did you hear if they caught the man?" is the last line of dialogue in the story. The narrator responds silently by thinking that she "did not want to know" (91). The invisibility that draws together the fiancé and the murderer might be seen as the grotesque embodiment of the invisibility that characterizes most of Clarke's immigrant characters and the communities they inhabit. Yet, despite the two men's invisibility, traces of their physical presence pervade the story. The missing men are certainly part of the phallic system that afflicts the drab fates of the women in the story, part of what "encourage[s]" the female narrator to have murderous and castrating fantasies about men (88), but neither of them is, I believe, the missing ninth man.

I am not suggesting here that the conundrums of this story can be resolved by reading it through its presence or absence in Clarke's introduction. My aim, instead, is to show how his introduction unwrites the gender signature of "A Short Acquaintance" while it inscribes itself in the other narratives to which it attempts to introduce us. Not preparing the reader for this story about women, then, is an aporia that points to Clarke's position as author/reader in the introduction. Despite the didactic tone of the introduction, this and other lacunae undermine Clarke's authority, thus illustrating the contingent relation of his function as author of the stories to his function as reader of them. To reckon with this contingency is to reckon with the contaminating effects each function has on the other.

Which brings me back to my argument as to why neither the fiancé nor the murderer can be the missing ninth man. Unlike the other male characters, they remain invisible precisely because they are still in control of their actions, beyond the grasp of the system's forces. All of the nine men, Clarke has told us, "exist on the periphery of rewards, and suffer from unfair chastisements" (1). The missing ninth man, then, can only be one who resides "on the periphery": the man who speaks the introduction, who locates himself in the margin of his text proper.

The slippage between author and reader now occurs between author and character. Clarke insinuates this when he says that "the nine men ... are, in a metaphorical sense, me" (3). My reading, however, of Clarke as the ninth man does not depend on such a metaphoric interpretation. His relationship to his characters depends on the trope of metonymy. It is a relationship that is possible because of the contiguity of those characters, because of the contingency that at once enables Clarke as author to circulate freely in the stories and that determines his position as the odd man out. This is precisely the paradox that defines him as character. "[T]he problematic of contingency," as Bhabha says, "strategically allows for a spatial contiguity—solidarity, collective action" (187). As the ninth man, then, Clarke unsettles the polarity of author and character, of self and other. He is, in effect, the man who embodies contamination. As the figure of the contingent itself, he is a split and ambivalent subject: he represents the margin that the characters in the centre of the book inhabit, but he turns this margin into a site of authorial surveillance.

Not unlike the character Clarke refers to as "the unnamed man in the story 'Canadian Experience'" who "has forgotten who he is" (2), Clarke himself forgets for a few pages that he is the author. In writing an introduction, Derrida says, "while pretending to turn around and look backward, one is also in fact starting over again, adding an extra text, complicating the scene, opening up within the labyrinth a supplementary digression, which is also a false mirror that pushes the labyrinth's infinity back forever in mimed—that is, endless—speculation" (27n27). As the narrative that supplements the nine stories, Clarke's introduction is a text that dislodges the dichotomy of centre and margin, of us and them.

V

If the writer of the introduction is the missing ninth man, as I am suggesting, it remains now to examine what kind of character he is. His function as character is iterative. He is a man who replicates many of the other characters' "tick[s]" (4). For example, as does the narrator of "A Short Acquaintance," who stresses the fact that she "spoke from the heart"—that is, in her "Trinidadian accent" (77)—but narrates the story in straight English, Clarke himself, as mentioned earlier, forsakes accent. Similarly, like the invisible men in the same story, Clarke cannot be pinned down—arrested as a stable figure.

His instability as character is nowhere more apparent than in another instance of ironic repetition. Posing as author, reader, and character, Clarke confounds the reader by the way he reads the only story to which he pays particular attention. This is, then, what happens in *Nine Men Who Laughed* when a character who plays author interprets a story he has written. Clarke tells us that the central character in "Canadian Experience" is "'unchristened,' nameless, because he has himself forgotten to exert his identity" (2). While Clarke is correct about the man's forgetfulness, he is wrong when he says the man lacks a name. For the character in question receives a Christmas card from Pat, another tenant in his boarding-house, an unemployed white actor, that clearly states: "To George, at Xmas" (47). This is the only instance in the story where this character, who is about to kill himself, is referred to by name. Far from being "nameless," he is unnamed by Clarke's statement. Perhaps Clarke's own forgetfulness here is yet another ironic clue to his function as a figure that is neither author nor character. He is neither, for his mis/reading is a disavowal of the knowledge that either role would confer on him.

Given the fact that George's alleged namelessness is the central point of Clarke's reading, the latter's forgetfulness produces yet another aporia in the introduction. Clarke attributes George's, and the other characters', forgetfulness to the system's insidious and appropriating power over them: "they forget or are made to forget that their former status, the aristocratic status they held at home, should be the stamp of their presence on the university and on this foreign landscape" (1-2). Not all of the male protagonists possess what Clarke loosely calls "aristocratic status," nor do their debilitating social and psychological experiences always derive, as he would have us believe, from the Canadian system. George "did not come to this country to attend university. Experience of the world, and his former life at home in Barbados were his only secondary education. He had come here against his father's bitter wishes" (35). The story's impetus rests on his incongruous reasoning that he ought to get a job at a bank on Bay Street—notwithstanding the fact that he "knew nothing about banks" (32)—but we are told very little, if anything, about why he emigrates. We do, however, get to hear what his father thinks of his decision to come to Canada:

> You call yourself a son o' mine? You, a son o' mine? With all this property that I leaving-back for you? You come telling me you going to Canada as a' immigrant? To be a stranger? Where Canada is? What is Canada? They have a Church o' England up there? Canada is no place for you, man. The son of a Barbadian plantation owner? This land was in our family before Canada was even discovered by the blasted Eskimos and the red Indians. Seventeen-something. A.D.! In the year of our Lord, anno domini. Who do they worship up there? And you come telling me that you going up there, seeking advancement as a' immigrant? In Canada? Your fortune and your future is right here! In this soil. In this mud. In this dirt. 'Pon these two hundred and eighty-something acres o' cane and corn!" (48)

Perhaps it is the collusion in the father's discourse between his pitch for authentic origins and his rhetoric contaminated by colonialism that spawns the inner drama of George's desire to emigrate. The otherness of Canada that the father at once constructs and derides is, ironically, George's object of desire. Canada seizes hold of his "imagination," a faculty that enables him to revise the script of his life, that endows him with "cleverness of nuance," what his actor friend defines more aptly as "something called a euphemism for lies" (35).

It is virtually impossible to penetrate this veneer of "nuance." One could surmise, though, that George's desire, which "others" him in Canada, is synonymous with his unacknowledged wish to disobey his father, his wish to defamiliarize himself with the presumed authenticity of origins. By disowning the land that is "naturally" his, George resists his own subjectivity as an essential entity. While both he and his father comply with the system that contaminates their consciousness, George, unlike his father who accepts the comfort of his plantation, disavows his identification with land, thus renunciating the name of the father, and by extension authority. He seems to operate according to Bhabha's formulation that "[t]he recognition of authority ... requires a validation of its source" (112). What possibly distorts his perspective during his eight years in Canada, while he awaits "amnesty" for his illegal immigrant status (36), is his ironic exchange of one colony for another as the site at which his desire might materialize. In effect, he becomes both us and them. In other words, the agency of his predicament lies partly with him, and not, as Clarke claims, with the Canadian system alone. George denaturalizes himself both from the system and from himself.

In a way that is reminiscent of this story's contaminating strategies and that typifies his own ambivalent positioning, Clarke remains heedless of this plausible scenario of George's desire. He does so, I would like to argue, because this kind of contamination is infectious. That he forgets George's name reflects, then, his own attachment to a desire to disempower the system that "others" him, a desire, however, that backfires since it can operate only within the economy of contamination. In this respect, the alleged namelessness of George might very well be connected to the fact that the only person addressing him by name is Pat—a white, and a woman at that. By unnaming George, Clarke takes away the power of the white namer (thus aligning himself with the authority George's father represents) and silences the woman at once. This is yet another ironic strategy, since the white actor is as pitiful and abject a figure as George.

If, then, the purpose of Clarke as the ninth man is to rewrite the stories so that the reader is left with no alternative but to follow the thread of his reconstituted narrative, which the introduction is, he fails to do so. What he succeeds in doing, however, is delineating how both the place of origin and the foreign landscape of these immigrants are equally uncomfortable and disturbing sites, how the reality they embody is a liminal one.

VI

There remains to be examined one more trope of contamination before I conclude my reading of Clarke as a figure that resides on the threshold of boundary lines. If, as I have shown, his elision of George's name is effectively his erasure of Pat's identity, it does not come as a surprise that he employs a similar strategy when he directly addresses the system. Despite his ambivalence about Canadian culture, or perhaps because of it, Clarke immediately locates himself and the other characters within it. "Canada" is the first word of his introduction.

"Canada," we read, "is the home of most of the characters in this collection" (1). The dislodging of origins as stable sites takes on a different guise now, for *Nine Men Who Laughed* operates as a text whose beginning and ending are disseminated into each other.

The introduction begins the book, but it is not the proper beginning since it was written after the stories were composed. The opening story constitutes the beginning, but its title parodies its inaugural position in the book: "A Funeral." These deferrals and renunciations prefigure the uncertainty of the book's end. The last story, "How He Does It," is not the end since the introduction was presumably written after it. The deferral of conclusion is also inscribed in the trope with which this last story ends, namely the set of ellipses that mark not so much the story's open-endedness as its self-reinscription, its desire to repeat itself by holding tight a truth of similitude that only the repetition of lies can enunciate. Here is the dialogue that gives a formal ending to the story, a dialogue between Joshua Miller-Corbaine (a man who has duped everyone, perhaps even himself) and his Jewish mistress after the latter's confrontation with Joshua's wife, whom he denounces as his maid:

> "I should have doubted her! Something, you know, about her appearance told me that a man in your position, wouldn't be associated with such a dowdy woman, such an ordinary—looking person!"
>
> "I told you I don't have a wife."
>
> "I'm sorry I didn't believe you."
>
> "Would I lie to you?"
>
> And he and she sit down to his dinner of lamb chops, brussel sprouts, Romaine salad and expresso coffee. (225)

The import of this passage rests on its last spoken line, but, because it is uttered by Joshua, its meaning collapses upon itself. Joshua is not just an incurable and intrepid liar. He is an itinerant character, for he travels from "A Man" to "How He Does It" with the same aplomb that he moves from one mistress to another. He "does it" by lying: by functioning as the spectral figure of the border-line separating truth from fiction.

There is here, then, a synchronicity of beginnings and endings that both articulates and misstates the function of their names. There is also an overlapping of origins that belies their claim to authenticity. Within the site that these disjunctions produce, there is, too, the splitting, and split, figure of contamination. For this jarring of formal and structural origins mirrors the dissolution of boundaries that construct the contesting ground of cultural and racial differences. This might not be what Clarke had in mind, but it is certainly what the text speaks as it develops its own strategies that militate against its author's "prepossessiveness."

It is when Clarke ventures to deal directly with "the prepossessive, less of the new culture" that his character best reveals itself:

> [Canada] was an attitude that became so much like ice water in the veins, that it ceased to be merely an attitude, but became the person who confronted me with her prepossessiveness, the woman, the system. The person was now a microcosm of all the words, bad conclusions and faulty definitions of "immigrant" and became a metaphor for arrogance.
>
> She, the attitude, the system, knew my meaning. Knew the meaning of the nine men who are, in a metaphorical sense, me. And since she knew

my meaning, the meaning of my writing and its importance, she assaulted me. It was an assault that was all the more reprehensible because it was based on personal knowledge. And the more so because its timing was deliberate, to catch me off-balance.

In their hearts, these men have refused to accept the various categorizations and all the conclusions that ... define them as "immigrants." ... They cannot sleep with the system or with the attitude.

But they do accommodate. They succumb to the assault. (2-3)

The excessive use of mixed metaphors and non sequiturs in these paragraphs is a sign of Clarke's style as character. He is the only "man" in the book whose laughter, if he laughs at all, is not inscribed in his discourse except as the trope par excellence that he chooses to interpret for readers. If laughter, as he tells us, is these immigrants' "only available weapon against resentment" (2), his own weapon is the image of "woman" that he constructs, or, to be more accurate, his emasculation of Canada as a hegemonic sign.

In an interview with Terrence Craig, Clarke said that the experience of immigration contributes to a "systematic draining" of male immigrants' "manhood" (118). This is exactly what Clarke defies here: he inverts the identity of the emasculated subject while, at the same time, blurring the signs of masculinity and emasculation. The dialectic structure of centre and margin is still operative, but it undergoes a series of crucial substitutions. Canada as centre is reconstituted as "woman," traditionally a sign of marginality; the immigrant still speaks from the margin but is imaged exclusively in masculinist, therefore traditionally dominant, terms.

Clarke does not exactly impede the dynamics that sustain the dialectical process whereby a centre maintains its position by defining itself against an excluded site. Because his dramatization of the conflict between centre and margin is extended to include gender conflict, the centre/margin dialectic goes awry. The chiastic relation that emerges from the performativity of Clarke's strategy helps to disclose the symptom of his colonial anxiety and desire, a symptom not unlike that characterizing George's condition in "Canadian Experience." Bhabha articulates that kind of anxiety and desire in the context of his reading of Frantz Fanon: "the very place of identification, caught in the tension of demand and desire, is a space of splitting. The fantasy of the native is precisely to occupy the master's place while keeping his place in the slave's avenging anger" (44). Clarke seeks to expose, and hopefully dissolve, the system's "prepossessiveness," its mastery over him. More importantly, he wants to do so without compromising his masculinity—a sign that he obviously values and identifies with a certain authenticity of the male immigrant subject. In order to maintain his manhood (that is, to avoid a same-sex encounter), he tropes Canada as "woman."

Interestingly enough, the centre in Clarke's gender-encoded script is a site that is contingent with, and therefore contaminated by, the woman/margin that he has insinuated into its space. As such, it is a space that he both covets and resists. By resisting the seductive, appropriating ploys of the system, he vouches for the intactness of his own masculinity. Apparently, though, the remaining men do not. Although Clarke tells us that "[t]hey cannot sleep with" her ("the attitude, the system")—thereby rendering her reprehensible assault on them ambiguous within the figurative schema he has constructed—he does admit later on that they "embrac[e] " the system (3, 5). He seems to avoid seduction as "man"[7] but not as writer, for he explains the intimate relationship between the nine men and the "system" by stressing that her "personal knowledge" of him applies to "the meaning of [his] writing" (3). This unwieldy intimacy and breach of boundary lines, this appropriation of his writing, is perhaps what best accounts for the logic of contamination inscribed in *Nine Men Who Laughed*—for those instances when the text speaks with and against its author.

VII

My employment of contamination as the operating code in this essay is not intended to undervalue the specificity of historical conflicts. Rather, I use it to accentuate the space within which these conflicts are enacted. In the introduction to *Nine Men Who Laughed*, Clarke performs a reading both of his stories and of the cultural conditions they rise from in a manner that elucidates, at least for this reader, the incommensurability of the colonial and diasporic experiences. He translates these experiences into a pathology of the immigrant subject, while showing that the source of this condition, the system, is not entirely immune to it. This does not mean that the system shares the immigrant's plight. In trying to construct its image of the Other, the system has to wrestle with its growing awareness that it is itself "othered" in the process. The conflictual encounter of system and immigrant not only brings to the fore the heterogeneity of each, but it also ensures that neither remains undifferentiated from the other.

Clarke's strategy of self-location thematizes the marginalized position of immigrants and asserts their differences. Yet, its multiple inversions, the relentless splitting that occurs in its discourse, reveal difference to be a matter of contingency. Not unlike the other men in this collection, Clarke practises a double gaze: as an immigrant, he looks backward to his homeland; as a writer, he rereads and rewrites his stories. In both cases, however, the origins that he traces are adulterated, their authenticities diffused. He encounters a similarly disturbed image when he gazes at the system that he both detests and embraces. This is why his writing himself into his own narratives both affirms and curtails his authority. The only stable figure that reveals itself to his gaze is that of ambivalence.

Endnotes

1. I am alluding here to Marlene Nourbese Philip's argument against Bissoondath's *A Casual Brutality* (see Nourbese Philip).
2. See her book *Oppositional Aesthetics*, and her essay "The Exclusions of Postcolonial Theory."
3. This is a liberal rendering of Gates' comments in his chapter "The Trope of the Talking Book" (137).
4. The pun I am attempting here obviously alludes to the elaborate process of signifyin(g) as it is practised in the Afro-American vernacular tradition (see Gates).
5. I am indebted for the formulation of this question to Lorna Jackson (a student in my graduate course on Canadian ethnic writing, University of Victoria, spring 1992).
6. They are, respectively, the Prime Minister, who manipulates the carnivalesque atmosphere of a

gravedigger's funeral in order to increase his waning popularity; the man who commits suicide; the "green hornet," who intends, at all costs, to break the "all-time record" for ticketing cars, especially those owned by "Wessindians" (59, 56); the Barbadian student at Trinity College who, as the title "If Only: Only If ..." suggests, regrets that he misjudged the potential of his Barbadian girlfriend; and the fake lawyer in "A Man" and "How He Does It," who mystifies his male friends as to how he manages to live a life of deceit.

7. One of the questions raised by Clarke's personification of Canada as woman involves, of course, the figure of the interracial couple, but I do not have the space to develop this point here.

Works Cited

Behdad, Ali. "Traveling to Teach: Postcolonial Critics in the American Academy." McCarthy and Crichlow 40-49.

Bhabha, Homi K. *The Location of Culture*. London: Routledge, 1994.

Brown, Lloyd W. *El Dorado and Paradise: Canada and the Caribbean in Austin Clarke's Fiction*. London: Centre for Social and Humanistic Studies, U of Western Ontario; Parkersburg, IA: Caribbean, 1989.

Brydon, Diana. "The White Inuit Speaks: Contamination as Literary Strategy." *Past the Last Post: Theorizing Post-Colonialism and Post-Modernism*. Ed. Ian Adam and Helen Tiffin. Calgary: U of Calgary P, 1990. 191-203.

Clarke, Austin. "Interview with Austin Clarke." With Terrence Craig. *World Literature Written in English* 6.1 (1986): 115-27.

_____. *Nine Men Who Laughed*. Markham, ON: Penguin, 1986.

Collier, Gordon. Introduction. *Us/Them: Translation, Transcription and Identity in Post-Colonial Literary Cultures*. Ed. Collier Amsterdam: Rodopi, 1992. xiii-xv.

Derrida, Jacques. *Dissemination*. Trans. Barbara Johnson. Chicago: U of Chicago P, 1981.

Foucault, Michel. "The Confession of the Flesh." *Power/Knowledge: Selected Interviews and Other Writings, 1972-1977*. Ed. Colin Gordon. Trans. Gordon, Leo Marshall, John Mepham, and Kate Soper. New York: Pantheon, 1980. 194-228.

Gates, Henry Louis, Jr. *The Signifying Monkey: A Theory of African-American Literary Criticism*. New York: Oxford UP, 1988.

Lionnet, Françoise. "Of Mangoes and Maroons: Language, History, and the Multicultural Subject of Michelle Cliff's *Abeng*." *De/Colonizing the Subject: The Politics of Gender in Women's Autobiography*. Ed. Sidonie Smith and Julia Watson. Minneapolis: U of Minnesota P, 1992.

McCarthy, Cameron, and Warren Crichlow, eds. *Race, Identity, and Representation in Education*. New York: Routledge, 1993.

Mukherjee, Arun P. "The Exclusions of Postcolonial Theory and Mulk Raj Anand's 'Untouchable': A Case Study." *Ariel* 22 (1991): 27-48.

_____. "Ironies of Colour in the Great White North: The Discursive Strategies of Some Hyphenated Canadians." *Double-Talking: Essays on Verbal and Visual Ironies in Contemporary Canadian Art and Literature*. Ed. Linda Hutcheon. Toronto: ECW, 1992. 158-71.

_____. "South Asian Poetry in Canada: In Search of a Place." *World Literature Written in English* 6.1 (1986): 84-98.

_____. *Oppositional Aesthetics: Readings from a Hyphenated Space.* Toronto: TSAR, 1994.

Nourbese Philip, M. "Immoral Fiction." *Frontiers: Selected Essays and Writings on Racism and Culture 1984 - 1992.* Stratford, ON: Mercury, 1992. 190-200.

Spivak, Gayatri Chakravorty. "Can the Subaltern Speak?" *Colonial Discourse and Postcolonial Theory: A Reader.* Ed. Patrick Williams and Laura Chrisman. 1993. New York: Columbia UP, 1994. 66-111.

Trinh, T. Minh-ha. *Woman, Native, Other: Writing Post-coloniality and Feminism.* Bloomington: Indiana UP, 1989.

West, Cornel. "The New Cultural Politics of Difference." McCarthy and Crichlow 11-23.

Experiences of Arrival: Jewishness and Caribbean-Canadian Identity in Austin Clarke's *The Meeting Point*

SARAH PHILLIPS CASTEEL

... the Jew must see that he is part of the history of Europe, and will always be so considered by the descendant of the slave. Always, that is, unless he himself is willing to prove that this judgment is inadequate and unjust. This is precisely what is demanded of all the other white men in this country, and the Jew will not find it easier than anybody else.

> —James Baldwin, "Negroes Are Anti-Semitic Because They're Anti-White," 1967

As a child, in what seemed to me a hostile country, the Jews were the only minority group discussed with reference to exploitation and racialism, and for that reason, I naturally identified with them. At that time, I was staunchly indignant about everything from the Holocaust to the Soviet persecution of Jewry. The bloody excesses of colonialism, the pillage and rape of modern Africa, the transportation of 11 million black people to the Americas, and their subsequent bondage were not on the curriculum, and certainly not on the television screen. As a result I vicariously channelled a part of my hurt and frustration through the Jewish experience.

> —Caryl Phillips, *The European Tribe*, 1987

I begin with these two epigraphs from James Baldwin and Caryl Phillips not in order to debate their truth value or to enter into the minefield of American race relations, but rather to illustrate the range of associations that Jewishness may carry in the black diasporic imagination. From the late 1960s perspective of the African-American writer James Baldwin, Jews are white oppressors, and to suggest otherwise is to excuse their participation in all manner of economic exploitation of African Americans. By contrast, for the Caribbean-born writer Caryl Phillips, reflecting twenty years later on his British childhood, Jewishness connotes the racial persecution of minorities, and in a certain sense stands in for blackness itself. In *The European Tribe*, Phillips cites the same passage from Baldwin that I have quoted above, remarking that he has always been puzzled by the anti-Semitic strain in African-American thought. As a child, Phillips identified strongly with Jews as fellow victims of European racism, and in *The European Tribe* he presents the oppression of Jews and blacks as being coextensive. While visiting the Anne Frank House, Phillips contemplates an anti-Semitic banner from a 1924 Berlin demonstration: "I have seen banners carrying such messages in London, but for 'Jew' read 'black'. Very little seems to have changed in the heart of Europe" (69). He asserts that for many "the Jew is still Europe's nigger" and cites Fanon's warning that "Whenever you hear anyone abuse the Jews, pay attention, because he is talking about you" (5354).[1]

The conflicting readings of Jewishness that Baldwin and Phillips put forward from their diverging cultural and historical perspectives testify to the instability of Jewishness as a signifier in the black diasporic imagination. The connotations of Jewishness for the black author

vary across not only time (in this case the civil rights era
vs. the late 1980s) but also space (Baldwin's Harlem vs.
Phillips' tribalized Europe). Indeed, if the figure of the
Jew in North American and European literatures more
generally is typified by its racial ambiguity,[2] this ambiguity may be traced across numerous black diasporic texts
as well. An illuminating case in point is Caribbean-
Canadian author Austin Clarke's Toronto Trilogy. The
first volume of the trilogy, *The Meeting Point* (1967),
which was published in the same year as Baldwin's essay,
elaborates a black Canadian reading of Jewishness that
may be compared with other black diasporic images of
the Jew such as those advanced by Baldwin and Phillips.
The Meeting Point hinges on a complex analogy between
the Caribbean and Jewish immigrant experiences in
Canada, which works at various points to both associate
and dissociate the two diasporas, In particular, Clarke
capitalizes on the racial ambiguity of the figure of the Jew
in order to highlight his Caribbean immigrant characters'
unstable relationship to blackness in post-war Toronto.

Tensions between blacks and Jews in twentieth-
century America (powerfully evoked in Art Spiegelman's
controversial 1993 New Yorker cover image of a Hasidic
Jew kissing a black woman) have tended to texture even
those discussions of black-Jewish relations that extend
beyond the borders of the United States. As Caribbean-
Canadian writer Marlene NourbeSe Philip remarks, it is
"difficult not to be aware of the allegations and counter-
allegations south of the [Canada-US] border between Jews
and African Americans" (66). While remaining sensitive
to such tensions, however, her discussion of black-Jewish
relations more closely echoes Caryl Phillips' account of his
adolescent identification with Jews. She recalls:

> At twelve, possibly, thirteen, I was outraged and upset
> at what had happened to the Jews. In the silence
> surrounding my own history and my own memory,
> I took to myself the pain of what had happened to
> Jewish people in Europe. Perhaps—I am sure that at
> some deeper level I knew what had happened to my
> own people ..., and that I was on the journey to my
> own past albeit through a surrogate issue. It matters
> not how we come to understand oppression, provided
> we take the lessons to heart and apply them to our
> lives. (65)

As a Canadian and a Briton of Caribbean descent respectively, Marlene NourbeSe Philip and Caryl Phillips stand
at a certain remove from the American scene, as do Paul
Gilroy and Derek Walcott, to cite two other notable
examples of black authors who have written sympathetically on Jewish themes.[3] These instances of Caribbean
diasporic identifications with Jewishness suggest that the
figure of the Jew carries significantly different associations
in the Caribbean and its diasporas in Britain and Canada
than it does in an African-American context.[4] I would
like to hold on to this distance, and to the alternative
symbolic associations of Jewishness that it opens up, in
order to enable a less polarized reading of the meeting of
Jews and Caribbean immigrants in the Canadian setting
of Austin Clarke's fiction.

The Meeting Point as Au Pair Narrative

Set in the early 1960s, *The Meeting Point* tells the story
of post-war Caribbean immigration to Canada through
the eyes of Bernice Leach, a Barbadian woman who
works as a domestic in Toronto. While a few Caribbean

immigrants had trickled into Canada earlier in the century to work in coal mines or as railway porters, black immigration was on the whole severely restricted by what one scholar has described as the "White Canada policy," so designated because it gave preferential treatment to northern European applicants in an attempt to maintain the British character of the population (Knowles 152). In the fifties and early sixties, Canadian officials continued to discourage Caribbean immigration, but limited numbers of Caribbean immigrants gained entry as a result of labour shortages in nursing and domestic work. In 1955, the federal government introduced the West Indian Domestic Scheme in response to the growing need for childcare that resulted from the movement of white Canadian women into the workforce.[5] Bernice and other female characters in *The Meeting Point* were modelled on these Caribbean domestics, with whom Clarke socialized as a student (Algoo-Baksh 36).

The Meeting Point, which focuses the reader's attention on the life of the Caribbean domestic, is an early instance of a genre that Bruce Robbins has labelled the post-colonial "au pair narrative" (143). According to Robbins, au pair narratives serve as "allegories of upward mobility" in which the metropole is problematically privileged as the site of the self-realization of the third-world subject (137). *The Meeting Point*, however, performs a powerful critique of this promise of self-fulfillment in the metropole by presenting Bernice's response to her new environment as deeply ambivalent. Throughout the novel, Bernice vacillates between a strong antipathy towards her inhospitable adoptive country and a hedonistic enjoyment of the material benefits that Canada offers. Bernice's relationship with her employers is equally conflicted. She feels exploited by them and frustrated by her powerlessness to demand higher wages, and yet she is moved to sympathy by their occasional acts of kindness and their own personal sufferings. Bernice's ambivalence manifests itself in her perpetually shifting ethnic, racial, and religious identities.

Bernice finds employment as a domestic for the Burrmanns, a wealthy Jewish family in Forest Hill for whom she must prepare blintzes as well as grilled cheese sandwiches. In keeping with the parameters of the au pair narrative, *The Meeting Point*'s focus is primarily on the dynamics between Bernice and the Burrmanns within the narrow confines of the domestic space that Bernice occupies: "It was a life, which, although restricted by virtue of her being a domestic in Forest Hill Village, nevertheless, was an interesting perspective into the world around her, the world of riches in Forest Hill itself" (131). The bulk of the novel takes place in the Forest Hill home of the Burrmanns, ensuring that both Jewish and Caribbean concerns are constantly in view. Since Bernice's entertainment consists in large part of observing the eccentricities of the Burrmanns, we are given as much insight into the Burrmanns' psychological drama as we are into Bernice's condition. At the same time as it explores Bernice's ambivalent relationship to blackness, Clarke's novel also exposes significant ambiguities surrounding the ethnic and racial identities of Bernice's Jewish employers.

Clarke's treatment of the Caribbean immigrant experience and rendition of the au pair narrative is particularly striking in its heavy emphasis on the Jewish presence in Toronto. In the first two volumes of the trilogy, virtually all of the non-Caribbean characters are Jewish, with the notable exception of Brigitte, an anti-Semitic German domestic. Moreover, in the course of juxtaposing the Jewish and Caribbean experiences of arrival,[6] Clarke devotes considerable attention to his Jewish characters' anxieties surrounding their racial and social status. Clarke's nuanced investigation of his Jewish characters' experience of assimilation has been obscured, however, by the critical literature's tendency to conflate Jewishness and whiteness. Horace Goddard, for example, describes Bernice's predicament in terms of an opposition between white and black: "Working for the Burrmanns [Bernice] is in a white world within which she is relegated to the black's perpetual state of slavery" (39). As a consequence, he argues, "Bernice builds up an inner hate for *the Burrmanns and whites in general*" (40; my emphasis). Clarke's biographer Stella Algoo-Baksh also subsumes the Jewish characters under the category of whiteness even as she emphasizes that whiteness has ethnic content.[7] There is no doubt that Bernice views the Burrmanns as an oppressive presence, but the standard reading of the Burrmanns as white oppressors does not in and of itself account for Clarke's decision to incorporate Jewish characters into his novel. On the whole, then, bell hooks' observation "that we lac[k] a complex language to talk about white Jewish identity in the United States and its relationship to blackness and black identity" (230) would seem to apply in a Canadian context as well.

    To a certain extent, the critical assumption that there is a basic and insurmountable hostility between blacks and Jews in Clarke's novel reflects the influence of American readings of race. Jewish-American writer Cynthia Ozick has described the deep suspicion with which the possibility of black-Jewish alliances is often regarded in the United States: "what has surprised some Jews, perhaps many, is that this Jewish assumption—this quiet tenet, to use a firmer word, that wounds recognize wounds—is not only not taken for granted by everyone else, especially by blacks, but is given no credibility whatsoever. Worse, to articulate the assumption is to earn the accusation of impudence" (46). This atmosphere of mistrust between blacks and Jews in the US informs one critic's conclusion that Jewish characters predominate in *The Meeting Point* because the Jew is the most visible oppressor of North American blacks, "for Jews are as important in the West Indian community of Canadian domestics as they are in the black slums of the United States" (Brown, "West Indian Novel" 102).

Clarke is in fact much more equivocal on the question of black-Jewish relations than the critical literature would suggest. His treatment of Jewishness calls into question static, binary constructions of black and white and thereby also works against the conflation of the American and Canadian contexts. For if *The Meeting Point* resists a reading of the Jewish characters as straightforwardly white, it also resists the absorption of Caribbean-Canadian experience into a larger discourse about African-American culture that would rely on an undifferentiated category of North American blackness.[8] Just as labelling Jews "white" obscures their problematic relationship to whiteness, labelling Caribbean Canadians as uncomplicatedly "black" elides their difference from African Americans and other black populations in Canada. A reading that posits black and white as stable and homogeneous categories makes it possible to treat *The Meeting Point* as though it takes place in Harlem rather than Toronto and to neglect the considerably different historical experiences of Caribbean Canadians.[9]

Challenging this "American" reading, *The Meeting Point* emphasizes through its engagement with Jewish as well as Caribbean diasporic themes that both whiteness and blackness are unstable categories that are profoundly conditioned by local and national contexts.

Jews and Whiteness

> *[Sam Burrmann] did not have what Bernice came to know as "the typical Jewish features"; and she felt that had he so wished, he could pass as an Italian, in summer; a very clear-skin washed-out Negro in winter.*
>
> —Clarke, *The Meeting Point*

When we first meet Bernice's employer Mrs. Burrmann, she is reading *Herzog*, Saul Bellow's acclaimed 1964 novel of modern Jewish-American alienation. In many respects, the project of *The Meeting Point*, which appeared six years after Herzog, parallels that of Bellow's novel. Like Bellow, Clarke is attempting to expand the scope of the post-war North American novel to make space for the representation of a diasporic group that is situated outside the mainstream. Towards this goal, for example, both authors infuse the established literary language with the cadences of a vernacular idiom. The 1950s have been dubbed "the Jewish decade" of American literature because of the unprecedented recognition gained by Jewish-American writers during this period (Harap 21), and Clarke's reference to Herzog suggests that he may have drawn inspiration from Jewish writers' breakthrough into the mainstream during the decade that preceded the publication of *The Meeting Point*. Similarly, for Clarke's Caribbean immigrants, the Jews provide a precedent for successful integration into Canadian society, but in this case the Jewish example proves to be a cautionary one.

Rather than equating Jewishness and whiteness in *The Meeting Point*, Clarke consistently draws attention to the racial ambiguity of Jewishness. In an early scene in the novel, Bernice serves as the unwilling moderator of a discussion of race among the children under her charge. When the son of a Jewish neighbour taunts Bernice for being black, the Burrmanns' daughter defends her:

> "You're not even white, wise guy," Ruthie said. "You're just a lousy little Jew, like all of us."
>
> "Oh God, man! you shouldn't call your friend by them hard words." And Bernice shook her head in sorrow.
>
> "I'm not a Jew. I am white. And, and-and-and ... she's black then, anyhow." (27)

In this revealing passage, Clarke exposes connections between the racism that the Jews direct towards the Caribbean immigrants and their anxieties about their own racial status. The boy's response to Ruthie's reprimand suggests that, for the Forest Hill Jews, emphasizing the blackness of their Caribbean servants is a means of insisting on their own whiteness in a country with a long history of de facto discrimination against Jews.[10]

The period in which the Burrmanns would have grown up was an intensely xenophobic one in Canada's history. In the Toronto of the twenties, thirties, and forties, Jews were subject to discriminatory hiring practices, quotas for university students, anti-Semitic riots, and various forms of racial segregation (see Hiebert). In particular, anti-Semitic immigration practices demonstrated that Jews did not form part of the white Canada envisioned by Mackenzie King and Frederick Blair, his deputy minister of immigration. In the early twentieth century, Jews, along with other eastern European immigrants and their southern and central European counterparts, were not considered desirable members of the Canadian nation, which had long been imagined as a home for the "northern races" (Andersen et al. 8-9). By the mid-1960s, however, the Burrmanns and their Jewish friends are able to make a firmer—if still anxious—claim on whiteness and Canadian belonging.

In tracing this shift towards an expanded definition of Canadian whiteness, Clarke highlights what a number of scholars have documented in the US context: the extent to which Jews exemplify the unstable and contested character of whiteness in the early and mid-twentieth century. In *How Jews Became White Folks*, American anthropologist Karen Brodkin shows that, in the United States in the early twentieth century when Jews were concentrated in industrial labour, they were racialized as non-white and underwent a "temporary darkening" (76). After World War II, however, in the US (as in Canada) suburban expansion and post-war prosperity facilitated the incorporation of Jews into whiteness and the middle class. Matthew Frye Jacobson opens his book *Whiteness of a Different Color* with an excerpt from Jewish-American author Philip Roth that explores the "seemingly natural but finally unstable logic of race" (2). As Jacobson notes, the Jewish experience is closely connected to that of numerous other European immigrant groups—including the Irish, Italians, Poles, and Greeks—who were initially racialized as non-white upon their arrival in the New World.

This historical context accounts for Clarice's Jewish characters' conviction that they are not quite white.[12] Moreover, as the children's conversation with Bernice suggests, if the Jews are not white in the eyes of the Wasp establishment, they console themselves that at least they are more white than the Caribbean immigrants they employ. As Jews, they exhibit a sense of marginality with regard to whiteness but a sense of whiteness and belonging with regard to blackness (see Brodkin 2), consolidating their claim to whiteness at the expense of Bernice and the other Caribbean immigrants. It is this contrastive logic that explains Mrs. Burrmann's decision to hire a Caribbean domestic. Initially, Bernice cannot fathom why Mrs. Burrmann employs her and then persists in doing much of the housework herself: "Sometimes I wonder why, with me here, she still killing herself over the house," Bernice confides to her sister Estelle who is visiting from Barbados. "You think it is because she must have somebody beneath her?" (163). Bernice eventually concludes that her presence in the household enables Mrs. Burrmann to assert her newfound social status, the security of her place in Toronto society. Bernice's presence signals that Mrs. Burrmann is both more white and less of an outsider than Bernice. Thus Mrs. Burrmann purchases Bernice's labour much as Bernice purchases clothes at Eaton's: not out of need but rather by way of assimilating to Canadian society and claiming a place in it;[13] yet it is precisely this desire to assert her Canadianness that makes Mrs. Burrmann's gesture of hiring Bernice such an anxious one. Mrs. Burrmann's family had arrived penniless from Poland only one generation prior; for her and her husband, the difficulties of immigrant life and the sense of exclusion are painfully fresh.

The Burrmanns' adoption of racist postures constitutes another such assimilationist gesture, a claim to membership in the white majority. While one critic has argued that the Jewish characters' "identification with the prevailing norm of white prejudice" falsifies their claim "to some special status of brotherhood in suffering" (Brown, "West Indian Novel" 100-101), I would suggest that the Jews' very prejudice bespeaks their anxieties about their own integration, and thus paradoxically aligns them more closely with the Caribbean immigrants. Clarke's emphasis is not so much on the Jews' forfeiture of their claim to fellow victimhood as it is on the insecurities that inform their racist gestures. Accordingly, the racism that the Burrmanns direct towards Bernice is continually offset by the racism that they direct towards themselves. Jewish self-hatred is a prominent feature of the Burrmanns, whose cocktail parties are punctuated by anti-Semitic jokes, much to Bernice's astonishment: "Bernice was puzzled, even after having witnessed so many times how these people could laugh at jokes about Jews, when they were all Jews themselves" (13). In this regard, too, the Jews' behaviour is echoed by the Caribbean immigrants, who exhibit their own forms of self-hatred and occasionally flirt with anti-Semitism, as when Henry paints a swastika on the door of a woman who has angered him in *Storm of Fortune*.

By highlighting behavioural parallels between his Caribbean and Jewish characters, Clarke resists slotting them neatly into a black/white binary. Instead, he periodically reduces the distance between the two groups, both literally and figuratively, even as he draws attention to the power imbalance between them. Toronto is indeed a "meeting point" for Clarke's Jewish and Caribbean characters, who engage in a variety of troubled friendships and cross-cultural relationships, one of which results in a pregnancy. In particular, Agatha, a Jewish acquaintance of the Caribbean immigrants, brings the Caribbean characters into close contact with Jews through her inter-racial romance with Henry, a Caribbean immigrant, and her somewhat one-sided friendship with Bernice's sister Estelle. The most positive image of black-Jewish relations in the novel is that of a black woman and a Jewish man holding hands and leading an anti-racism protest march.[14] Agatha's volatile relationship with Henry is, however, more typical of the uneasy and vexed relations between Jews and Caribbean immigrants in Clarke's novel. Agatha is resented by the Caribbean women and her clumsy attempt to commiserate with them as a Jew is rebuffed. Nonetheless her attachment to Henry appears to be genuine, and she suffers considerably as a result. When Agatha becomes engaged to Henry in *Storm of Fortune*, she is informed by Bernice and her friend Dots that she has now become "one o' we," "a Wessindian"—a gesture of friendship that is subsequently withdrawn (149).

In his discussion of the au pair narrative, Robbins notes that writers such as Jamaica Kincaid and Bharati Mukherjee abandon the marriage plot between master and servant that served as the end-point for nineteenth-century antecedents of the genre such as *Jane Eyre*. *The Meeting Point* similarly refuses the narrative of class mobility through marriage. A deeply troubled affair between master and servant unfolds in *The Meeting Point*, with Estelle substituting for her sister Bernice as the recipient of the master's attentions. Sam Burrmann initiates a sexual relationship with Estelle in a scene that highlights the power differential between the two protagonists. Sam "stand[s] over her like a landlord and not a lover," with "a criminal's grin" on his face (190), while in her interior monologue Estelle expresses both fear and a desire for revenge. The language of conquest and physical aggression permeates this and later scenes between Sam and Estelle. Subsequent to the rape scene, however, they are described as having an "affair" and even a "friendship." Several times they profess their love for each other, but the words ring increasingly hollow and a more violent undertone returns as the relationship deteriorates. When Estelle becomes pregnant, Sam disowns the child, and Estelle's botched attempt to abort the pregnancy results in a miscarriage and her hospitalization at the end of the novel.

Even as the relationship between Estelle and Sam in many respects confirms the Caribbean immigrants' perception that they are trapped in a twentieth-century form of slavery, Clarke also probes deep into Sam's past in order to complicate the image of him as the white master. Sam, who is strongly associated with blackness throughout the novel, is in fact the figure who most obviously disturbs the black/white binary. Sam is "the poor Jew, who had brains, but no social acceptability" (5), the son of a peddler who could not afford to move his family out of their downtown Toronto immigrant neighbourhood when the rest of the Jews left. In his "Spadina days," Burrmann had imitated the mannerisms and pastimes of "the Harlem-like men" he met in the jazz clubs he frequented (181). In the present time of the novel, while endeavouring to maintain an image of Anglo respectability that meets his wife's rigorous standards, Sam is irresistibly drawn to aspects of black culture that are familiar to him from his youth. He conceals these parts of his past from his wife for fear she will disapprove:

> Mr. Burrmann really never felt at home, at home. Not even when [he was] a boy growing up on Palmerston Boulevard in the guts of old downtown Toronto, in the days when Jews inhabited and ruled that entire section. ... He used to spend those days in a "gang." Some of the "gangsters" were young "coloured boys," sons of West Indians who had come to Canada to work as porters on the railroads, and as domestics in white, rich kitchens and homes. ... Bernice did not know (not even Mrs. Burrmann from whom he hid it ...) that he had been close to black people throughout his adolescence and university days. (147-48)

Sam later becomes the first Jew to attend Trinity College at the University of Toronto and subsequently a successful lawyer. Yet his preference for jazz over his wife's Beethoven and his deeply troubled affair with Estelle bespeak his incomplete assimilation. Perhaps the most striking indicator of Sam's failure to achieve a secure sense of Canadian identity is Bernice's characterization of his physical appearance. Bernice notes that her employer does not have "the typical Jewish features," that "he could pass as an Italian, in summer; a very clear-skin washed-out Negro in winter" (210). Rather than identifying Sam as white, Bernice's description signals the ambiguity of his racial status. The description locates him somewhere on a continuum between black and white and suggests the possibility of sliding between racial assignments.

As in other au pair narratives such as Jamaica Kincaid's *Lucy*, in Clarke's novel the domestic worker's proximity to her employers functions to deflate the myth of the harmonious North American family; yet in *The Meeting Point*, not only marital infidelities and domestic discord are brought to light by Bernice's intense scrutiny of the Burrmanns, but also their incomplete assimilation. Because Bernice is subject to some of these same anxieties, she is particularly sensitive to the unease that Mrs. Burrmann's socialite persona masks: "She saw Mrs. Burrmann put down her glass of port; pass her hands over her cheeks as if she was removing a stain, or pain; look purposely frustrated, and alien amongst the happiness" (11). The Burrmanns' insecurity about their status in Canadian society is evidenced by the lengths to which they go to anglicize themselves. Mrs. Burrmann likes to remind others that she comes from respectable Jewish stock, from "one of North America's best diasporas" (5). She "was brought up in an orthodox Jewish home with Christian dispositions" (185) and prefers the Unitarian Church to her local synagogue. For his part, Sam is being suffocated by an Anglo-Canadian society that demands cultural conformity.

While for Clarke's Caribbean immigrants the Burrmanns offer a model to be emulated insofar as they have achieved economic success, in moral and spiritual terms their example is a negative one. When Bernice observes the drunken behaviour of some of Mrs. Burrmann's cocktail party guests, she judges them morally deficient: "And this was when Bernice, like a tablet of ten commandments, flounced away in great disgust: these people are doomed doomed doomed, she told God" (66). Recalling the debauched scene sometime later, she distances herself from her Jewish employers and their friends: "lawlessness to the height! I too glad I is a poor black woman!" (66). In this allusion to the Exodus story,

Bernice figures as the Burrmanns' moral conscience, condemning the Jews who have escaped from bondage only to relapse into idolatrous behaviour; but the critique is not unidirectional. The Burrmanns' "Egyptian" decadence serves as a warning to her against the dangers of an empty materialism to which the Caribbean immigrants are also susceptible.

Bernice and her friends are jealous of their employers' wealth but at the same time recognize the cost of that success: self-alienation and the partial effacement of their identity. The Burrmanns' dysfunctional marriage and sexual problems are symptomatic of the emotional ruin and the costs of assimilation that lie behind the glitzy façade of their economic achievements. As we discover with Boysie and Dots in *Storm of Fortune* and *The Bigger Light*, the Caribbean immigrants soon follow the path of the Burrmanns, sacrificing emotional and marital fulfillment to material ambition.

Caribbean Canadians and Blackness

> *Bernice had not then liked the word "black" used to describe her colour. It was before she began reading the Black Muslim newspaper, Muhammad Speaks.*
>
> —Clarke, *The Meeting Point*

Clarke's emphasis on the Burrmanns' incomplete assimilation draws attention to Bernice's own efforts to adjust to her host society, efforts that—while far less successful than those of the Burrmanns—nonetheless in many ways parallel them. Bernice's anxious consumption of clothes from Eaton's echoes the behaviour of the

Burrmanns, who compensate for their insecurities by drowning themselves in material goods and alcohol. Like Mrs. Burrmann, Bernice attempts to anglicize and whiten herself, straightening her hair and applying to her skin a complexion-lightening cream purchased in Harlem. Mrs. Burrmann facilitates this process, transferring to her a collection of Avon cosmetics and various articles of clothing that help her to appear more "Canadian." The two women embark on a joint programme of intellectual and spiritual improvement as well. Mrs. Burrmann's return to university inspires Bernice to start reading *Life* and *Time*, and both women look to religion as a means of assimilating. Mrs. Burrmann, who never visits the synagogue, goes so far as to use Bernice as a decoy to bring Christian missionaries into her house. Mrs. Burrmann's abandonment of the synagogue is echoed by Bernice's departure from the Negro Baptist Church in favour of the Unitarian Church to which Mrs. Burrmann had once belonged:

> This was a much better church, she felt. ... It was a cleaner and wealthier church than her old Negro Baptist Church; and the congregation was all white—or mostly white; and they did not come to church to moan and groan, and exchange experiences about white people and about racial discrimination. Bernice felt purged, in a way. She chopped an inch off the hemline of her dresses; stopped wearing nylon stockings with seams and began stepping out into the pearly white, white virginity of winter and broad-minded liberal Christianity, clickitty-clacketty, in a pair of Italian three-quarter heels. (29-30)

The Burrmanns' repression of their ethnic identities and their anxious attempts to identify as white Canadians thus serve to echo and amplify Bernice's and the other immigrants' own assimilationist gestures. The Burrmanns construct their whiteness in opposition to Bernice's blackness, fixing her racial identity in order to become more secure in their own. For their part, Clarke's Caribbean immigrants also polarize racial identities when it suits their needs, tending to identify as "black" and to adopt anti-Semitic views when they feel most oppressed. At one point in the novel after a particularly unpleasant encounter with Canadian racism, Bernice listens sympathetically to the German domestic Brigitte's complaints against her Jewish employers: "Working for these Jews is terrible. I was a Nazi. I am German. I confess to you, Bernice darlink, that as a German, I know what Nazis had in their heart about these people." "Girl, I understand," Bernice responds (205). In this scene, Bernice endorses Brigitte's anti-Semitic views as a gesture of solidarity with a fellow domestic and fellow immigrant; yet Bernice herself never spouts anti-Semitic rhetoric despite her tremendous frustrations with her working conditions in the Burrmann household. She has none of Brigitte's ideological conviction, instead altering her opinion of the Burrmanns according to her mood and their behaviour.

In much the same way, Bernice lacks a coherent conception of blackness. In the scene in which the children argue about whether Jews are white, Bernice is upset by the young Jewish boy's repeated insistence that she is black not only because of the boy's naïve racism but also because she does not at this point in the novel use the term "black" to describe herself. It is only after visiting Harlem and subscribing to *Muhammad Speaks* that she comes to briefly identify herself as a black Muslim. Her radicalization is fairly limited, however, and the rhetoric of American blackness remains foreign to her as she continues to distance herself from Harlem-style constructions of blackness. At the end of *The Meeting Point*, Bernice appears to shed any residual identification with American blackness when she prevents her sister Estelle from joining an anti-racism protest march: "But this is Canada, dear, not America. You and me, we is West Indians, not American Negroes. We are not in that mess. Leave that damn foolishness to them, you hear?" (306).[15]

Bernice's negotiation of a variety of racial, ethnic, and religious identities illustrates the processual nature of "blackening," a term that Rinaldo Walcott introduces to denote both the imposition of discourses about blackness onto subjects and these subjects' own inscriptions of those discourses.[16] *The Meeting Point* calls attention to the performative dimension of Canadian blackness and other racialized identities in a series of scenes in the trilogy in which the Caribbean characters impersonate not only African Americans but also Jews. Bernice and the other Caribbean immigrants repeatedly adopt African-American tastes, attitudes, and idioms but then dispense with them as swiftly as they do hairstyles and clothing. A black childhood acquaintance of Sam's laces his speech with Harlem jive talk, and Henry similarly favours a "Harlem American slang" (274). Elsewhere in the novel, by contrast, Dots mimics Mrs. Gasstein, a Jewish neighbour, and in *Storm of Fortune*, Dots' husband Boysie wears a nylon stocking on his head that resembles Mr. Burrmann's skullcap. Similarly in *Storm of Fortune*, Bernice fantasizes that she has taken the place of her employer so that she has now become "Mistress Bernice Burrmann," the "black Jew" (94).[17] These impersonations of Jews are brief and farcical, but they nonetheless point to a larger pattern of behaviour exhibited by Clarke's characters, who over the course of the trilogy assume a variety of ethnic identities and postures that expose the instability of racial assignments.

Through the Caribbean immigrants' erratic engagements with African-American culture, we witness how the valency of race changes according to local and national contexts. As Bernice moves between Barbados, Toronto, and Harlem, her religious and ethnic identities shift as a result of the racial categories imposed on her and according to her attitude towards her environment and her employers:

> "I happy as hell in Canada," she once told Dots; and Dots had to wonder whether it was the same person who had said last week, "Canada, Mississippi, Alabama, South Africa, God, they is all the same thing!" And when Dots asked how, Bernice added, "As far as a black person is concerned." This made Dots very unhappy and confused. But it was this ambivalence which Bernice entertained even with the Burrmanns: on Monday morning, she hated Mrs. Burrmann for what she had done to her over the weekend, and by Friday, she was in Mrs. Burrmann's corner, blaming Mr. Burrmann for his wife's drinking. And she would say he was giving his wife a dog's life. And sometimes too, she would say, "Child, it is Canada that liberate me, you hear?" (131)

In this passage, Clarke links Bernice's volatile view of Canada to her feelings about the Burrmanns, both of which are subject to dramatic fluctuations. When Bernice is feeling most exploited, she draws on American conceptions of blackness, likens her situation to slavery, and identifies as a Muslim. Alternately, when she feels comforted by the Britishness of Canada, she becomes "coloured" and Unitarian.

In general, Clarke's Caribbean immigrants maintain a highly ambivalent relationship to Harlem and the alternative, more militant conception of blackness it represents. Estelle initially wishes that she were coming to the United States rather than Canada, enthusiastically declaring that "America is a place of places! ... America is really God's country on earth" (81). Dots' husband Boysie, in contrast, argues that Canada is more integrated than the United States (a position he later revises): "That is one reason why I like this country, and hate Amer'ca so blasted much. Things tough, here. That is true, 'cause I been trying to track-down a job for eight months now. Still, you could see a star o' progress, here" (82).

Part of the appeal of Canada for the Caribbean immigrants lies in its colonial flavour. Bernice has only heard Negro spirituals on the radio and has little sense of connection to African-American culture. By contrast, she prizes her cheque-book from the Royal Bank of Canada for the British lion that is emblazoned on it, and feels that her money is secure in a bank that she associates with the British monarchy: "The word, Royal, gave it that special flavour and prestige" (134). On the drive into Toronto from the airport, Estelle is impressed to see a sign for Cadbury chocolate as well as the Palmolive building: "We uses to use that same soap, back home" (90). Thus both Bernice and Estelle exhibit what Katie Trumpener identifies as a "transcolonial consciousness," an awareness of linkages among Britain's colonies resulting from the "circulation of goods and customs, ideas and ideologies, languages and literary tropes" (244).

In Bernice's case, this transcolonial sensibility at times supersedes racial identifications, her sense of affiliation with Canada as a former British colony overriding a racially based identification with African Americans. When her feelings of kinship with Canada are not reciprocated by her host society, however, an alternative identification with African Americans becomes more appealing to her. Bernice's ambivalent relationship with Canada and her fluctuating identifications with American blackness can therefore be understood in terms of the contradictions that ensue from Canada's transcolonial but asymmetrical relationship to the Caribbean.

In addition to the transcolonial, another basis for identification that Clarke explores in *The Meeting Point* is gender. Closely observing the marital travails of her employer, Bernice at regular intervals identifies with Mrs. Burrmann as a fellow victim of male oppression and experiences "spasms of affection" for her employer (154). At one of the Burrmanns' parties, both women suffer the indignity of being pinched on the behind by a drunken guest, and they often commiserate over the failings of men. It is striking that the moment of greatest closeness between Bernice and Mrs. Burrmann is also that at which Mrs. Burrmann reverts to her Jewish identity. When Bernice receives news of her mother's death, Mrs. Burrmann comforts her and murmurs some words in Hebrew (or possibly Yiddish), "a language Bernice had heard spoken very seldom in the house" (232). Mrs. Burrmann recalls European relatives whom she has lost, and the two women are united by their common experience of suffering: "Black woman and Jew woman together, in grief and sorrow, feeling the same sorrow and feeling the same grief, experiencing the same emotion, as if I were her sister, and she were my sister," Bernice affirms (245). In this passage, both gender and ethnicity are cited as the basis for a rapprochement; yet the news of Bernice's mother's death proves to be false, and the intimacy between the two women is quickly broken.

Clarke's presentation of Bernice's various attempts to define her identity and of her shifting relationship to blackness reminds us of the necessity of situating *The Meeting Point* in both its national and transnational/transcolonial contexts. Bernice's and the other Caribbean immigrants' efforts to establish their identities and to secure their place in Canada expose a tension between transnational categories of race, religion, and gender on the one hand, and national and local contexts on the other. Transnational racial affiliations are potentially empowering for the Caribbean immigrants, who are radicalized by their cross-border identification with African Americans. Racial categories can also be mystifying, however, when they function to obscure the particularities of the national or local setting. Clarke resists such a mystification by stressing the ways in which moving between national contexts puts pressure on and transforms his characters' ethnic and racial identities.

Clarke's Analogic Strategy

In his 1982 essay "In the Semi-Colon of the North," Clarke recalls a train journey from Toronto to Timmins, the town to which he moved five years after his initial arrival in Canada in 1955. Clarke introduces a Jewish motif towards the end of the essay when the train passes through a town improbably named Swastika. This jarring event prompts him to reflect on both the victims of the

Holocaust who were transported across Europe in trains and their "namesakes in Toronto [who] could not rent a cottage in the weekended lakes" (36). As he waits for the train to reach his destination, he contemplates how a Jew might respond to arriving in the town of Swastika: "I try to imagine how a namesake of those European times, would feel entering this northern Ontario town with its brazen name, for the War is still raging in our painful memories" (37). Thus as in his fiction, here Clarke reads the Caribbean experience of arrival (in this case his own) against an earlier Jewish encounter with Canadian xenophobia. Like *The Meeting Point*, Clarke's essay is informed by a sense, not of an equivalence, but of a resonance between Caribbean and Jewish experiences of arrival.

Having refused a polarized or "American" reading of black-Jewish relations, *The Meeting Point* would seem to open up the possibility of cross-cultural alliances. The instability of racial assignments and the resonances between the Caribbean and Jewish immigrant experiences that Clarke highlights suggest that there is a potential for solidarity between the two groups, as in the image of the black woman and Jewish man leading the anti-racism pro-test march. Indeed, Sam Burrmann's childhood memories recall a time when Jewish and Caribbean immigrants had lived in much closer contact in Toronto's downtown.[18] However, while there are isolated moments in the novel in which a rapprochement seems possible, more typical of *The Meeting Point* are the failed attempts of a Jewish student, Agatha, to claim kinship with the Caribbean immigrants on the basis of her Jewishness. The Caribbean women are generally dismissive of Agatha's overtures, and her relationship with Henry collapses under pressure from both sides to "stick to their own kind." The anti-racism protest march is shunned by Bernice, and the Burrmanns' habit of singing Negro spirituals at their parties is ridiculed by the Caribbean immigrants, who regard the practice as patronizing. Most critically, the affair that develops between Sam Burrmann and Estelle is a source of anguish to both, and is intermittently represented as rape and a return to the days of slavery.

Clarke suggests that Sam's distorted relationship with Estelle has its origins in the consuming guilt that he carries with him because, as an adolescent, he had once let a black friend take the fall for a petty crime that he himself had committed. This adolescent betrayal symbolizes the moment at which Canadian Jews' fortunes began to diverge yet more sharply and decisively from those of their Caribbean counterparts. Sam's ability to capitalize on his lighter skin and to secure his future at the cost of his friend's incarceration anticipates the post-war economic rise of Canadian Jews and their incorporation into a newly expanded category of whiteness that opens its doors to Jews while continuing to firmly exclude blacks. Sympathetic relationships between Jews and blacks in the novel are obstructed by class and power divisions that result from this post-war shift in the definition of Canadian whiteness, and Clarke finally pulls back from alternative possible configurations of relationships between these two groups.

While the friendships and romances between the Jews and the Caribbean immigrants in *The Meeting Point* sour, however, the analogy between the two diasporas remains the key device that enables Clarke's investigation of the Caribbean-Canadian experience of arrival. The characters' inability to forge cross-cultural alliances should not therefore blind us to the ways in which the analogy is a productive one. Ultimately, Clarke reads the Caribbean immigrant experience against the earlier Jewish experience of arrival and assimilation in order to call attention to the protean character of the Caribbean immigrants' racial identities. If blackness is "a sign which is never closed and always under contestation," a sign that "allows for a certain kind of malleability and open-endedness" (R. Walcott xiv-xv), what I have suggested here is that Jewishness as presented by Clarke both shares in and underscores the malleable character of racial categories. Jewishness, which is perceived by Clarke's characters as neither white nor black but as occupying an ambiguous space between these two poles, demonstrates the degree to which racial categories are constructed on contrastive grounds. Because of what Brodkin terms its "racial middleness," Jewishness has a fluidity that undermines the black-white binary, as becomes evident when we juxtapose Baldwin's and Phillips' conflicting readings of Jewishness with which I opened this discussion. It is not by chance, then, that Clarke explores the instability of Bernice's racial and religious identities against the background of the Jewish experience of assimilation, for Jewishness thematizes the slipperiness of racial categories and in particular the contested character of whiteness. In *The Meeting Point*, the unstable sign of Jewishness serves to draw attention to Bernice's volatile relationship to the various constructions of blackness to which she is exposed in Barbados, Toronto, and Harlem.

Certainly the racial assignments imposed on Clarke's Caribbean immigrants are far more rigid and fixed than those imposed on the Jews; indeed, it is in part by racializing the Caribbean immigrants as non-white that the

Jews lay claim to whiteness. If Clarke's Jews for the most part are able to pass as white, there is little question as to how the Caribbean immigrants are viewed by their host society. For this reason, the Caribbean immigrants have great difficulty following the path of integration into white Canadian society that their Jewish employers have taken. When Bernice's friend Dots amuses herself by mimicking Mrs. Gasstein, she stops herself short: "she realized she had exhausted the performance, and she had to face an audience of reality. 'This country could never be home, gal'" (268). By interrupting Dots' performance, Clarke points to the limits of the comparison that he has drawn between Jewish and Caribbean Canadians and the profound power and class differential that divides them in post-war Toronto. Nonetheless the presence of the Jewish characters, who are neither fully white nor fully assimilated, serves as a reminder that racial categories are always constructed and therefore—at least potentially—subject to negotiation and contestation.

Endnotes

I would like to thank the editors of this special issue for their very helpful comments on an earlier draft of this article.

1. See also Phillips' treatment of these themes in his novel *The Nature of Blood* (1997).
2. See Brian Cheyette for a more general discussion of what he describes as the "protean instability of 'the Jew' as a sign" (11) in British and American literature.
3. In *The Black Atlantic*, Gilroy identifies some of the parallel motifs and concerns of the Jewish and African diasporas: the idea of a return to a point

of origin, the condition of forced exile, and the redemptive power of suffering (208). Jewish motifs appear throughout Derek Walcott's poetry, and most extensively in *Tiepolo's Hound* (2000), a book-length verse biography of the Jewish Impressionist painter Camille Pissarro, who was born in St. Thomas.

4. According to Sue Greene, the symbolic association of Jews with homelessness and wandering accounts for the disproportionate representation of Jews in Caribbean literature (151). Greene argues that Caribbean novelists are not interested in depicting Jewish characters per se, but introduce Jewishness strictly as a means of elucidating aspects of Caribbean identity. This is indeed one part of what Clarke's novel accomplishes. However, Clarke also gives considerable dimension to his Jewish characters, so that Jewishness is never merely a device.

5. The scheme initially allowed one hundred Caribbean women to enter Canada and subsequently expanded. The women were recruited in the Caribbean by Canadian immigration officers: potential domestics had to be eighteen to thirty-five years of age, single, and in good health, and they were required to have a grade eight education. By 1965, they numbered 2,690, which was more than the total number of Caribbean immigrants to Canada prior to 1945 (Walker, West Indians 10). Many women with other aspirations used the scheme as a means of gaining entrance to Canada; they were only bound to domestic work for one year, and after five years could apply for citizenship. As a consequence of the scheme, women predominated among Caribbean immigrants between 1955 and the late 1970s (19).

   See Makeda Silvera's valuable collection of interviews with Caribbean domestic workers.

6. "The Experience of Arrival" is the title of part 1 of *The Meeting Point*.

7. For example, Stella Algoo-Baksh writes, "The thematic content of [*The Meeting* Point and its sequel *A Bigger Light*] relates in the main to the black immigrant but its emergent application to whites is evident as well. Though the black experience is inevitably of central importance to Clarke, such content is often embedded in the writer's probing of the relationships between blacks and whites in general, or specific associations between black men or women and whites of the opposite sex" (97). Greene, while generally more attentive to constructions of Jewishness, reads the novel in terms similar to the approach of other critics: "For the West Indians of Clarke's trilogy, the Toronto Jew is simply a contemporary version of 'massa.' Inasmuch as the author's sympathies seem to lie with the West Indians, this view is apparently Clarke's as well" (159).

8. For a critique of this kind of homogenizing critical practice, see R. Walcott (ch. 1). See also Malcolm Gladwell's article "Black Like Them," which describes the dramatically different reception of Caribbean people on either side of the US-Canada border. While Caribbean immigrants to the United States have often been perceived as "good" blacks or even "black Jews" because of their perceived emphasis on education and frugality, Caribbean Canadians have not had large pre-existing black populations with whom they could be favourably compared. As a consequence, Caribbean Canadians have tended

to be regarded less sympathetically than Caribbean Americans.

9. One example of this tendency to Americanize *The Meeting Point* is Brown's reliance on James Baldwin in his reading of Clarke's novel in "The West Indian Novel" (102) and in his book-length study of Clarke, *El Dorado and Paradise*, where he writes, "Beyond the sexual issue, contact between Jews and blacks in the novel reflects the same tensions and similarities that have been noted by James Baldwin in the United States" (67).

10. This history of discriminatory practice culminated in Canada's tragic failure to rescue Jewish refugees from the Nazis (see Irving Abella and Harold Troper). See John Boyko (ch. 3) for a concise account of the history of Canadian anti-Semitism.

11. See Andersen et. al.'s introduction to their edited collection *Painting the Maple* for a general discussion of the racially exclusive subtext of dominant images of the Canadian nation.

12. Historically, Jews have often been represented as racially ambiguous, as neither black nor white or alternately as being both black and white simultaneously (Cheyette 11). Literary examples abound that ascribe black skin and "African" traits to Jews, or associate Jewish characters with blacks and Moors, as for instance in *The Merchant of Venice* (3.5). Cheyette suggests that it is because of their very racial ambiguity that Jewish difference "is often projected onto a supposedly unambiguous blackness" in English and American literature (9). See also Gilman (ch. 7) on the perception of Jews as black.

13. A related but slightly different example of this phenomenon is Mrs. Gasstein's decision to employ a German domestic. In this case, a Jewish woman hires a German servant both to take revenge for the Holocaust and to assert that as a Canadian Jew, she is no longer vulnerable to anti-Semitism.

14. This image records Canadian Jews' significant role in anti-racism movements in the first half of the twentieth century. See James W. St. G. Walker ("The 'Jewish Phase'") for a detailed account.

15. Here, Bernice unwittingly echoes Mrs. Burrmann, who earlier in the novel had expressed relief that Canada had been spared the racial disturbances besetting its neighbour to the south: "As Bernice served the ice, the announcer was saying that the Reverend Dr. Martin Luther King had led 2,500 Negroes in the shadow of the State Capitol here today.... 'Praise God, it doesn't happen here,' Mrs. Burrmann said, a noticeable relief in her voice. 'We're even better than Britain'" (16).

16. Relevant here is Brodkin's distinction between "ethnoracial assignments," which are imposed by society, and "ethnoracial identity," which is constructed by individuals within the context of ethnoracial assignments (3).

17. For their part, the Jewish characters also occasionally mimic black culture. Agatha reproduces Caribbean speech patterns in her desire to identify with the Caribbean immigrants, and we learn that earlier in his life, Sam had imitated the mannerisms of the "Harlem-like men" with whom he socialized (181).

18. This account is substantiated by the memoir of Harry Gairey, a Jamaican who came to Canada in 1914.

Gairey recalls that Caribbean-Jewish contact and collaboration was common in Toronto during the period that Sam Burrmann describes.

Works Cited

Abella, Irving, and Harold Troper. *None is Too Many: Canada and the Jews of Europe, 1933-1948*. 3rd ed. Toronto: Lester and Orpen Dennys, 1991.

Algoo-Baksh, Stella. *Austin C. Clarke: A Biography*. Toronto: P of the U of the West Indies, 1994.

Anderson, Joan, Avigail Eisenberg, Sherrill Grace, and Veronica Strong-Boag. "Constructing Canada: An Introduction." *Painting the Maple: Essays on Race, Gender, and the Construction of Canada*. Ed. Joan Anderson, Avigail Eisenberg, Sherrill Grace, and Veronica Strong-Boag. Vancouver: UBC Press, 1998. 3-15.

Baldwin, James. "Negroes Are Anti-Semitic Because They're Anti-White." *New York Times Magazine* April 9, 1967. *Blacks and Jews: Alliances and Arguments*. Ed. Paul Berman. New York: Delacorte, 1994. 31-41.

Boyko, John. *Last Steps to Freedom: The Evolution of Canadian Racism*. Winnipeg: J. Gordon Shillingford Publishing, 1998.

Brodkin, Karen. *How Jews Became White Folks and What That Says about Race in America*. New Brunswick, NJ: Rutgers UP, 1998.

Brown, Lloyd. *El Dorado and Paradise: Canada and the Caribbean in Austin Clarke's Fiction*. London, ON: Centre of Social and Humanistic Studies, 1989.

_____. "The West Indian Novel in North America: A Study of Austin Clarke." *Journal of Commonwealth Literature* 9 (July 1970): 89-103.

Cheyette, Brian. "Introduction: Unanswered Questions." *Between Race and Culture: Representations of "the Jew" in English and American Culture.* Stanford: Stanford UP, 1996. 1-15.

Clarke, Austin. "In the Semi-Colon of the North." *Canadian Literature* 95 (Winter 1982): 30-37.

_____. *The Bigger Light.* 1975. Toronto: Vintage Canada, 1998.

_____. *The Meeting Point.* 1967. Toronto: Vintage Canada, 1998.

_____. *Storm of Fortune.* 1971. Boston: Little, Brown, 1973.

Gairey, Harry. *A Black Man's Toronto, 1914-1980: The Reminiscences of Harry Gairey.* Ed. and introd. Donna Hill. Toronto: Multicultural History Society of Ontario, 1981.

Gilman, Sander. *The Jew's Body.* New York: Routledge, 1991.

Gilroy, Paul. *The Black Atlantic: Modernity and Double Consciousness.* Cambridge: Harvard UP, 1993.

Gladwell, Malcolm. "Black Like Them." *New Yorker* April 29-May 6, 1996: 74-81.

Greene, Sue. "The Use of the Jew in West Indian Novels." *World Literature Written in English* 26.1 (1986): 150-69.

Harap, Louis. *In the Mainstream: The Jewish Presence in Twentieth-Century American Literature, 1950s-1980s.* New York: Greenwood P, 1987.

Hiebert, Daniel. "Jewish Immigrants and the Garment Industry of Toronto, 1901-1931: A Study of Ethnic and Class Relations." *Annals of the Association of American Geographers* 83.2 (1993): 243-71.

hooks, bell. "Keeping a Legacy of Shared Struggle." *Blacks and Jews: Alliances and Arguments*. Ed. Paul Berman. New York: Delacorte, 1994. 229-38.

Jacobson, Matthew Frye. *Whiteness of a Different Color: European Immigrants and the Alchemy of Race*. Cambridge, MA: Harvard UP, 2000.

Knowles, Valerie. *Strangers at Our Gates: Canadian Immigration and Immigration Policy, 1540-1997*. Toronto: Dundurn P, 1997.

Ozick, Cynthia. "Literary Blacks and Jews." *Blacks and Jews: Alliances and Arguments*. Ed. Paul Berman. New York: Delacorte, 1994. 42-75.

Philip, Marlene NourbeSe. "Black-Jewish Relations." *Border/Lines* 29-30 (1993): 64-69.

Phillips, Caryl. *The European Tribe*. Winchester, MA: Faber and Faber, 1987.

Robbins, Bruce. "Upward Mobility in the Postcolonial Era: Kincaid, Mukherjee, and the Cosmopolitan Au Pair." *Modernism/Modernity* 1.2 (1994): 133-51.

Shakespeare, William. *The Merchant of Venice*. New York: Cambridge UP, 2003.

Silvera, Makeda, ed. *Silenced: Talks with Working Class Caribbean Women about Their Lives and Struggles as Domestic Workers in Canada*. 2nd ed. Toronto: Sister Vision, 1989.

Spiegelman, Art. Valentine's Day. Cover image. *New Yorker* February 15, 1993.

Trumpener, Katie. *Bardic Nationalism: The Romantic Novel and the British Empire*. Princeton: Princeton UP, 1997.

Walcott, Derek. *Tiepolo's Hound*. New York: Farrar, Straus, and Giroux, 2000.

Walcott, Rinaldo. *Black Like Who? Writing Black Canada*. Toronto: Insomniac P, 1997.

Walker, James W. St. G. "The 'Jewish Phase' in the Movement for Racial Equality in Canada." *Canadian Ethnic Studies Journal* 34 (Spring 2002): 1-30.

_____. *The West Indians in Canada*. Ottawa: Canadian Historical Association, 1984.

Clarke vs. Clarke: Tory Elitism in Austin Clarke's Short Fiction

GEORGE ELLIOTT CLARKE

Perusing Austin Chesterfield Clarke's short stories, one catches, now and then, the distinctive odour of the entertaining *and* tawdry James Bond spy adventures authored by British writer Ian Fleming (1908-64). Too, both authors stud their pages with references to pricey autos and shapely women. (Or should that be shapely automobiles and pricey women?) Then there is their mutual attentiveness to high-stakes card games and horse races. (Clarke works *both* species of gambling into his short story, "Give It a Shot" [1987]) Conceivably, if Fleming were still alive, he would make an apt partner for Clarke in one of those racially two-toned, "buddy" films that Hollywood insists we must have. Think of Fleming, with his tux, Roosevelt-style cigarette holder, and priceless presidential endorsement (from suave J.F.K.), then think of Clarke, with his (occasional) pinstripes, pipe, and Errol Barrow-style, prime ministerial poise. Perhaps the resemblance has something to do with both writers having a fondness for splendour—and *fascinante* women. Assuredly, Fleming's Bond is constantly sizing up the "merchandise" in *Moonraker* (1955):

> As she bent over the table her black skirt brushed
> Bond's arm and he looked up into two pert, sparkling
> eyes, under a soft fringe of hair ... then she whisked
> away. Bond's eyes followed the white bow at her waist
> and the starched collar and cuffs of her uniform as she
> went down the long room. ... He recalled a pre-war
> establishment in Paris where the girls were dressed
> with the same exciting severity. (38-39)

In Clarke's "How He Does It" (1986), the ogling is explicitly commercial:

> ... when the door open, Jesus Christ! the most
> prettiest, the most best-dress, the most sexiest, the
> most beautiful Jewish woman from outta Israel and
> Judea ... was standing up, full in the door, full in the
> breasts, full in the hips, solid as the best securities in
> the stock market down Bay Street, and on the loveliest
> pairs o' legs these two eyes o' mine have ever had the
> pleasant pleasure tainted with lust to rest on. (217)

Fine loving requires, irreducibly, fine living. Fleming provides, obligingly enough, this gourmet detail:

> Bond helped himself to another slice of smoked
> salmon from the silver dish beside him. It had the
> delicate glutinous texture only achieved by Highland
> curers—very different from the dessicated products
> of Scandinavia. He rolled a wafer-thin slice of brown
> bread-and-butter into a cylinder and contemplated it
> thoroughly. ... He stirred the champagne with a scrap
> of toast ... (39-41)

And Clarke models this sartorial moment in "A Man" (1986):

> He was dressed as if he was going to a wedding ... tall
> in a long black woollen winter coat, three-piece-suit

> usually of dark brown and worsted, and made with
> a hint of London's fashion and cut ... and he would
> climb into the long, expensive luxury car after flipping
> back the tails of his winter coat to avoid sitting on
> them on the seat. (120)

A mail-order catalogue of the wares retailed in Clarke's
récits would include, for starters, a subscription to the
Globe & Mail (the *haute couture* Toronto daily), meer-
schaum pipes, black leather attaché cases, Bally shoes and
slippers (also black), Dom Perignon champagne (Bond
sips it too), pinstripe suits (dark blue), Chanel Number
17, Oxford shoes, Turkish tobacco, dry martinis (another
Bond favourite), Mario Palomino Jamaican cigars,
Martini & Rossi vermouth *secco*, Bombay Gin, and
lubricated condoms. These are the rewards of Clarke's
bourgeois heaven. Fleming's Bond can purchase such
items readily (given his government salary, his consum-
mate skill at cards, and his white male privilege), but
Clarke's black immigrant characters are either would-be
or used-to-be aristocrats. Their access to the status symbols of the (WASP) Canadian Establishment is frustrated
by a polite, tight, *white-iste* caste system. Occasionally,
they earn their way to the good life (at high personal
cost); usually, they lie or cheat to advance; frequently,
they fail, becoming addicts or suicides. In spite of such
social(ist) realism, Clarke launches few polemical assaults
on racism. His writings are not anti-white (though white
women attract some venom). Rather, like Fleming,
Clarke nudges us toward accepting conservative notions
of social class implicit in the admiration of state spectacle
and market commodities. Hence, Clarke's protagonists
pursue fine liquors, luxurious habilements, prized tobac-
cos, and envy-spurring accessories (including mates and

lovers). Although their failures (or compromised successes) suggest a critique of racism, their narratives preserve the *main* determinant of social stratification: class. Clarke has read his Marx and Fanon (and Fleming?) only as a means of finding a fresh route into *Burke's Peerage*.

1

Born in Barbados in 1934, Clarke has lived, since 1955, in Canada, where his first novel, *Survivors of the Crossing*, appeared in 1964. Despite assertions to the contrary, he was neither the first nor the second African-Canadian novelist, but the *sixth*, though he was the first to publish a novel *in* Canada.[1] Known principally for his novels, Clarke has, nevertheless, published five collections of short stories, from his first—and best—collection, *When He Was Free and Young and Used to Wear Silks* (1971), to his most recent, *There Are No Elders* (1993).[2] The *nouvelles* articulate, against Caribbean and metropolitan Toronto backdrops, yearnings for independence, cultural assertion, masculine agency, and élite acceptance. Though Clarke's black protagonists produce stolid broadsides against empire, nostalgic paeans to lost Island paradises, romantic poems of cultural pride, and even wry deconstructions of icy Canadian racism, they are, for all that, defrocked gentry, anxious to assume classy places in Canada's ruling class. Impeccably educated, often of Brahmin backgrounds, they do not emigrate to Canada to become peons or to serve as slaves. Problematically though, as Clarke posits in his Introduction to *Nine Men Who Laughed* (1986), "immigrant life" is tantamount to "slavery" (7). Tragedy—or Juvenalian satire—in Clarke's *oeuvre* requires, then, not the mere event of racism, but rather the bracing plunge into a lower standard of living. This fact explains the curious repetition of a striking *ur-*moment in two of Clarke's texts. In "If Only: Only If ... ," a 1986 story set in mid-50s Toronto, the narrator lists the range of stereotypical jobs then open to black men: railway porter, "a janitor somewhere," or "a man who does handout towels in washrooms down Yonge Stree [sic], in bars and clubs that don't let-in no black or coloured or Negro men" (100). Six years later, Clarke opened his essay *Public Enemies: Police Violence and Black Youth* (1992) with a like remembrance of Original, Socio-Economic Sin:

> How should I react to the man ... dressed in a white butler's jacket and black trousers ... and in the shine of whose shoes I could see, if I had been so disposed, my disappointment and embarrassment? This man, in this sparkling men's room, its four walls of polished white, squared tiles, dwarfed by two white porcelain urinals. In his silent blackness, this man, with a skin polished high as the marble, standing with an ironic dignity handing out white towels to *me* ... (1)

Clarke is moved to confession in this moment of, to employ a phrase from Richard Sieburth, "uncharacter-istic autobiographical explicitness" (53): "I disappeared before he could extend his hand. I disappeared in order to obliterate the man, his status and his memory from touching and *tainting my status*" (*Public* 1, my italics). Clarke feels such disdain that, though he shares the same colour as the washroom attendant, the latter's abjection renders him an Untouchable. Though Clarke tried to "obliterate" the man, his spectre haunts characters and narrators who are, with their champagne tastes and beer budgets, the most pronouncedly class conscious of any in Canadian fiction (save for Mordecai Richler's Duddy Kravitz and Dany Laferrière's Vieux). Clarke's *comédiens* are Lears. Though Clarke later embraces the totem of the washroom attendant as his link to the indigenous African-Canadian past, this too-visible man personifies *Failure*.

Perceptively, Clarke's short fiction delineates a Neo-Darwinian struggle in which the geographically-displaced become class-misplaced, regardless of their ability, their training, their morality, their pedigree. Whatever their current shabby, shoddy, even shitty positions here, his protagonists, at home, enjoyed "aristocratic status" (Introduction 1).[3] In "They Heard a Ringing of Bells" (1971), for instance, Sagaboy, stricken with tuberculosis, remembers that, at home, he had dreamt of being "*the governor o' the whole blasted West Indies*" (29). In "If the Bough Breaks," Caribbean women in a Toronto beauty parlour exclaim: "Back home, we'd be ruling the roost. We'd be women with men and husbands that make decisions and run things" (22). Enid, the heroine of "Waiting for the Postman to Knock" (1971), relates the degradation that immigration has wrought:

> I came into this country as a decent middle-class person in Barbados. ... [I]t is only in Canada that I am known as a labourer, or a working woman ... because back home I never lifted a straw in the way of work, for my parents were rich people. We had servants back home. (32)

Now in Canada, Enid awaits eviction from her barren apartment, her hydro and telephone service have been disconnected, and her landlord and creditors harry her relentlessly. Enid's mother declares that, had Enid remained in Barbados, she would be "a high school mistress, or a doctor or a lawyer, anything but being in that cold, ungodly place, Canada, working for white people and servanting after people who don't know how to treat you as a human being" (37). This theme returns in a Lord Chesterfield-like, advice-to-my-son-abroad, epistolary fiction, "Letter of the Law of Black" (1992), in which a father, Anthony Barrington St. Omer Edgehill, advises his son, now resident in Canada, that "the colonial is the fact that transcends blackness" (59). His son's colonial roots will permit him to evade the racism of Canadian life. For one thing, he comes from superior stock—and a proven culture.

According to Clarke, it is immigration, that is to say, a precipitous, economic decline, that creates a negative blackness. The apartheid of immigration, its relegation of vast classes of people to poor-paying jobs or no jobs, fosters the postlapsarian "slave." Clarke states explicitly, then, that "the men [in *Nine Men Who Laughed*] are black only because they live in Toronto, in a society which has officially branded them 'immigrants' from the West Indies" (Introduction 7). Clearly, Clarke has studied his Fanon, perhaps *Peau noire, masques blancs* (1952), where Fanon theorizes that "le Noir n'a plus à être noir, mais à l'être en face du Blanc" (90) and that "le nègre infériorisé va de l'insécurité humiliante à l'auto-accusation ressentie jusqu'au désespoir" (50). The effect of the Manichean division between black and white is to rigidify class categories. Thus, "on est blanc comme on est riche, comme on est beau, comme on est intelligente" (43); blackness is the infernal inverse. One is not born "black"; blackness is a socio-economic hell into which one is plunged. Hence, the "I" in Clarke's polemical *cri de coeur, Public Enemies,* is, simultaneously, "slave, Negro, coloured, black, colonized" (15). Asking rhetorically: "How long are we to remain immigrants?" (*Public* 19), Clarke demands, in effect, how long are we to remain black, to remain slaves? In *Black Man in a White Land,* (1967),[4] a frustrating, frank, reckless pamphlet, Clarke, using the pseudonym, Ali Kamal Al Kadir Sudan, proposes that "the black man in a white society is a minority—subhuman" (4-5). Likewise, in "Letter," Edgehill instructs his son in how to subvert negative constructs of blackness:

> But if you are seen ... reading Pushkin ... *they* will say you are an intellectual. Even if they call you a colonial intellectual, as they have a habit of doing, such as black writer, a black artist, or black doctor, it would be different. You would, by this intelligence, be more dangerous to them, and *they* would not be able to despise, or worse still, ignore your presence, and call you a visible minority. (60)

Thus, blackness is fluid, and can be applied—like paint—to anyone who lapses in class and morality. Clarke affirms the unreality of constructed blackness when he unveils his desire "to discover something which a former black student at Yale University called a 'black aesthetic', a black way of seeing black things, a blackening of the consciousness" (Introduction 6). This blackening denotes a sardonic trope. Any group can be or become black—that is to say, low-class or no-class. Hence, the father in "Letter" warns his son: "Beware of the lower classes of all races. They spit on you because they grew up spitting on the ground" (61). Likewise, in

"If the Bough Breaks," one of the women emphasizes the class jealousy that Euro-Canadians project towards their immigrant equals and superiors. When she and her husband buy a new car, she reports, the neighbours stare "'from behind their curtains. We shouldn't have those things. We shouldn't live the way *they* live. We shouldn't'" (20). In the same story, a woman remembers calling an uppity, white security guard a "'nigger-man'" ("If" 13). Whiteness is, then, an unstable *sign*. Clarke—as Ali— comments, for instance, that "the black West Indian has been educated by colonialism to think of himself as *a white man*; in more fortunate cases as a black Englishman, or a black Frenchman, or a black Dutchman" (*Black* 8, my italics). White racists presume, wrongly, that *race* ordains excellence (or *not*), but, as Clarke insists, class and heritage determine that quality: "cultural ancestry is a greater force than ... colour or the branded status of 'immigrant'" (Introduction 7). With this thesis, Clarke is equipped to defend class privilege, even as he indicts the operations of racism. Nevertheless, his apology for class-ism necessitates a repetition of caste-supporting, sexist, white-fostered images of beauty and success.

2

Jean Baudrillard theorizes in *Seduction* (1979, 1990) that "the strength of the feminine is that of seduction" (7) and that the secret of this irresistible power is its presentation of an alluring absence, or blankness, whose indeterminacy annihilates masculine attempts at definition. Seduction, "by producing only illusions, obtains all powers" (70). Crucially, Baudrillard aligns this alluring absence with a cinematic whiteness, "the spectral whiteness of the heavenly stars, after which they [film stars] are so appropriately named" (96). In his short fiction, Clarke agrees, tacitly, with Baudrillard: women, whiteness, and, hence, white women symbolize attractive, glistening surfaces that can entrap and destroy the unwary,[5] meaning, for Clarke, black male immigrants. Thus, Clarke considers the psychological threat posed to self-conscious blackness by the omnipresence of white-supremacist imagery in North American society. Speaking as Ali in 1967, he asserts: "Because of the contemporary idiosyncrasy of white advertising media, I do not think the white man understands the dignity of the human body as an object of love" (*Black* 6). The pervasiveness of this spectacular whiteness ensures that "the black man's future in a white society will always be in terms of white society's schizophrenia about blacks" (4). Pursuing this argument, Clarke creates protagonists who view white women as symbols of Canada—that is to say, of a vamp who entices "her" thralls with phoney promises of *bourgeois* comfort.[6] Whore-like, the Canadian "system" encourages "laughter and seduces the 'immigrant'" (Introduction 5). This sexed perception is accented by Clarke's metonymization of Canada as "this *fucking* system" (Introduction 5, my italics) and by his autobiographical recollection of a female exemplum of white racism. Damnably, she is "the *person* who confronted me with her prepossessiveness, the woman, the system ... now a microcosm of all the words, bad conclusions and faulty definitions of 'immigrant' and ... a metaphor for arrogance" (Introduction 3). He upholds his conflation of *woman* and *system* in the next paragraph: "She, the attitude, the system, knew my meaning" (Introduction 3).

The Canada-as-white-whore metaphor recurs, then, throughout Clarke's *oeuvre.* For instance, in "Canadian Experience" (1986), the unemployed protagonist, George, a high-school-educated Barbadian immigrant, about to be dislodged from his abysmal room for non-payment of rent, is succoured by a white sometime actress who shares the same grimy building. Hearing the woman take her shower, George imagines "the red-faced ugly blackheads painted red at the bottom of the spine" (38), an obvious red-and-white symbol of Canada (given that the blemishes are scarlet *cold* sores). Suitably, she is, *de temps en temps,* a prostitute, for following her shower, she states that she has washed herself "clean" to attend "an audition in an hour": "You never know what directors're going to ask you to do" (39). This cheerless passage ends with the actress wrapping a towel about herself, but leaving "the two small nipples of her dropped breasts" bare to "his undesiring eyes" (40). He resists this temptation, but there is no escape from predatory whiteness. Hence, in contemplating applying for a job in a ritzy bank, George is frightened away by the "blue eyes ... like ice-water" of a female employee (43). Ashamed of his failure to find work, haunted by his alienation from paradisal Barbados ("where he was born in a smiling field of comfortable pasture land" [47]), the immigrant commits suicide by leaping in front of a subway train. Naturally, the train's "ugly red" colour recalls the actress' "red-corpuscle sores" (50-51).

In "The Motor Car" (1971), Calvin, the protagonist, objectifies the requisite white woman as "this Canadian thing" (102). She is "this blasted white woman humbug-ging him about sex" (103). As Calvin scrimps and saves to buy a Ford Galaxie automobile, so does he plan to acquire the "Canadian thing" as the perfect accessory for the vehicle. Eventually, he succeeds, but, during his triumphant spin, the woman continues, though he has commanded her to stop, to sing along with a calypso playing over the car radio. Thinking angrily to himself: "Well, who tell she she could talk back to Bajan man like Calvin?" (109), Calvin brakes abruptly, thereby pitching, fatally, the seatbelt-less woman against the windshield. Notably, this killing results after the folksy, omniscient narrator discusses Canadian economic imperialism in Barbados, stating "they was more *Air Canada* planes all bout Seawell Airport in Barbados in them days that you would have think that Barbados did own *Air Canada*" (95). In truth, it is "the other way round" (95). Calvin's assault on "this Canadian thing" is metaphorical revenge for Canada's raping and pillaging of Barbados.

In "Not So Old, But Oh So Professional" (1993), Max, a bachelor and Caribbean immigrant, who spends his nights shyly ogling a young prostitute, Linda Pearl Mason, accepts her proposal that she visit his downtown Toronto home. As her middle name suggests, Linda's skin exudes "a porcelain white sheen" (82). After spending a lyrical evening conversing and drinking, in a kind of casual symposium, Max becomes aroused when Linda passes her fingers through her hair:

> She was not caressing herself the way I have seen some women pass their hands over their breasts, squeezing the nipples a little to stimulate them and the eyes of the man watching; or how I have seen some women pass their hands over their thighs, slowly, slowly, rubbing faster and then faster still, and slapping them; or even as I have seen some women pass their fingers through their public hair to their vaginas,

> even opening the lips, and doing little stimulating,
> destroying things to a man's balance. ... She was
> just drawing her hands through her hair, a natural
> function, and that naturalness made it more enticing
> and betraying and seducing. (97)

Max's voyeuristic, pornographic pleasure (or self-seduction) in watching Linda and his resultant, destabilizing *aporia* mirrors the vertigo that a too-prolonged gazing upon a provocative Canada also induces. (The "system" also does "little stimulating, destroying things" to Black Caribbean immigrants.) Max climaxes under the ministrations of the "pearly" white Linda while nostalgic dreams of his Island past fill his mind. But, this is callous, tough Toronto. And Linda's cash-driven response to his orgasm returns Max sharply to the mean, capitalist world: "Now you owe me, motherfucker!" (101). Linda is as cold as the glass-sheathed skyscrapers of Bay Street. Clarke's tale allegorizes the Caribbean male's morbid mating dance with the "albino" widow spider of Canada. For this reason, Linda's siren-like whiteness receives photographerly attention:

> She was wearing white tonight. I have no defense
> against that color. ... For better *and* for worse: white
> dominates me. ... Her breasts were half-covered in
> white lace, worked into the top of her outfit, and that
> too was made of white, soft cotton. It was oppressive,
> irredeemably seductive ... (88-89)

Linda is "overpowering" (89), just as the white coldness of Toronto's business district, Bay Street, overwhelms the protagonist of "Canadian Experience." Too, disillusioningly, given her French Canadian roots (her true surname is Maisoneuve), Linda is an archetype of Canada's "two founding peoples." This fact suggests that no real *rap-prochement* is possible between them and recent claimants of Canadian citizenship. Indeed, another white woman, Susan Cole, the protagonist of "In an Elevator" (1993), voices, eloquently, the basic white supremacist Canadian attitude: "I was here first, and I work here, and no god-damn immigrant or cleaning woman or black sonofa-bitch, nobody's gonna make me feel threatened and live like a victim in my own fucking country, province, in my city." (60). Cole offers her frank revelation after recalling that she had consistently been bested, at a top private school in Ontario, by the black daughter of a Barbadian prime minister.

The seductive, white female/system/nation tricks, turns tricks on, and fucks black male slaves/colonials/immigrants. "Her" "prepossessiveness" (Introduction 3),[7] her ownership of and first claim to commodities that she does not want, ever, to share, engenders in her black vassals a degree of desperation (sometimes violent), self-hatred (sometimes suicidal), and, in the best of them, a passionate cunning. Nevertheless, Clarke's imagery revivifies sorry, nasty, stodgy, and flat-out reactionary notions about the damning consequences of female sexuality. Khalid Kishtainy writes that the teachings of St. Cyprian of Carthage included the influential precept that "if a woman invited the eyes of men, called forth their sighs and offered them matter for their lust and fuel for the flames of passion, she must be held guilty of their ruin" (21). It is impossible to differentiate Clarke's figurative language from this ayatollah-like vision. The "seductiveness" of the Canadian "system" thus dooms its "tricked" immigrants. But the dilemma posed by Clarke's sexist imagery is complicated when one recalls that, for

Marx, "prostitution is the most logical career for the capitalist way of life" (Kishtainy, 46).[8] If one accepts this insight, then Clarke's moralistic condemnation of whorish (white) women makes no sense. However, Clarke's real target is the seductive nature of capitalism itself, a "system" that must be regulated by a meritocracy based, scrupulously, on heritage and talent.[9]

If some of Clarke's white female characters are purveyors of dangerous allure, of treacherous—if radiant— promises, black women inspire an alternative constellation of metaphors, mainly involving notions of nurture. A perpetual contest between "mothers"—the Canadian "Whore of Babylon" and the pseudo-Anglican "Mary of Barbados"—occurs in Clarke. The white harlot offers *fausse* enticements; but the poorer, saintlier, black mother calls on her children to preserve their dignity, to strive for advancement (without giving way to rank materialism), and to honour their heritage. Clarke's employment of the Messalina/*mater* trope highlights his conservatism, for a primal division in his work is the split between the love of the Mother Country—a nearly incestuous desire for that country—versus lust for the stepmother, the new country, a passion expressed in terms of desire for material gain at any price. This essentialist difference is exemplified by the Afro-Barbadian mother in "An Easter Carol" (1971). She is an idealized, earthbound goddess, a neo-Marian figure. Preparing her son to accompany her to church, she declares: "Christ! boy, you look real good! You look just like a little doctor. Now, I want you to grow up fast, and be a doctor, hear?" (9). The injunction contrasts starkly with the desires expressed and solicited by the gallery of white female characters surveyed above. Instead, in a kind of neo-natal nationalism, the mother incarnates the *voice* of Barbados—the "motherland" itself—instructing the boy to succeed. If her words do not suffice to spur the boy to achievement, there is her physicality, her seductiveness:

> I looked up at her, so large, so beautiful, so lovely, and so black—a mysterious queen or something, from Africa, with her hair braided neatly and long; with her old white dress which she washed three times a week, clutching to the feminine twists and turns of her full body. She looked at me, and she looked at my thoughts; and she smiled. She drew me close close to her breasts and her rolling soft stomach, where I could feel the love and blood pumping through her body. (10)

Not only does the mother's body bear the usual romanticized, black nationalist inscriptions of Africa, it is also associated with the topography of Barbados: "I listened to the beautiful mountains and valleys of her surging voice ..." (1). Whiteness, in this story, is redemptive, unthreatening: "... I could see women dressed in the white of angels, white hats, white shoes, as if they were proud to be part of this great resurrection morning, as if they had remained new brides, new virgins, all their lives" (13). Despite such conceptualizations, the figure of the black mother still shades into that of the white whore, for both are *obscure objets de désir*; both pose the threat of psychological castration. In fact, the mother anticipates the white prostitute, Linda, in a crypto-sexual detail: she uses "Evening-in-Paris perfume" (9), while Linda *is* "the scent of Evening in Paris, which is just a way of saying that she is overpowering me" ("Not So Old, But Oh So Professional" 89). Even in the paradisal setting of

Barbados, then, a woman can menace masculinity, just as Linda imperils Torontonian Max's sense of maleness: "... I was sitting in a house with a woman whose presence in the house was the consequence of the myth that I was a man. Am a man" ("Not" 98). Vertiginously then, the white whore and the black mother both endanger self-conscious black manhood.

To avoid this trap, Clarke's protagonists—like Max in "Not"—quest for true masculinity. However, this search is fraught with difficulty. For instance, in *Black Man in a White Land,* Clarke, as Ali, argues, "it is a bit naive to suggest ... that the black man in North American society can ever have a future as a MAN" (3). Clarke's 1973 essay, "Some Speculations As to the Absence of Racialistic Vindictiveness in West Indian Literature," notes the "emasculating psychological effects of slavery" (169) and suggests that the dream of a redeemed masculinity is now implicated with a regressive *macho* posture:

> It seems that the West Indian writer, a man from a society free of the worst pathologies of racialism, a man from a society into which Black nationalism had to be imported from American Blacks ... , could do nothing more than couch his literary expression in the pathology of self-identity and crisis, personal crisis, and the concept *machismo* (related to the conquest of women) within the social framework of the island in which he lived. (180)

His frustrated aristocrats are, then, tinder for the Revolution, but they also represent a tired, effete, black macho nationalism. They are men who "have forgotten, at that most critical point in their lives, the moment of their *contact* with hostility [discrimination]"; each "has forgotten who he is" (Introduction 2). Later, Clarke returns to this theme, asking whether his fellow and sister African Canadians "see themselves as victims, and behave as victims of this racism, without remembering and acknowledging that they are men and women" (*Public* 8). Memory, particularly that anchored in the "Motherland," is a guarantor of the "national" soul, a conservative nostrum that George Grant articulates in *Lament for a Nation: The Defeat of Canadian Nationalism* (1965). Therein, Grant claims, chasteningly, that "memory is never enough to guarantee that a nation can articulate itself in the present" (12).[10] This assertion proves devastatingly true for the male protagonist of "Canadian Experience." His memories of his privileged life in Barbados—"eight, healthy, well-fed Barbadians, squinting because the sun is in their eyes, standing like proprietors in front of a well-preserved plantation house made of coral stone, covered in vines so thick that their spongy greenness strangles the windows and the doors" ("Canadian" 47)—do not preserve him from suicide. Nor do the get-rich-quick schemes of Pat in "Give It a Shot" or the "playerism" of the protagonist of "A Man" yield viable supports for a progressive masculinity.

But Clarke is not bereft of such images. For this reason, the masculinist scopophilia that influences Clarke's descriptions of female characters also determines his accounts of spectacles and the accoutrements of wealth and power. Thus, in "An Easter Carol," the boy-narrator records, nearly without irony, the majestic images of "The Lord Bishop, with his robes fluttering like the Union Jack in the breeze ... the Prime Minister of the island ... and the lords and ladies of the island, all untitled, but all rich and white" ("Easter" 14). This admiration of pomp and circumstance is not a unique, narrative oddity. Clarke exalts the image of then-Ontario Lieutenant Governor Lincoln Alexander "adorned in vice-regal raiment, plumed and epauletted in Elizabethan finery to resemble a Lord of the Fleet" (*Public* 5). Clarke even bemoans the supposed truth that African Canadians disparage ostentation, "particularly as that prominence is bestowed by the media and the establishment": "It is as if we want to remain, each and every one of us, oppressed ..." (*Public* 5). Oppression is best countered, in this scheme, by honouring and rewarding the meritorious, especially those who have demonstrably *overcome* oppression: "He who is now being lauded and recompensed, and made a chancellor of York University, Oscar Peterson, was [once] barred from entering the Towne Tavern, because on his arm was a white woman" (*Public* 13). Derek Walcott is celebrated as being "one of our heroes from another discipline, equal in importance to being a first black Mayor, or a first black Lieutenant-Governor: a poet" (*Public* 6). (This comparison is a rather curious way to toast a Nobel laureate.) In any case, Clarke's admiration for acceptable public figures is akin to his ease with comfortable—and comforting—commodities. Ownership has its privileges. Thus, Clarke distinguishes little between recording the tastes of gourmet food or the aroma of an exquisite cigar or inscribing a woman's body: "She puts the dress on and runs her hands over her hips, and she smoothes the rich material which covers her luscious body for a moment from my eyes" ("Beggars" 68). Such images figure the pleasure and import of Tory voyeurism, of seeing one's way clear to what one desires.

3

Clarke drafts a political vision riven by contradiction. His critique of racism is blasted by his defence of privilege. One cannot very well exult "aristocratic status" (Introduction 1) to ward off racism, then have a character praise a white mistress because "her movement was aristocratic" ("Man" 144). Sexism compromises Clarke's criticism of Canadian "prepossessiveness": the depiction of a sluttish society reproduces the hoariest (whoriest?) gender clichés. Worse, Clarke's anti-racist utterances occasion a hint of rebarbative ethnocentrism. In his Ali persona, he proffers this analysis of the state of the Civil Rights Movement, *circa* 1967:

> The Jew is a Jew because WASP (whites in general) say he's a Jew. The same thing is true for the black man, but with greater visciousness [*sic*]. In the civil rights struggle, the Jew is not doing anything to ease the pressure on the Negro: if there were no Negro, there would be a Jew! The bad publicity that the black man gets today can be ascribed to the Jews because they control the communications. (*Black* 4)

There is, here, a fundamentalist ascription to essences, yet, simultaneously a realization that no true, "pure" blackness can ever be recovered. To wit: "the Canadian black man is obsessed with an irrational Negritude: he hates the white man partly because it is fashionable to hate him" (3). When one is free from such faddish irrationalities, one can even, support one's local police:

> I will admit that the same policemen we sometimes accuse of violent discrimination, make my life safe

> and secure in a city bordering on the American
> syndrome of ghettoized crime. [T]his city is still *north*
> of the border of America and of racism. (*Public* 18)

Ingeniously, perhaps even with opportunistic *élan,* Clarke
has always coupled assaults on Canadian racism with
a strong endorsement of Canadian anti-Americanism.
Speaking as Ali, in 1967, he bemoans the fact that
"Canada is an American satellite" (*Black* 5) and that
"the CANADIAN BLACK ATTITUDE [is] derived
from the Black-White clashes in America" (2). Twenty-
five years later, Clarke was still able to allege that one
reason for the riot of May 4, 1992, in Toronto, was that
"American racism had taken root in Canada in the minds
of black Canadians" (*Public* 3). This argument recurs
in "Initiation," a satire of black radicalism, in which
Clarke's *nom de guerre,* Ali Kamal Al Kadir Sudan, is
recycled, as the *nom de guerre* of a character whose "real"
name is "Terrence Washington Jefferson Lincoln Lucas,
the *Third*" (43). Ironically, Clarke lampoons a character
bearing his ex-cognomen for doing what he had once
done, namely, play at U.S.-style radicalism in a setting
where it could not apply. Toronto, for better or worse, is
not Harlem ("Initiation" 29).

Positioning himself, in his short fiction, as a sane,
reasonable, good, Tory writer, Clarke upholds *bourgeois*
Canadian nationalism; stands by the police, enforces age-
old, Puritan attitudes regarding women; regards racism
as an American phenomenon (exercising a hazardous
influence *only* on Black Canadians); exalts the virtues of
good breeding, good living, and good gin; and even sub-
scribes, shamefully, to the tenets of a conspiracy theory.
This version of a "Common Sense Revolution" could

be subscribed to, one imagines, by many conservatives, from Ian Fleming to the Canadian prime minister John George Diefenbaker (1895-1979).

For all Clarke's dexterous writing in support of his ideology, though, one must question the efficacy of a literary politics which holds, in stentorian tones, that Utopia is a location where professionals—and other deserving members of the elect, indigenous or immigrant, black or white—can join hands and drink Johnny Walker (gold), tack "QC" suffixes or "Hon." prefixes to their names, and debate the merits of Combermere School versus those of Bishop Strachan (while police club the envious rabble in the streets?). The ideal is not, however, a convincing prescription of societal happiness. Given his status as social satirist, pomp-loving politico, conservative idealist, pissed-off but loyal subject of Elizabeth II, and mild foe of robber-baron capitalism, perhaps Clarke must be classed as Canada's answer to V.S. Naipaul. Yet, despite the blind spots in Clarke's social vision, there is much that is salvageable, commendable too, in his largely sympathetic overview of the (black) immigrant's plight and in his principled, though limited, attacks on the *de facto* caste system which impedes their upward mobility. Clarke's work reminds us that, as scholar Aubrey McPhail has said of the martyred Nigerian writer Kenule Saro-Wiwa, "every serious writer is, on some fundamental level, a moral writer" (69). Clarke is strikingly so. (Note the fierce, cryptically Christian aesthetics of his Toryism.) Although, his short stories can seem, like those of Saro-Wiwa, "unsure, unclear, and sometimes morally suspect" (McPhail 84), he knows that "the technique of honesty is not always utterly simple" (Pound, "Troubadours" 96). One can read Clarke's fiction with some relish (or perhaps Grey Poupon mustard), and its underlying elitism remains difficult to digest, but it is, nevertheless, a feast of (social) instruction.

Endnotes

1. In his thoughtful review of Stella Algoo-Baksh's *Austin C. Clarke: A Biography* (1994), "Survivor of the Crossing," Brian John Busby, relying on a mistaken claim by Lorris Elliott in *Literary Writing by Blacks in Canada* (1988), writes that a novel by one Brian Gypsin, namely, *To Master, a Long Goodnight,* published in New York in 1946, "is very likely the first black Canadian novel" (11). But "Brian Gypsin" was a misprint for Brion Gysin, a white American writer, whose purported novel is really a biography. The first African-Canadian novel was, arguably African-American writer Martin Robinson Delany's *Blake,* inked in Chatham, Ontario, and serialized in two magazines, between 1859 and 1862. Next in line was Amelia Etta Hall Johnson, who was born in Canada West (now Ontario) in 1858 and who published *Clarence and Corinne; or, God's Way* in Philadelphia, Pennsylvania, in 1890. (Another potential contender—and Canada West native—Lucretia Newman Coleman published her novel, *Poor Ben: A Story of Real Life*, in Nashville, Tennessee, in either 1890 or 1891.) Born in Canada West in 1859, William Haslip Stowers co-authored *Appointed: An American Novel,* with William H. Anderson, and published it under the pseudonym, Sanda, in Detroit in 1894. The third novelist, John Hearne, was born in Montréal in 1926, grew up in

Jamaica, and published his first novel in London in 1955. The fourth novelist was, arguably, Jan Carew, a Guyanese native, who published his first novel, *Black Midas*, in London in 1958 and later acquired Canadian citizenship.

Busby's point that Clarke's "literary career stretches back farther than [that of] any other black Canadian" (11) also requires amendment. When Clarke's *Survivors of the Crossing* appeared in 1964, Gérard Étienne had already published, in his native Haiti, *six* books of poetry and prose; after arriving in Canada, he published another book of poetry in Montréal in 1966. Similarly, Anthony Phelps had published three books of poetry in Haiti by 1964, and issued other poetry and drama in Montréal in 1966 and 1968. With three Haitian-published texts to his credit by 1964, Franck Fouché published his drama, *Bouki non paradi,* in Montréal in 1964, thus becoming the first, published African-Canadian playwright. Another playwright, the Trinidad-born Lennox Brown, began to publish his prize-winning dramas with the Ottawa Little Theatre in 1965. New Brunswick poet Anna Minerva Henderson released her book of poems, *Citadel,* in 1967; while the Jamaican-born Gershom Williams self-published a novel in Toronto in 1968. Though Clarke was a fairly isolated figure, *qua* novelist, in African-Canadian literature in the mid-1960s, he was not the only publishing writer, or the only pioneer, and his relative loneliness was short-lived. See my "A Primer of African-Canadian Literature," *Books in Canada* 25.2 (March 1996): 5-7 and "Africana Canadiana: A Select Bibliography of African-Canadian Authors,

1785-1996, in English, French, and Translation," in *Canadian Ethnic Studies.*

2. The others are, in chronological order, *When Women Rule* (1985), *Nine Men Who Laughed* (1986), and *In This City* (1992).

3. Clarke's black male "aristocrats" would fit splendidly into this passage in Fleming's *Moonraker*: "There were perhaps fifty men in the room, the majority in dinner jackets, all at ease with themselves and their surroundings, all stimulated by the peerless food and drink, all animated by a common interest—the prospect of high gambling, the grand slam, the ace pot, the key-throw in a 64 game at backgammon. There might be cheats or possible cheats amongst them, men who beat their wives, men with perverse instincts, greedy men, cowardly men, lying men; but the elegance of the room invested each one with a kind of aristocracy." (43)

   Think, for instance, of J.M.G.M.-C. in "A Man," or Mr. Joshua Miller-Corbaine in "How He Does It," or the Jamaican in "Give It a Shot," or Anthony Barrington St. Omer Edgehill in "Letter of the Law of Black." These gentlemen have their flaws, *oui,* but their commitment to elegance mitigates their sins.

4. Stella Algoo-Baksh does not include this pamphlet, an interview with Ali (Clarke) conducted by Nazzam Al Sudan (Marvin X), in the bibliography she compiled for her monograph, *Austin C. Clarke: A Biography* (1994).

5. Here is yet another point where Clarke attains a strange, accidental *entente* with Fleming, who regularly pimps, in his tales, beautiful—and drop-dead deadly—(white and "exotic") women.

6. This vision of white woman as vampire also occurs in African-Canadian writer Darius James' campy satirical novel *Negrophobia* (1992). Here the white female protagonist, Bubbles, exclaims: "Without the vampire beauty of my whiteness, without the definition of my skin, without my *emblematic significance*, I was presence without appearance, a being without basis, a creature without context—*an invisible*—a colorless network of organs and entrails in translucent casing" (167-68). Her self-definition is resonantly Baudrillardian—and Fanonesque.

7. Note Clarke's utilization of a quasi-economic term as a synonym for "racism." His critique of Canadian "prepossessiveness"—not racism—accents his class concerns.

8. An interesting irony pertains to Clarke's Canada-as-harlot paradigm. Kishtainy points out that "prostitutes over the centuries were inwardly religious and conservative and were rightly represented in literature with a royalist mentality" (49). This description of the political orientations of prostitutes squares nicely with accounts of Canada that accent its religious, Tory, and monarchical predilections.

9. In this reading, Clarke's characters resemble black knights (or Bond figures?) endangered by Canadian "*belles dames sans merci.*" In their existentialist, noble failings, they uphold masculinist and conservative ideals of chivalry. Thus, in "An Easter Carol" (1971), the Bajan Easter churchgoers consist of women wearing "the white of angels," while the men sport "suits of long ago black, which fitted them like coats of armour" (14).

10. Clarke's disdain for greed aligns him with Canadian Red Toryism, as defined by Grant, who maintains

that, in traditional, Canadian conservative thought, "the good life [makes] strict demands on self-restraint" (Grant, *Lament* 70). Hence, in "The Motor Car," then, Calvin's greed is viewed as a kind of displacement of nature: "But the bank account was mounting and climbing like a woman belly when she in the family-way" (98).

Works Cited

Algoo-Baksh, Stella. *Austin C. Clarke: A Biography.* Toronto: ECW Press; Barbados, Jamaica, Trinidad and Tobago: The Press of the University of the West Indies, 1994.

Baudrillard, Jean. *Seduction.* Trans. Brian Singer. Montréal: New World Perspectives, 1990. Trans. of *De la séduction.* Paris: Éditions Galilée, 1979.

Busby, Brian John. "Survivor of the Crossing." *The Literary Review of Canada.* 4.6 (June 1995): 11-12.

Clarke, Austin. "Beggars." *There Are No Elders.* Toronto: Exile Editions, 1993. 63-80.

_____. [as Ali Kamal Al Kadir Sudan, pseud.] *Ali Kamal Al Kadir Sudan: "Black Man in a White Land."* Interviewed by Nazzam Al Sudan [pseud. of Marvin X]. Burlington ON: Al Kitab Sudan, 1967. [interview transcript]

_____. "Canadian Experience." *Nine Men Who Laughed.* Toronto: Penguin, 1986. 31-51.

_____. "An Easter Carol." *When He Was Free and Young and He Used to Wear Silks.* Toronto: House of Anansi, 1971. 1-15.

_____. "Give It a Shot." *A Shapely Fire: Changing the Literary Landscape.* Ed. Cyril Dabydeen. Oakville, ON: Mosaic, 1987. 37-59.

_____. "How He Does It." *Nine Men Who Laughed*. Toronto: Penguin, 1986. 205-225.

_____. "If the Bough Breaks." *There Are No Elders*. Toronto: Exile Editions, 1993. 9-28.

_____. "In an Elevator." *There Are No Elders*. Toronto: Exile Editions, 1993. 46-62.

_____. "Initiation." *In This City*. Toronto: Exile Editions, 1992. 25-54.

_____. Introduction. *Nine Men Who Laughed*. Toronto: Penguin, 1986. 1-7.

_____. "Letter of the Law of Black." *In This City*. Toronto: Exile Editions, 1992. 55-74.

_____. "A Man." *Nine Men Who Laughed*. Toronto: Penguin, 1986. 117-152.

_____. "The Motor Car." *When He Was Free and Young and He Used to Wear Silks*. Toronto: House of Anansi Press, 1971. 90-111.

_____. "Not So Old, But Oh So Professional." *There Are No Elders*. Toronto: Exile Editions, 1993. 81-101.

_____. *Public Enemies: Police Violence and Black Youth*. Toronto: HarperCollins, 1992.

_____. "Some Speculations As to the Absence of Racialistic Vindictiveness in West Indian Literature." *The Black Writer in Africa and the Americas*. Ed. Lloyd W. Brown. Los Angeles: Hennessey & Ingalls, 1973. 165-194.

_____. "They Heard A-Ringing of Bells." *When He Was Free and Young and He Used to Wear Silks*. Toronto: House of Anansi, 1971. 16-29.

_____. "Waiting for the Postman to Knock." *When He Was Free and Young and He Used to Wear Silks*. Toronto: House of Anansi, 1971. 30-50.

Clarke, George Elliott. "A Primer of African-Canadian Literature." *Books in Canada* 25.2 (March 1996): 5-7.

Fanon, Frantz. *Black Skin, White Masks.* Trans. Charles Lam Markmann. New York: Grove, 1967. Trans. of *Peau Noire, Masques Blancs.* Paris: Éditions de Seuil, 1952.

Fleming, Ian. *Moonraker.* 1955. London: Pan Books, 1964.

Gilroy, Paul. *The Black Atlantic: Modernity and Double Consciousness.* Cambridge MA: Harvard University Press, 1993.

Grant, George. *Lament for a Nation: The Defeat of Canadian Nationalism.* Toronto: McClelland & Stewart, 1965.

Kishtainy, Khalid. *The Prostitute in Progressive Literature.* London: Alison & Busby, 1982.

McPhail, Aubrey. "The Short Fiction: *A Forest of Flowers* and *Adaku and Other Stories.*" In *Ken Saro-Wiwa: Writer and Political Activist.* Ed. Craig W. McLuckie and Aubrey McPhail. Boulder, CO: Lynne Rienner Publishers, 2000. 69-86.

Pound, Ezra. "Troubadours: Their Sorts and Conditions." *A Walking Tour in Southern France: Ezra Pound among the Troubadours.* Ed. Richard Sieburth. New York: New Directions, 1992. 87-98.

Sieburth, Richard. Introduction. *A Walking Tour in Southern France: Ezra Pound among the Troubadours.* Ed. Richard Sieburth. New York: New Directions, 1992. vii-xxi.

Philosophize or Indict: A Comparative Look at Narrative Tone in Sam Selvon's and Austin Clarke's Immigrant Fiction

VICTOR J. RAMRAJ

In a tribute to Samuel Selvon on his death in 1994, Austin Clarke acknowledges his literary debt in his early career to Selvon; he conveys that they were kindred artistic spirits: "Sam and I were very close, probably because he realized I was copying his style" (50), particularly Selvon's use of demotic Caribbean language in his immigrant novel *The Lonely Londoners* (1956), which Clarke startlingly came to realize was the only "psychological language" for evoking the Caribbean psyche and "for getting to the heart of the matter" ("Sam Selvon" 51). An additional hallmark of Selvon's style is his use of humour. In his Toronto immigrant novels, Clarke employs humour as well, but there is a major difference in the way he does this that would suggest they are not such close kindred artistic spirits after all. This is the comparative issue that I address in this essay. Humour, theorists have noted, is employed with tonal differences that can be identified as satire, comedy, and farce. As satire it serves to chastise and reprimand with the intention of initiating reform, while as

comedy it points out shortcomings but with an awareness of the sad undercurrents of life, and as farce with no
intention other than to elicit purposeless laughter.[1] If we
accept this distinction, Selvon can be seen as a writer of
comedy, as a "laughing philosopher"; Ismith Khan notes
that Selvon "found humour in the simple, the ordinary,
the plain. ... His ability to laugh, talk, joke, and listen
to the people he immortalized was a genuine one. If he
laughed, he laughed with them because he felt one with
them, and he knew them well" (59). Clarke's humour
is much more militant; he wants to bring about reform
in the treatment of his Toronto-Barbadian immigrants
(the counterpart of Selvon's lonely Londoners) and to
persuade them to modify their way of life, values, and
outlook in their adopted environment.

This difference in their tonal approaches to the
immigrants' experience in their particular locales—
London and Toronto—is most starkly pointed up if
we juxtapose Selvon's concluding pages of *The Lonely
Londoners* and Clarke's introduction to his collection
of stories *Nine Men Who Laughed* (1986). Both authors
make illuminating theoretical observations on the nature
and function of their protagonists' (and by implication,
their own) laughter. Selvon's novel depicts the hard life
of the first batch of West Indian immigrants to post-
World War II London, particularly their inability to
cope with the trauma of racism. The protagonist of the
novel, Moses, a contemplative, philosophical individual,
feels the pain and despair of his fellow immigrants and
offers us his melancholic musing throughout, but particularly and poignantly at the end. Here once more is
the oft-quoted passage from the end of the novel that
captures the reflective voice of the narrator-protagonist

that underscores the function of laughter to hold despair in check:

> Under the kiff-kiff laughter, behind the ballad and the episode, the what-happening, the summer-is-hearts, he could see a great aimlessness, a great restless, swaying movement that leaving you standing in the same spot. As if a forlorn shadow of doom fall on all the spades in the country. As if he could see the black faces bobbing up and down in the millions of white, strained faces, everybody hustling along the Strand, the spades jostling in the crowd, bewildered, hopeless. As if, on the surface, things don't look so bad, but when you go down a little, you bounce up a kind of misery and hopelessness and a frightening—what? He don't know the right word but he have the right feeling in his heart.

"Kiff-kiff laughter," a Caribbean demotic term, is defined in the *Dictionary of the English/Creole of Trinidad & Tobago: On Historical Principles* (2008) as "describing a laugh usually at someone else's expense." There are instances in the novel where characters make fun of each other but it is harmless fun. Selvon portrays recurringly his Londoners as availing themselves readily of revitalizing companionship at gatherings. At one lively fête, there is some high-spirited and good-natured taunting of the affected host, aptly named Ladela Harris, which, however, never moves beyond raillery. Moses, the acknowledged mentor of the immigrants, observes of someone's humorous digs at Harris: "It does only he fun he making, for he not a malicious fellow at heart" (51). Selvon has said elsewhere: "The comedy element has always been there among black people from the Caribbean. It is their means of defense against the sufferings and tribulations they have to undergo. I always felt that this is a very strong element indeed and it is too easily brushed aside by well-meaning critics who feel that the funny story has its place but it just so much and nothing more" ("Interview with Nazareth" 423). The laughing philosopher-novelist, conscious of the underlying sadness of their lives, encourages his protagonists to employ laughter as a coping mechanism.

The last sentence of the novel evokes kindly rather than satiric laughter. "It was a summer night: laughter fell softly: it was the sort of night that if you wasn't making love to a woman you feel like you was the only person in the world like that."

Selvon's portrayal of Moses and his fellow immigrants resorting to laughter, wit, and humour as coping and survival mechanisms in stressful social and economic situations is antithetical to Clarke's harsh condemnation of what he dismisses as his protagonists' escapist laughter in *Nine Men Who Laughed*. To drive home his point, Clarke includes an author's "Introduction" to the stories and, in unrelentingly harsh language, Clarke rails against his protagonists' amnesiac laughter to their racial and economic exploitation, which he dismisses as "the weapon of fools" (9). Clarke depreciates laughter as a coping mechanism:

> When a character says "this fucking system" or "This system makes me laugh" (out of frustration or, more realistically, because he has become lazy, too lazy to think clearly), he is trying to reduce either the seriousness of the hurt inflicted upon him by the system or to make the system's racism less abrasive: he is confessing to his own inadequacy to take a strict moral position and

> destroy the system. All nine men laugh because they
> are perhaps, already morally dead. (5)

He acknowledges that laughter can be used as a means of defusing and lessening their frustration when confronting "racial and cultural tension" (4), but such "laughter becomes demeaning criticism of the individual's worth":

> The men who laugh in these stories are doing
> so because they represent the powerless and the
> colonized. They are not laughing because they
> are amused that a policeman beats them in cell or
> that they see a greenhorn friend being beaten or
> even that they are discovered in a tricky situation
> of sexual infidelity. They are laughing because they
> have become accommodating to a hostile society, and
> their laughter is therefore a "tick," an idiosyncratic
> adaptation to the society. (4)

The stories show the dire consequences of amnesiac laughter. The protagonists all meet dismal ends: they either lock themselves away from society, go mad, commit suicide, or are brutalized and murdered.

"Canadian Experience" is representative of the indicting tone of these stories. The protagonist, George—Clarke says in the Introduction that he is unnamed to indicate his generic immigrant experience, but his name appears unobtrusively on a greeting card the protagonist examines—is not blessed with self-knowledge or with self-expression. His responses and reactions are conveyed by his constant laughter. Clarke's use of laughter both literally and figuratively obtrudes in the story; the word "laughter" and its inflexional variants occur at least thirty times. The metaphor conveys the conflicting feelings and responses of the confused protagonist—and it calls for explication. Once or twice, it conveys the protagonist's paltry attempt at mocking the system, his occasional sense of satisfaction on some minor accomplishment, and his nostalgic pleasure on recalling pleasanter days in Barbados. But pervasively, it reflects his fears and insecurities, his overwhelming prejudicial treatment. Towards the end of the story, it shows his ennui and confusion, as he laughs "but does not know why" (50). And when he throws himself under the wheels of a train, it indicates his self-abnegation and his knuckling under the system. Clarke clearly rejects such laughter.

The form of laughter Clarke endorses is the purposeful, militant kind, characteristic of satire, which springs from a firm conviction and desire to reform. And to illustrate the difference between laughter of this and the self-abnegating kind, he puts as the first story of *Nine Men Who Laughed* a satirical piece on Barbadian politicians, entitled "A Funeral." The narrator of this story does not temporize with the ugly sociopolitical system of Barbados that he perceives to exist; instead, he relentlessly pokes fun at its members. The angry, mocking laughter of this story is much like that of *The Prime Minister* (1977), the "roman à clef" in which Clarke indicts the government of Barbados after he was unceremoniously relieved of his responsibility as general manager of the Caribbean Broadcasting Corporation for criticizing the then Barrow government, a consequence, Clarke would say, that those invoking satiric rather than temporizing laughter against the system should expect.

In his Toronto trilogy of novels—*The Meeting Point* (1967), *Storm of Fortune* (1973), and *The Bigger Light* (1975)—Clarke examines the black working-class immigrants' struggles in an inhospitable white society. He shows them living bleak lives, the victims of racial prejudice, and he captures well their intense feelings of alienation. Like Selvon, his unerringly sharp ear for Caribbean speech patterns and rhythms contributes much to the richness of his characterization. Clarke's strident anger against the unaccommodating white society, his overt plot manipulation to support his stand, and his inability to keep sufficient authorial distance from protagonists make his humour a mixed bag of censure and understanding; but his understanding is muted and never enough to mitigate his indictment of his Barbadian character and even less so his bitter portrait of white individuals and institutions. Indubitably Clarke's narrators are at one with the Barbadian newcomers but at the same time they are one removed from them; they are more responsible, more educated and more ambitious— components that temper the tone of camaraderie.

The title of *The Meeting Point* is ironical; there is really no chance of these divergent communities meeting. Clarke's work stands in contrast to Nadine Gordimer's early short story "Is There Nowhere Else Where We Can Meet?" (1947) that records the narrator's anguish that there may be no place for the races of apartheid South Africa of the 1940s to meet, yet she resolves at the end of the story to keep persevering. *The Meeting Point*, like the other two novels of the trilogy, is a serious sociological study if void of the humour of Selvon's fiction that imparts—for good or bad—a philosophical perspective on the lot of these immigrants. The portraits are all grim and grave with little narratorial contemplativeness. The protagonist, Bernice Leach, is a black Barbadian immigrant who works as a maid in the home ironically of a Jewish family in Toronto whose relations have experienced the holocaust. She and her fellow Barbadian maids feel threatened by the exclusive whiteness of the environment, symbolized by the recurring snow imagery. Perceiving herself as a twentieth-century slave and never comfortable in her adopted home, she is nevertheless hesitant to return to her impoverished peasant life in Barbados. Her male Barbadian friends, chronically unemployed, attempt futilely to achieve acceptance through sexual relationships with white women. These characters have to contend with inner as well as outer conflicts as they try to retain their black pride and identity and come to grips with self-hatred and beckoning materialism. In *Storm of Fortune*, the same group of Barbadian immigrants reappears. No longer fresh immigrants, they still feel alienated and unaccommodated. Some are managing to improve their fortunes (although the ways by which they do so often strain the reader's credulity). The characters who have achieved a measure of economic success and feel they deserve acceptance into the system now have to cope with more sharply felt social alienation that heightens their self-doubt and self-hatred.

One critic notes that *The Bigger Light* has an air of "solemn analysis that is not typical of Clarke's earlier novels" (Algoo-Baksh 1997, 32). This may be valid, but when the work is set next to Selvon's novel it is possible to say that Clarke's has a solemnity absent in Selvon's immigrant novels (though not in the Trinidad novels that includes *A Brighter Sun* [1952], *An Island Is a World* [1955], and *The Plains of Caroni* [1970][2]). *The Bigger Light,* the concluding volume of the Toronto Trilogy, focuses on the experiences of Boysie, one of the immigrants who has achieved relative financial success (like the landlord Moses of *Moses Ascending*). His social life is wanting, however, and he suffers from intense depression, which is pointed up by Clarke's use of recurring death imagery. Boysie's is the most probing psychological portrait that Clarke has undertaken and perhaps best affirms Clarke "solemnity." Desperate to belong in Canada, Boysie gradually becomes estranged from his wife and his West Indian identity as he attempts whatever tenuous assimilation is afforded him. He writes letters to prestigious Toronto newspapers, wears three-piece suits, avoids West Indian parties, and rejects calypsos for Judy Collins' songs. The novel ends with Boysie driving his car across the Canada-American border to seek refuge in Harlem where the narrator (and Clarke) unabashedly says he will "find out some answers" (218), but there is little to suggest that he can rally himself and arrest his malaise. While Selvon portrays Moses in *Moses Migrating* as a zany individual and ends the novel at the no-man's-land setting of Heathrow, where Moses is not sure he will be readmitted to Britain, Clarke offers a closure which some have seen as too convenient, too solemn.[3]

The difference in tone is noticeable when we compare two aspects of Selvon's and Clarke's fiction: their treatment of those immigrants (like Boysie) who have achieved some measure of relative success and their representation of the man-woman relationship in the migrant community. Selvon's irony is compassionate compared to Clarke's, as in this passage from early in *Moses Ascending* that records Moses' passionate poetic lament—which Moses himself describes as "taking an objective view" (5)—on the pre-dawn labours that are exclusively the black man's in London:

As he stands, mayhap, in some wall-to-wall carpeted mansion (resting, dreaming on his broom or hoover) and looks about him at mahogany furniture, at deeply-padded sofas and armchairs, at myriading chandeliers ... at Renoirs and Van Goghs and them other fellars, what thoughts of humble gratitude should go through his mind! Here he is, monarch of all he surveys, passing the wine, toasting the Queen, carving the baron of beef, perambulating among distinguished guests, pausing, perhaps, for a word on the fluctuation of guilt-edge shares or the new play in the West End.

And the black man is the chosen race to dream such dreams, and to enjoy the splendour and the power whilst the whole rest of the world is still in slumberland. Oh, the ingratitude, the unreasonableness of those who only see one side of the coin, and complain that he is given only the menial tasks to perform? (As I became objective, I was mad to jump up and put on my clothes and go straight to work!) (6-7)

What really is the author's tone here? As the last sentence signals, Moses appears to be taking both literally and ironically what he says here about the opportunities available to blacks in London. Selvon prefaces the passage with this comment by Moses that sets in motion doubts about the likelihood of unambiguous irony in the narrator-protagonist's tone: "One of the things that gave me great delight was to be able to stay in bed and think of all them hustlers who had to get up and go to work" (5). Revealingly, earlier in *The Housing Lark*, the narrator, whose voice is as ambivalent as Moses', would appear to both share and censure the women's judgement of their pleasure-seeking, irresponsible male partners: "Look at these dreamers, and imagine that characters like these could get serious" (43).

This can be compared with Henry's unambiguous rage against the system in *The Storm of Fortune*, the second novel of the Toronto trilogy:

> You want to know something? I feel like getting up outta this bed right now, and walking down Yonge Street and smashing every goddam store window down there. Then I'm heading for Queen's Park, and I killing every blasted politician there. And when I finish doing that, I have my gun, and be-Jesus Christ, I am killing every cop that pass. (51-52)

Henry has the good sense not to put his words to action, but his vitriolic sentiment passes muster for a narrator who takes to task the amnesiac laughter of the feckless. In *A Bigger Light*, Boysie, like Moses in *Moses Ascending*, has achieved a measure of material success. He owns a cleaning business and is financially better off than his West Indian counterparts with whom he does not want to be identified. But this is not a playful response, unlike Moses' to Galahad that it is "the parting of the ways" for them: "To be seen talking with them on the street would be to mark himself as one of them; and he couldn't have that for he was moving up" (96). He dissociates himself from the black militants, very much like Moses initially does, but Clarke's portrayal is not characterized by Selvonian amusement:

> Nobody was going to brand him as a Black Power advocate, or a Black Militant. He was a businessman. And he had to make a living, buy a house, and move away from this slum, to the suburbs, from this blasted place on Ontario Street which seemed to be the final

resting place on earth for the aged, the prostitute, and the wino. (175)

In an essay "The West Indian Immigrant in Canada," Clarke speaks reprimandingly of what he calls this "inverted snobbishness and intra-segregation among West Indians" (6; qtd. in Isaacs 109). Camille Isaacs notes that Clarke pinpoints this aspect of the West Indian immigrants in the Toronto trilogy (which Boysie comes to repudiate): "This pride in ethnicity is ... evident in Austin Clarke's work. His characters are proud of, and want to emphasize their distinct West Indianness. The characters in Clarke's Toronto trilogy ... want to make sure that everyone knows their ethnic identification. Henry wants to stress he is 'a goddamn Wessindian' (*Storm of Fortune* 281)" (87). Boysie's self-doubt, his quest for acceptance in the white society, his shunning of his fellow West Indians and of West Indian culture are reflected in the main character of Clarke's story "Four Stations in His Circle" (in *When He Was Free and Young and He Used to Wear Silks*), in which Clarke shows with biting humour how the protagonist isolates himself in a mansion he has purchased in a white neighbourhood. Ironically, his neighbours assume that he is just the caretaker.

For Selvon, the man-woman relationship is often problematic in the émigré community but he plays up the humour and plays down the sadness that underlies the lonely Londoners' lives. In "Brackley and the Bed" (1957), one of Selvon's most anthologized stories, Brackley, desperate to avoid marriage to Teena, immigrates from Trinidad to London; when Teena follows him there, afraid to confront her, he agrees to let her stay with him in his barely habitable flat, letting her have his bed.

Eventually to get his bed back, he somewhat reluctantly marries her, only to learn that she knew his aunt is coming to London and will share the bed with Teena, relegating him once again to sleeping on the floor even on their wedding-night. Selvon understands the circumstances of Brackley's harsh life in a society where he feels alienated, and he is aware of the practicality rather than the romanticism of working-class West Indian man-woman relationships in which women basically want their partners' economic support and men expect sexual gratification and domestic service. He reveals with warm irony the subtle power women wield in this pre-feminist novel. For Selvon, this is an incident of confidence-man meeting confidence-woman, and he retains a light-heartedness without averting the young Trinidadian's difficulty to find decent work and accommodation and his resignation to his fate that results in his induced passivity yet his readiness to comply with Teena's demands for economic security. Selvon mentions that Brackley comes from a part of Tobago where "Robinson Crusoe used to hang out with Man Friday" (374) but this appears to be incidental rather than intentional of postcolonial militancy as Clarke might have elected to accentuate. If there is any significance to the Friday-Crusoe allusion in the story, it is to feature amusingly that Brackley domestically is Teena's Man Friday. In *Moses Ascending*, Selvon does invert with telling irony the Crusoe-Friday relationship in portraying Moses' relationship with his English handyman but the political intent is mitigated by the comical re-inversion of the handyman's dictating to an ineffectual Moses how to cope with demanding tenants.

The Housing Lark (1965), which relates the financial misadventures of a group of West Indian men and women when they decide to pool their paltry resources to buy a house in London, is perhaps Selvon's most hilarious immigrant novel. Selvon resorts to farce in depicting the men's relationships with their partners, dodging any moral judgement however slight that informs his other comic novels; here he takes the position that boys will be boys; immature men will be immature men. He leaves their irresponsible, sexist, and impractical behaviour unindicted, instead milking the zany incidents for merriment. The narrator appears both to share and to censure the women's judgement of their pleasure-seeking male partners: "Look at these dreamers and imagine that characters like these could get serious" (87). The authorial view of these women could be compared with Clarke's treatment of Bernice in the Toronto trilogy. Clarke is sympathetic to her lot; she is portrayed as a fighter, unlike the feckless men. Like Selvon, Clarke is aware of the emasculating society in which the men find themselves but unlike Selvon he expects them to try to do something about it rather than use laughter as escape.

Though Selvon features several women in his London stories and novel, he gives prominence to men, particularly companions of Moses, from whose point of view the events are generally narrated. Moses remains "one of the boys." This in large measure would explain the genial, tolerant, amused tone of the narrative. In Clarke's fiction, however, women are given more prominent roles. Bernice is in fact the dominant figure and the moral agent who tries to keep the men in check. Clarke admires this aspect of her but he also feels she is a bit too dictatorial, a judgement that does not diminish her censure of the often irresponsible men. In *When Women Rule* (1985), Clarke is censorious of this female dominance over men—men on both sides of the racial divide. He portrays poor and working white males (while not free of racial bigotry) as being similarly emasculated by domineering partners. Nick of "The Collector" harks back to a time when "this country was *clean*" (47) of immigrants; his wife fuels his narrow-mindedness. The war amputee Alexander in "On One Leg" creates the impression when he is with his "buddies" that he is a man's man but he is in fact virtually emasculated by his tyrannical wife. Little humour informs these portraits; the tone of the collection stands in glaring contrast to that of Selvon's *The Housing Lark*.

Selvon was proud of his reputation of a humorist and as a writer who uses skilfully Caribbean demotic, which, intertwined with his humour, became the hallmark of his style. But he later lamented the fact that critics' preoccupation with his humour and his use of the demotic blinkered them to other aspects of his fiction, and that his reputation as a novelist appeared to rest on certain novels to the exclusion of others. It is true that more than half of Selvon's fiction uses humour sparingly and employ standard English. It is true also that whether his novels use demotic or standard English, warm humour is an inescapable feature of his writings. He was particularly fond of *An Island Is a World*, which not only employs standard English but, in its examination of the young protagonist's thoughts on such large issues as life, death, love, nationhood, friendship, and race, has a much more serious, "solemn" tone than his comic fiction set in London. Yet Selvon does not mute the voice of the laughing philosopher. His later novel *Moses Ascending* perhaps more than any of his London fiction embodies the warm awareness of the sadness beneath human laughter. Though politically uncommitted, unlike what Clarke demands of his protagonists, Moses is humanly concerned with the lot of his fellow men.

In this novel, Moses has bought a house and is leaving the basement apartment he has shared with Galahad for many years. He tells Galahad that this is "the parting of the ways" (2); Galahad counters accurately: "You can't erase me like that. ... I am part and parcel of your life" (3). One of the moving passages in the book is his lament (saved from mawkishness by wit) for his fellow immigrants with whom he associated when he first moved to London (as related in *The Lonely Londoners*):

> Where have they gone? What are they doing? Somewhere out there, somewhere among the millions of whites; in the bustling traffics and the towering buildings and the confusion and pandemonium of the city, they are scattered and lost. I only hear stories of their plights and sorrows, tales of tragedy whispered on the wind. I hear that Big City has gone mad, walks about the streets muttering to himself, ill-kempt and unshaven, and does not recognise anyone. It is as if the whole city of London collapse on him, as if the pressures build up until he could stand it no more and had to make a wild dash around the bend. (9-10)

What particularly endears this mildly eccentric narrator to the reader is his constant self-examination. He is conscious of his eccentricities and worried that he may be, as Galahad, a friend, harshly tells him, "heading straight for the madhouse" (43). At the end of the novel, he undergoes an extended period of self-probing and makes a discovery that he describes as an epiphany, though humorously: "I suppose, really, this is what is meant when one sees the light, like how Saul become Paul. I try out Moses-Roses, and it come to me in a flash, like a revelation" (117). What Moses comes to realize is that he need not become a political militant to help his fellowman. The solution is not in politics but in traditional values, in doing good to others, in being generous and philanthropic. Moses' philosophy is a romantic one, in keeping with his character that *The Lonely Londoners* defines as having "the right feeling in his heart" (126). And this generates his (and his author's) genial rather than amnesiac humour.

In *Moses Ascending*, Selvon, a decade after Clarke's activist theorizing in the Introduction to *Nine Men Who Laughed*, appears to examine such militancy and activism but with expected Selvonian geniality. Moses is confronted with political activists, full of passionate intensity, who are persuading him to take a stand politically and are making his life miserable by ridiculing his apolitical stance. In depicting Moses' experience with these activists, Selvon pokes fun in both novels at the politically zealous and militant, but his treatment of this theme varies considerably between the two novels. In *Moses Ascending*, he shows Moses besieged by Black and Asian militants who make him feel guilty because he steers clear of their radical actions, desiring to be left alone to "live in peace" (3), practising a "philosophy of neutrality" (97). Caught between commitment and passivity, he experiences excruciating ambivalence. When he briefly and naively experiments with political activism, Selvon employs him effectively as an ingénu to poke light-hearted fun at the militants and tellingly of himself. Armed with his notebook and clipboard, this novitiate activist gets himself into awkward racial and political situations in his effort to obtain material for his sociopolitical study. Selvon introduces the episodes relating these incidents as much to define Moses' naivete as to poke fun at the militants' narrowness and biases.

In his last novel, *Moses Migrating* (1983), Selvon remains true to his humorous perspective on immigrant life even when they return home on a ship for a holiday. Moses' character undergoes a sea-change resulting in the humour in the main shifting from comedy to farce: he is less contemplative, less bothered by inner conflicts. The novel opens with him preparing to leave Britain for Trinidad, and though initially he claims to be fleeing racial prejudice in Britain, he perceives himself more and more as an unconflicted ambassador of British culture. An eccentric, his eccentricity becomes zanier and zanier as the novel progresses. As such, the novel is less a continuation of *Moses Ascending* than a disparate work, even though there are brief initial references to some minor issues and situations in the earlier novel. Moses' political antics elicit farcical laughter. Selvon does not invite serious considerations of his views. He does not portray Moses pondering why he has decided to return to Trinidad or engaging in serious discussion with his cabin mates about what lies in store for them after so many years abroad—as would be expected of Moses of *Moses Ascending*. Instead, what the author emphasizes about the journey home, in a long farcical episode, is Moses' and Jeannie's love-making in the same room where Jeannie's husband lies prostrate from seasickness. Similarly, the episodes set in Trinidad, such as the hilarious extended beach scene where Jeannie loses her bikini, are not intended seriously. Selvon plays it and other actions by Moses simply for laughter as an end in itself. As a central aspect of the narrative, he has Moses participate in a prize-winning carnival band that features Britannia and her subjects. In a Clarke novel, it would be possible to take this as a satirical allegory; this would be in keeping with Clarke's artistic-militant perspective, but for Selvon it would be totally inconsistent with his philosophy of forbearance and the novel's portrait of Moses as a zany individual.

In his later immigrant fiction, Clarke continues to write militantly and whatever humour he employs has a sharp edge to it. In *Prime Minister*, which, as we have seen, Clarke wrote after a stint with the government of Barbados, the humour is satirical as he pokes fun at corrupt local politicians—which stands in contrast to Selvon's zany depiction of Moses' return to Trinidad. *Proud Empires* (1986) looks back in a similar vein to Barbados politics of the 1950s. Boy, a thirteen-year-old high-school student, prepares for a scholarship examination in the middle of a national election, which proves a rite of passage for him. It opens his eyes to the corruption and treachery of island politics. But Clarke is less concerned with Boy's development than with the reprehensible conduct of the politicians and the distorted values of the middle class. At the end of the novel, Boy, who has gone to study in Toronto (where inevitably, like Clarke's other immigrant characters, he experiences racism), returns to the island and allows himself to be persuaded to enter politics. But Boy's experiences are so cursorily given and his character so sketchily portrayed that it is not clear exactly what he has learned about politics and what he can contribute politically. Characteristically, *Proud Empires* has many fine episodes of scintillating dialogue, employing the rhythm and idiom of Barbados English, which helps considerably to bring the characters to life. But the novel confirms that Clarke's strength as a novelist lies not in his humorous perspective as in his indictment of the follies, foibles, and vices of his Barbadian characters whether at home or abroad.

His novel *The Polished Hoe* (2002) continues the solemnity of the immigrant novels but without their strident tone. There is a subtler ironical tenor; whatever humour is introduced has little of the cutting edge of the Toronto trilogy. In an interview, Clarke admits that he began writing this later novel "as a novice," throwing "out a lot of the things that I did in the previous novels" (Interview). He retains the demotic language, which he agrees with Selvon is so appropriate to the West Indian experience, using it to authenticate this community rather than to make it amusing—a credo that the Martinique writer Patrick Chamoiseau in his novel *Texaco* reaffirms for Clarke:

> ... [I]n that novel I saw the possibilities which [Patrick Chamoiseau] could—and did in fact—achieve. The broadening of the language which really is wonderful. One would refer to it derogatorily as Creole French. But he was able to use that and create a new language. And it's interesting that one of the most impressive reviews of the book was written by Derek Walcott himself. Having been born in St. Lucia, he would speak a patois version of French. And of course, English, too. (Interview)

He acknowledges his influences may have been the writers "he had been reading" (Interview) before he put fingers to the keyboard: James Baldwin, Saul Bellow, Ian McEwan. V.S. Naipaul, Derek Walcott, Richard Wright, and Patrick Chamoiseau's *Texaco*. He now has achieved more ironic control, more aesthetic distance, and offers more incisive, less judgemental studies of the characters' psyches and is no longer just a literary activist protesting against injustice and discrimination. Perhaps, as he suggests, his mood at the time of writing the novel may have accounted for the less angry, indicting voice:

> I felt the freedom and the liberation from all of the things that could influence the writing of a book negatively. I was not anxious for anything. I was in a very good mood. I was healthy. I was cheerful. And I had retained my sense of humour. And I thought ... that they are the ingredients that an author must experience and realize if he or she is going to write something that is great and good (Interview).

Significantly some scholars have called attention to his personal sense of humour that makes him a kindred spirit of Selvon. Algoo-Baksh tells us in her biographical study that no matter what happens to him he retains "a delightful sense of humour" and that his letters to her were "often characterised by effervescence and wit" (188). And Harold Marshall reiterates that one of his appealing qualities is "his sense of humour" (qtd. Algoo-Baksh, 1994 189). In this regard, Clarke, speaking of the title of *The Polished Hoe,* told an interviewer that he was not aware of the possible double-entendre in the title.[4] Austin Clarke was more than likely tongue-in-cheek when he said this, exhibiting an authorial amusement that is more characteristic of Sam Selvon's than of Austin Clarke's early protagonists.

Endnotes

1. See, for instance, Highet, Kernan, Meredith, and Worcester.
2. *The Plains of Caroni* has an uncharacteristic satiric bite when Selvon exposes the merciless exploitation of sugar workers in 1960s Trinidad.
3. See, for instance, Henry.
4. He tells Linda L. Richards, editor of *January Magazine* (Nov. 2002), when she asked him if the double entendre was intentional: "You know, to be quite honest, it was not. This was brought to my attention when I went to the States and [when I was] introducing the book, everybody started laughing. My brother was in the audience, so afterwards I said to him: Why are the people laughing? And he said: Don't you know? Then he started laughing. And it was that certain black Americans pronounce the word 'whore' as 'ho.' As in: She's a ho. You see? So I said: Yeah, if anybody asks me, I'll say I intended the double entendre. [Laughs] But I did not. I never thought of it.

Works Cited

Algoo-Baksh, Stella. *Austin C. Clarke and His Works*. Toronto: ECW Press, 1997.

_____. *Austin Clarke: A Biography*. Kingston, Jamaica; University of West Indies Press; Toronto: ECW Press, 1994.

Clarke, Austin. *The Bigger Light*. Toronto: Little, Brown, 1975; Boston-Toronto: Vintage Canada, 1998.

_____. Interview with Linda L. Richards. Nov. 2002. *January Magazine*. http://januarymagazine.com/profiles/aclarke.html 10 Mar. 2013.

_____. *The Meeting Point*. London: Heinemann, 1967; Toronto: Vintage Canada, 1998.

_____. *Nine Men Who Laughed*. Toronto: Penguin, 1986.

_____. *The Polished Hoe*. Toronto: Thomas Allen, 2002.

_____. *The Prime Minister*. Don Mills, ON: General Publishing, 1977.

_____. *Proud Empires*. London: Gollanz, 1986.

_____. "Sam Selvon: A Celebration." In *ARIEL: Tribute to Sam Selvon*. Ed. Victor J. Ramraj. 27.2. (April 1996): 49-63.

_____. *Storm of Fortune*. Toronto: Little, Brown, 1973; Boston-Toronto: Vintage Canada, 1998.

_____. "The West Indian Immigrant in Canada." Unpublished ms. (McMaster), Box 20, Folder 14, 1962.

_____. *When He Was Free and Young and He Used to Wear Silks*. Toronto: Anansi, 1971.

_____. *When Women Rule*. Toronto: McClelland & Stewart, 1980.

Gordimer, Nadine. "Is There Nowhere Else Where We Can Meet." In *Voices of the Serpent*. London: Gollanz, 1953. 42-49.

Highet, Gilbert. *The Anatomy of Satire*. Oxford: Oxford UP, 1962.

Henry, Keith. "An Assessment of Austin Clarke, West Indian-Canadian Novelist." *College Language Association* 29 (1985): 9-32.

Isaacs, Camille. "A Binding of Community: Storytelling and Identity Construction in Black Canadian

Literature." PhD Dissertation, University of Calgary, 2006.

Kernan, Alvin B. *The Cankered Muse: Satire of the English Renaissance*. New Haven: Yale UP, 1959.

Khan, Ismith. "Sam Selvon: A Celebration." In *ARIEL: Tribute to Sam Selvon*. Ed. Victor J. Ramraj. 27.2. (April 1996): 49-63.

Meredith, George. *An Essay on Comedy and the Uses of the Comic Spirit*. 1877.

Nazareth, Peter. Interview with Selvon. *World Literature Written in English* 18 (November 1979): 420-37.

Selvon, Sam. "Brackley and the Bed." In *Ways of Sunlight*, 151-55.

_____. *A Brighter Sun*. London: Allan Wingate, 1952; London: Longman Caribbean, 1986.

_____. *The Housing Lark*. London: MacGibbon & Kee, 1965.

_____. *An Island Is a World*. London: Allan Wingate, 1955: London: Longman Caribbean, 1983; Toronto: TSAR, 1993.

_____. *The Lonely Londoners*. London: Allan Wingate, 1956; London: Longman Caribbean, 1986; Toronto: TSAR, 1991.

_____. *Moses Ascending*. London: Davis Poynter, 1975; London: Heinemann, 1984.

_____. *Moses Migrating*. London: Longman, 1983; Longman Caribbean, 1987.

_____. *The Plains of Caroni*. London: MacGibbon & Kee, 1970; Toronto: Williams-Wallace, 1985.

_____. *Ways of Sunlight (Stories)*. London: MacGibbon & Kee, 1957; London: Longman, 1973.

Winer, Lise. *Dictionary of the English/Creole of Trinidad & Tobago: On Historical Principles*. Montreal-Kingston: McGill-Queen's UP, 2008.

Worcester, David. *The Art of Satire*. London: Russell and Russell, 1960.

The Mother as Culinary Griotte:
Food and Cultural Memory in Austin
Clarke's *Pig Tails 'n Breadfruit*

BRINDA MEHTA

The Afro-Barbadian-Canadian writer Austin Clarke occupies a place of distinction in both Caribbean and Canadian literature. Born in Barbados in 1934, Clarke left for Toronto in 1955 where he has been living in a state of self-imposed exile after returning briefly to Barbados in 1975. The author of eight published books, including two personal memoirs, Clarke's *oeuvre* also comprises journalist and political essays. His earliest works, such as *Survivors of the Crossing* (1964) and *Amongst Thistles and Thorns* (1965), focus on the lives of the rural proletariat of Barbados whereas later novels such as *The Bigger Light* (1975) deal with the West Indian immigrant experience in Toronto. A 1977 work entitled *The Prime Minister* represents the culmination of a two-year appointment as General Manager of the Barbados Government's Broadcasting Company, a position from which he was unceremoniously fired in 1976 due to major political differences with the ruling government. This incident marked a turning point in Clarke's perception of the land of his birth, focusing on attitudes that have alternated between disappointment, rejection, and nostalgic idealization. Caught between the immediacy of his immigrant Canadian present and the ambivalence toward the Barbadian past, Clarke comments on the necessity of transcending the "anxiousness of duality in an interview with Frank Birbalsingh where he states:

> I have grown away not only in distance but in attitude from Barbados. At the moment, I am concerned with determining or defining an identity for the Caribbean man who has lived in Toronto for some time, in such a way that he will no longer consider himself an immigrant, an outsider, or a minority person, but would come to understand that his presence here, and the ease with which he continues to live here, is caused by the solid foundation that he got from the West Indies. (Birbalsingh 101)

Anxious to immortalize the foundational roots of his Caribbean identity mediated nevertheless by Canadian naturalization, Clarke uses the figure of the mother in his recent memoir *Pig Tails 'n Breadfruit* (1999) as the necessary catalyst who facilitates an engagement with the self as it confronts and accommodates its exilic disposition. However, it would be safe to assert that Clarke's memoir is written at a moment when he nostalgically remembers the past whose "authenticity" is put into question by several years of voluntary exile in Canada. The memoir consequently spans three timelines wherein the personal reflections of the adult Afro-Barbadian-Canadian writer transport the reader to the Barbados of his boyhood that is, in turn, inscribed within a larger framework of Barbadian colonial history. This essay asserts that the memoir contains a palimpsest-like structure where personal memory intermingles with cultural and culinary history to provide a narrative of economical cultural production that is so skilfully articulated that the women being described come alive on the page and the food that they provide spreads before us in a smorgasbord of sensory delights.

The author's most enduring ties to his Barbadian past are revealed through a personal homage paid to the mother who provides her son with an enduring ethics of living during his most formative years. As he admits in an interview: "It occurred to me that, from my early days in Barbados, I was surrounded by women who were perhaps more powerful and intelligent than I had been disposed to accept and that they really controlled things. ... They nurtured us and gave us an understanding of how to live" (Birbalsingh 93, 95). Ritualized cooking practices shared by the mother and other women of the community, as well as those willing to learn from them, reproduced cultural agents such as Clarke who were so steeped in their own cultural heritage that they performed as cultural agents in their own right.

The choice of a culinary memoir places Clarke in a position of uniqueness as a male Caribbean writer given the fact that the search for identity through the problematics of food production has primarily been the preoccupation of women writers from the Caribbean and the "third world" in general. The link between food, gender, and identity has been successfully explored in the writings of Caribbean, Latina, and South Asian women writers such as Ramabai Espinet, Rosanne Kanhai, and Lakshmi Persaud from Trinidad in "Indian Cuisine," "Soul Food," and *Butterfly in the Wind*, respectively;

Laura Esquivel from Mexico in *Like Water for Chocolate*; and Chitra Divakaruni from India in *The Mistress of Spices*, among others. On the other hand, Clarke's male peers living in the Caribbean diaspora such as the Barbadian George Lamming in *The Immigrants* and the late Sam Selvon from Trinidad in *The Lonely Londoners* have tended to focus on issues of identity through the prism of immigration and acculturation. The exploration of a predominantly "feminine" genre by a male writer reveals the tensions and contradictions inherent in a particular problematics of representation related to gender ideologies that simultaneously affirm and negate the subjective agency of Barbadian (Bajan) women. For this reason, Clarke's personal re-imaginings of the past are, at the same time, filtered through a blurry optic lens that both complicates and contradicts the positioning of gender ideologies in 1940s Barbados. This search for authenticity problematizes the representation of gender by immobilizing women in conventional culinary roles linked to cultural preservation on the one hand while simultaneously celebrating female cultural agency and its crucial role in the construction of cultural memory on the other. Through the adroit overlapping of cultural history and personal reminiscence, *Pig Tails 'n Breadfruit* highlights the ritualistic order of cooking as a site of female labour and as a means of finding a sense of place at "home" and in the diaspora through the mediation of women.

The memoir is a literary celebration of the culinary dynamism of Clarke's mother and other female members of his native Barbadian community. Establishing a close connection between cooking, orality, and women's history, the memoir pays tribute to a strong tradition of culinary matriarchs whose dexterity in the kitchen paved the way for the inscription of women in the collective history of pre-independence Barbados of the 1940s. The unrecognized labour of women in the domestic sphere of the kitchen has often resulted in their invisibility in public historical documentation. However, this study shows that, in Clarke's narrative, on the other hand, the women are presented as chroniclers of culinary history in which food production becomes a palimpsest to interrogate gender and class distinctions through the oral inventiveness of cooking. The kitchen becomes a politicized site of production and distribution activities to reveal the managerial skills of women within the privatization of the domestic. In other words, food production permits black Barbadian women to assert their selfhood through their subjective claiming of Caribbean history. Food becomes a signifier of cultural consciousness and a subsequent affirmation of a mode of cultural production that has its roots in a disenfranchising history of slavery and oppression. Consequently, the experiences of these culinary experts bring alive an obscured woman-centred historical past through narratives of resistance in the present. This resistance thematizes the symbolic dimension of food by expanding the realm of the symbolic to include food production and by exposing the political messages that can be represented in food discourse as symbolic production. This study makes the argument that food can be a signifier of political displacement by serving as a carrier of political messages, such as the anti-colonial discourse encoded in the culinary practices of the author's mother, and by exposing the latent sexism demonstrated by Clarke himself in terms of his nostalgia for maintaining the status quo of hard labour in the kitchen. In other words, by locating food as a site of symbolic action in which politics can be displaced, the memoir highlights the symbolic discursive insurrections that enable women to act politically even when they do not enter the public political arena explicitly.

To fully appreciate the importance of the mother in Clarke's memoir, it is important to situate the text within an historical context. Female historical subjectivity in the Caribbean has been largely ignored or misrepresented in "official" accounts until the recent scholarship of leading Caribbean feminists from the region. As Bridget Brereton states: "The exclusion of women from conventional history thus reflected systems of gender oppression and in turn reinforced them by encouraging the definition of women as 'Other,' the passive, there but not there, never the makers and movers of history" (124). Presented as passive victims of history in several accounts, women were either discounted or subjected to a racialized and gendered alterity in the colonial narrative of planters, immigration officers, and male historians. Stereotypical misrepresentations obscured the dynamism and complexity of women's lives under African slavery by relegating women's experiences to the "private" or domestic spheres of influence that were "unworthy" of public exposure. It has been the task of Caribbean feminists to resurrect women's history from the archives of oblivion by insisting that "personal life such as family relations and women's roles within the family is just as crucial and just as much part of history" (Brereton 124). By reconceptualizing and deconstructing the very notion of history as a masculinist narrative, feminist scholars have posited Caribbean women as active agents in history-making through their economic, cultural, and political contributions during slavery, the post-emancipation period and present-day living. In this way, the women in Clarke's narrative continue the tradition of Caribbean feminism initiated by their foremothers through their culinary activism in which they outline a blueprint of feminist action in 1940s Barbados through their control of the kitchen and food-related activities. Culinary production through the preparation of meals, subsistence gardening activities and participation in informal entrepreneurial networks in the local market facilitates the elaboration of a woman-authored testimonial narrative in which the experiences of black working class women receive prominence through communal participation and oral communication. Comparing the testimonial narrative to the oral life story, Carole Boyce-Davies states:

> Oral life story clearly exists in that same liminal space between the public and the private, between oral and written discourses. In its intertextuality, its open-ended, dialogic form, then, the oral life story form functions explicitly to facilitate empowerment for women who historically have been silenced, whose words are not accepted as having legitimacy in the realm of accepted public discourse. ... Life stories, viewed against this backdrop, are another of those sublimated women's articulations (15).

Women author these interstitial border narratives that provide the site for their culinary insurrections to contest marginal representation. The mother becomes the "subversive" history maker, the original female griotte who, through her culinary reimaginings, furnishes the necessary script for more affirming representations of Barbadian women through the intersectional positioning of food and women's oral culture.

The inscription of food in the Barbadian cultural imaginary establishes culinary history as a metonym for women-centred cultural traditions in which the mother's cooking techniques become a veritable memory bank of individual stories and experiences. Referring to his mother's sharpness of memory, Clarke affirms: "My mother, who says her age is between eighty-one and ninety-one … makes it her business to impress me with the sharpness of her memory. Using memory and greater age as weapons authority, she reminds me of the meals she cooked on Sundays sixty years ago" (29). The mother's memory establishes a certain genealogy of origin to locate women's histories within an enduring tradition of wisdom, creativity, and self-reliance in the kitchen.

The frequent references to slave food in the memoir establish the primacy of the slave culinary ethic as the very foundation of Caribbean cuisine. Food preparation becomes a medium of self-expression amid the exacting and dehumanizing circumstances of slavery whereby enslaved Africans "were able to exercise the human potentiality to taste, to compare, to elaborate their preferences. … The ability to render judgements of food, to develop comparisons, to calibrate differences in taste—and to be prevented from doing so—help to suggest that something of the taste of freedom was around before freedom itself was," according to Sidney Mintz (37). The tasting and preparation of food as a prerequisite to the "tasting" of freedom helped to establish the culinary autonomy of the slave kitchen when it came to choosing seasonings and flavours that would significantly "alter" the colonial menu. By engaging in a form of culinary bricolage "the slaves quickly displayed their readiness and ability to draw freely upon what was available in recreating with new content and in new form their own distinctive culture" (Mintz 42). The cultural creativity displayed in the colonial kitchen paralleled the political inventiveness of different resistance movements in the Caribbean that provided the necessary point of motivation to change existing patterns of being.

In the memoir, the kitchen becomes a microcosmic representation of a larger world view where food symbolizes a certain poetics of life and ethic of self-definition. Scornful of the loftiness of French colonial cuisine whose heavy sauces and overabundance of garlic were used to camouflage the nefariousness of the colonial politic in the Caribbean, the mother negates the self-proclaimed superiority of colonial food through an effective unmasking of the pretentiousness of "hot cuisine" (1). The subversive transformation of "haute cuisine" into "hot cuisine" upsets the binary distinctions between colonial and native food by reducing the former to an equal footing with the local cuisine characterized by its "hot" and simply flavourful nature. For the mother, food preparation corresponds with the transmission of important values as a key to self-awareness. As the narrator indicates:

> Food. It is a word that defines my life. Not food in the sense of "hot-cuisine," as my mother called that kind of French sophistication with sauces and garlic, in her characteristic dismissive prejudice against food cooked by Europeans, especially the French. "What do French-people know about cooking food?" It was her final judgement, and the last nail in the coffin of any pretentiousness I would have about food. (1)

Consequently, the kitchen becomes a school of informal learning and an important space to depoliticize colonial cultural values in favour of the local culture. The memoir thereby demonstrates how the mother is able to conduct her private revolution against colonial domination and its subsequent colonization of the Caribbean mind through the inventiveness of an indigenized culinary vocabulary that provides the necessary language for effective decolonization.

The mother's culinary "decolonizations of intent" are reflected in her cooking styles that affirm her colonial subjectivity as an independent agent who chronicles the history of colonial oppression in Barbados. In other words, the mother writes herself into history through the cooking of local dishes that are inscribed within the aesthetics of slave food preparation as the necessary counter script to the master narrative. Anne Goldman establishes the relationship between subjectivity and ethnicity through the use of the culinary metaphor. She states: "Figuring the development of an ethnic identity with the metaphor of domestic labour thus provides a means of associating struggle in the political domain with endeavours in the cultural space. Because it calls attention to the work involved in cultural production, the culinary metaphor provides writers with a means of reexamining power" (191). The mother's dominance in the kitchen as a means of controlling cultural space provides her and the women of her community with the opportunity to renegotiate their subaltern position of sexualized and racialized otherness within the colonial polity. These renegotiations include the acknowledgement of women's invisible labour within the confines of the kitchen as well as the association of cooking with a particular strategy of cultural documentation whereby the mother's culinary magic resurrects indigenous myths, legends, and aspects of local oral history that have been submerged under the weight of the colonial archives.

Caribbean feminists such as Rhoda Reddock, Bridget Brereton, Verene Shepherd, and others pay tribute to the founding efforts of enslaved African women who established their autonomy through their active contribution to labour production on the plantations as well as in the colonial kitchens. However, the gendered imbalance in task performance ascribed a lower social, economic, and political value to women's responsibilities over the centuries. Rhoda Reddock attributes this discrepancy to what she calls the "naturalization of women's work, in so far as it is reduced to the level of instinct or 'second nature'" (3). The feminization of the domestic labour force has been based on gender-determined essentialism that has characterized certain jobs as inherently feminine (re: inferior) in nature. As a result of gender-based typecasting, these jobs have been viewed as unskilled, non-technical labour with a low market value. The productivity of women has been undermined through the association of their domestic work with a long-standing "female tradition" of sacrifice and service to family and community. Reddock continues: "The reality of women working in the domestic/household economy usually unpaid and certainly underpaid, is that they provide a flexible body of potential wage-workers available for temporary, insecure employment, to be dismissed when this is no longer economically viable" (5). These inequities have reinforced the devaluing of women's undocumented (re: invisible) household labour. Moreover, the economic negation of women's work has also accounted for their larger historical and political marginalization in the collective psyche despite women's best efforts to convert passive victimhood into active empowerment through the politicization of space and the development of a strong sense of feminist consciousness to contest the status quo.

In Clarke's narrative, the kitchen becomes a site of contestation when the mother converts it into the necessary supportive space to facilitate new beginnings for women. She converts the kitchen into a site of creativity by enabling the women to perform everyday culinary magic, as a means of controlling their circumstances. The women's labour in the kitchen becomes an enduring element of cultural production to revise its previously unrecognized status. The narrator pays tribute to the culinary matriarchs in his family for whom cooking was both a way of life and a way of making history. As the novel reveals: "These women were always cooking. ... As these women cooked, they talked bout the food they were cooking and whether they should try a different assortment of spices, a different combination of ingreasement" (10). Kitchen talk provides the women with a sense of community where every woman's participation is valued for its ability to create a communal story of cooking as a validation of diverse experiences and styles. Kitchen talk as a form of oral conjure transforms the dynamics of the kitchen from a site of daily drudgery into a creative poetry workshop that stresses the inventiveness of women's oral narratives. The narrator situates his mother as the original "dub" poet of Caribbean cooking through her mastery of the language of cooking:

> "Lemme take out a little o' this water. Now, a pinch of salt. That would do. Lil salt meat. ... I have any salt beef? Or pig tail leave-back from the last time?

I have salt beef, man! Salt beef going–go better with the boil-chicken. Wash it off good, so that it won't have-in tummuch salt, to make the rice too salty. A little sprig o' thyme from offa my tree, and cover-she down … and that's that! Boy, we cooking!" I look at her and wonder. This woman is a poet. (217-18).

Orality, as a form of alternative knowledge, gives women the necessary power to elaborate other forms of literariness that do not conform to acceptable models of conventionality. Orality, as a model of underground female expression, refers to all forms of communication that have been repressed by canonical structures of "ordered rationality" and discursive transparency. Carolyn Cooper associates orality with a form of folk wisdom, "that body of subterranean knowledge that is often associated with the silenced language of women and the 'primitiveness' of orally transmitted knowledge" (65). Orality symbolizes the ancestral language of women who constantly resurrect their foremothers as enduring role models to establish a female heritage of intergenerational continuity.

Recreating a meal from memory facilitates a sense of community among the women who are free to demonstrate their improvisational skills in the kitchen. The narrator pays tribute to these culinary artists who perform transformational magic by conjuring a smorgasbord of local specialities: "As a boy I was surrounded by women—mother, countless aunts, women-cousins and all the neighbourhood women, my mother's friends—women who were all continuously involved in some confounding and miraculous feat in the kitchen. In all that time, and with all those women, I never once heard one of them use the word 'recipe'" (5). The narrator experiences a certain protective warmth in the company of these women. The traditional cooking and sharing of food provides a vital link between mother and child whereby the restorative power of food has a positive impact on the boy's development. This recuperation is a symptom of cultural rootedness that establishes a sense of belonging. Anne Goldman celebrates the culinary agency of women through the culinary metaphor which she posits as being "distinctly feminine. ... Such a recuperation of a female legacy enables self-assertion at the same time it celebrates the lives of women family members as role models" (191).

Goldman establishes a correlation between food, identity, and cultural development by identifying these factors as a prime motivator of female subjectivity. The women's culinary magic resembles the language of hieroglyphics whose successful decoding unravels a woman's story. The narrator discovers a feminist genealogy of strong matriarchs in his family who serve as his mentors and represent a primary model of Caribbean feminism, even before the term achieves political agency. He states:

> My mother was married to a man who lived with his mother—Gran, or Grans, we called her. ... Gran ruled the roost. Her own daughter, Verona ... had her children from three different men and had refused to marry any one of them, those "worthless men!" She lived her life in full feminist independence, even before anybody in Barbados knew anything about single parents or independently spirited women. Then there was Miss Edey, Gran's sister, another spinster ... [who] ... was morally reluctant to leave her profession of maid and housekeeper and wanted me, especially, to understand the importance of duty. (9)

The narrator finds his focus amid a group of exceptional women whose disregard for the rules of social conventionality and gender-determined decorum becomes the very source of their independence and strong mindedness. By elaborating alternative models of kinship ties that fly in the face of rigid colonial categorizations, these women claim ownership of their lives in the absence of male partners. Fuelled by their spirit of self-reliance, these women control their personal subjectivities through a particular transgendered "occupational input" that gives them simultaneous access to the public and private spheres of influence in their capacity as "domestic" and "professional" workers. The women create their own history through a particular "women's talk" whereby "women examine alternatives for talk in environments which often mute their voices or ignore their words" (Bate 15). While stressing the cooperative nature of such talk, Barbara Bate identifies four underlying elements that animate women's talk: the importance of communication, the need to respect diverse perspectives, the desire to identify with others and the pleasure of creativity. Women's talk as communal talk provides a multi-volume document of shared and individual experiences that create a valuable woman-centred time line. The memoir reveals this time line through the women's culinary productivity where "women's talk" is transformed into culinary dexterity based on an intimate understanding of the oral tradition of food. The narrator reminisces: "I can still see those women performing feats of culinary magic, with all the arrogance, intolerance to criticism, and competitiveness that is peculiar to persons whose knowledge is based exclusively on an oral tradition, on myth and on the inheritance of customs" (41). The parallel between the spoken word as "food for thought" and the oral ingestion of food as sustenance for the body leads to the creation of an historical text whereby oral accounts, which are either lost of forgotten, receive "concrete" articulation in specific dishes. In other words, food provides testimony for lived-out cultural experiences that have been ignored by the more conventional, Eurocentric narratives of colonial history that have obscured oral, undocumented, or "unpalatable" accounts of non-European realities.

The "mythical" proportions of these narratives reveal the women's powers of storytelling whereby cooking provides the necessary fuel to fire the imagination: "And always the women. Cooking, and telling stories that at night made my skin crawl with fear … about ghosts born in Barbados. Those women did not depend upon Grimm's fairy tales or Hans Christian Andersen to bring my heart into my mouth" (12-13). By focussing on local legends and myths, the women are able to resurrect the ghosts of the Barbadian past which have been buried under the weight of colonial fairy tales. Western fairy tales have created a false point of reference for Barbadian children by exposing their inapplicability to an Afro-Caribbean context. These stories seem displaced and out of context ensuring that the colonial subject will always fail in his/ her attempts to fathom this non-reality. The privileging of colonial referents that reveal their incongruity leads to a corresponding devaluing of local culture as a means to "discredit the histories, experiences and dreams of subordinate groups" (Giroux xv). By using European cultural references as much sought-after models to emulate, the forcible ingestion of the colonial ideal automatically infers that these models of exemplarity will always remain out of the reach of "native" children. Nativeness is immediately associated with imperfection and inferiority, creating feelings of low self-esteem and cultural shame. To circumvent internalized racism and psychological insecurities, the women's stories offer radicalized possibilities to initiate "a practice of liberation." The transformative potential of these stories can be compared to bell hooks' articulation of the "engaged" voice that she describes in the following manner: "The engaged voice must never be fixed and absolute but always changing, always evolving in dialogue with a world beyond itself" (hooks 11). The engaged voice, as a voice of transgression, destabilizes the authority of colonial discourses to reactivate collective memory from its state of imposed dormancy by initiating new beginnings in the same way that the women in Clarke's narrative refuse to limit themselves to the narrow scope of a recipe. Local histories are thus given new meaning through the politics of engagement that create the necessary space for alternative narratives. In other words, the erasure of parallel histories from hegemonically composed narratives is counteracted by new articulations of decolonized histories that reclaim their lost origins. The mother provides the voice for these new articulations. Her presence serves as a constant reminder of the importance of respecting the realm of orality and pre-discursive modes of communication as active sites of personal historicity to rectify the distortions created by colonial readings of Barbadian history. At the end of the memoir, the mother comes full circle in her question for subjectivity that finds its fruition in her backyard garden. As the narrator recalls: "She stands beside me as she used to stand so many years ago, in the backyard kitchen, and she repeats, almost word for word, the directions she used to order me about with fifty years ago" (248). The "earthiness" of her journey testifies to her physical and spiritual connection to her roots where "everything around us was smaller and more natural, and grown on trees in our backyard" (248).

At the same time, the mother's personal subjectivity embraces a larger diasporic solidarity through "food communion" with African-American soul food. The inscription of the personal within the collective through a shared history of food establishes a pan-African culinary consciousness to locate home within the expansiveness of the diaspora. The memoir refers to this connection: "Harslick and cou-cou is a cultural dish in Barbados, something like 'soul food' to African Americans" (27). If "Bajan" food provides the source/sauce for cultural identity, it simultaneously extends itself beyond geographical boundaries through a commonality of culinary expression found in the rootedness of plants and vegetables that are basic to African cuisine on the continent and in its diaspora. Culinary "roots" speak with a certain authority as food history reveals the well-known fact that roots themselves have known a long tradition of culinary mixing and trans-Atlantic migrations. The preservation of African culture through food can be accomplished by an effective "dialogue of roots" across various routes, as root foods provide the necessary common ground for different varieties of African, Afro-Caribbean, and African-American cuisine. Consequently, the narrator's mother becomes the original pan-Africanist whose cooking provides a primary text for discourses on race, class, and gender from a woman's point of view in which food preparation charts the migration of African food habits. The mother's culinary dynamism validates an important female legacy of oral culture that reclaims the past while securing its permanence in the cultural present.

The mother's culinary prowess leads to a position of distinction that endows her with shamanic powers to invoke and sustain the permanence of women-centred cultural traditions that maintain the social and spiritual equilibrium of the community. Food is endowed with a certain religiosity of meaning by providing sustenance for the soul to infuse it with a new poetry in the face of colonial hardships and cultural denigration. The narrator refers to his mother's position of authority within the household and the larger community and her crucial role in maintaining the holistic well-being of her people through her personal sense of historicity established through cooking: "She assumed that parental, superior attitude that left no possibility of independence of variation, of personal assurance, because my assurance was hers, my self-assurance came from her dignity of meaning, and from her memory of that history and her understanding of the myths that surround our ways of cooking" (246). The mother, as the backbone of racial pride and tradition, bridges the gap between the past and present while mediating the insecurities of the future. Her cooking establishes a culinary geography of diaspora that provides the essential link between West African cuisine as the origin of Afro-Caribbean food preparation and its creative adaptations in the Caribbean in the face of slavery, hard labour and economizing. At the same time, this culinary diaspora reveals the glaring disparities between colonial/native social and economic realities that reinforce the hierarchy of colonial culinary racism through the primacy of colonial cuisine, the unavailability of primary resources and the distribution of inferior food products to the "colonies," as will be discussed later.

Highly ritualized cooking techniques imported from West Africa during the Middle Passage established food as a cartography of location to circumvent the geographical dislocation experienced by the enslaved Africans. The preference for root foods, such as yam and tubers, provided a sense of stability and groundedness in the face of cultural displacement and psychic alienation in the new lands. The African's intimate knowledge of agricultural methods as a means of establishing a close connection with the land through food production was transplanted to the Caribbean to promote a sense of cultural continuity despite the violent severing of ties with the mother land. The high value placed on nutritious food that could be grown inexpensively, under less than favourable conditions, favoured the cultivation of staples such as rice, beans, peas that could creatively "expand" in the stomach to feed entire populations. As Christine Mackie explains: "The three main staples were yam, plantain and Indian corn; on these the African slave depended for his very survival in the New World, and they all had been part of the everyday diet in Africa. From the dishes made with them, one can see how very strongly Caribbean cuisine is rooted in African food" (Mackie 17). In other words, food patterns were based on strategies of survival and the ability to make the most of limited resources. The practical nature of food preparation enhanced the ingenuity of cooking as a symbol of improvisational survival skills that necessitated an ingrained knowledge of the land and its productivity. As the memoirs indicate: "In days of yore, your belly was usually sticking to your back through hunger. Slaves was always hungry. Food was always scarce. They had to learn how to 'cut and contrive,' how to improvise" (1). The need to maximize limited resources through the preparation of slave food was linked with the exigencies of the body instead of a well-articulated politics of race. Instead, the pragmatism of slave food established a legacy of culinary enterprise based on a commonality of experience to further promote a sense of belonging in an alien environment.

The memoir highlights this ethos of sharing through communal, culinary solidarities: "And it was the same meal, identical in almost every detail, in every home" (30). The cultivation of kinship ties around a shared meal provided a feeling of belonging as sustenance for the body and soul while, at the same time, laying the foundation for family and social organization around cooking rituals. The memoir establishes the "origin" of slave food rituals as a point of reference for future generations in the Caribbean and the African diaspora is revealed in the following quotation: "Barbadians have always known that the food we eat is 'slave food,' based on leavings or leftovers, the remnants of the better cuts of meat eaten by the Plantation owners. The Amurcans would call it soul food, but I would argue that we Wessindians, and Barbadians in particular, had come to soul food long before African Amurcans, African Canadians and Africadians. Slave food is an older concept of black aesthetics and black culture than is soul food" (60). By associating slave food with a sense of historicity, the narrator consequently claims the subjectivity of colonized Barbadians through a particular culinary genealogy that establishes the primacy of the Barbadian self. Genealogical documentation displaces the primacy of colonially imposed or false points of reference for colonized histories through a subjective (re)claiming of "indigenous" history as a counter point to hegemonic manipulations. As evidenced in Clarke's narrative, women engineer these subjective historical repositionings of intent through the cultural documentation provided by their kitchen labour as a chronicle of "our version of hot-cuisine born and bred in Barbados. Or, as my mother would say, 'our ways of cooking'" (41). The culinary, as a ritualized articulation of the historic, redefines the politics of cooking by positioning women as cultural historians through a gender-determined engagement with food that overrides their traditional exclusion in male-centred historical narratives. The narrator refers to these alternative women-centred narratives that question the legitimacy of the "officially-written" documents that lay claim to the absolute historical truth. Women displace the centrality of these written narratives through their oral insertions that convert uni-centred absolutisms into alternative pluri-centred reflections. The narrator admits:

> And I remember just in time, before I disrespect her rigid marking out of the boundary of mother and child, that she is my mother, and that perhaps she does not really have to know about Africa or Africanization or black Amurcan nationalism or soul food to know that a chicken needs the proper "seasning" to make the ingreasements palatable and sweet when they are cooked. And I listen. I have to listen. (247).

In other words, the mother's powers of intuition based on her worldly experiences in the kitchen provide a refreshing alternative to the loftiness of political ideology and dogma that provoke a certain existential indigestion that detracts from the simplicity and sweetness of home cooking.

The relationship to food expresses a society's cultural ethos. The women play the role of ensuring the preservation of this ethos through their participation in highly ritualized food patterns. The formalizing of food preparation is reflective of a corresponding "formalizing of the social" whereby the kitchen becomes the stage on which daily interactions are played out. Food offers microcosmic glances into a society's inner workings wherein, as Claude Lévi-Strauss affirms: "We can hope to discover for each special case how the cooking of a society is a language in which it unconsciously translates its structure or else resigns itself to revealing its contradictions" (595). In other words, the "language" of food provides a document of cultural history in which women provide the necessary script for the effective writing-out of this text. This documentation scripts the social organization of the kitchen as the site of a gender-based division of labour. While the memoirs establish cooking as a function of gender, they also situate the primacy of the kitchen as a locus of women's hard labour, thereby dispelling any myths about women's second hand contributions to cultural production. As the text indicates: "Kitchens were places where hard work was performed" (20). This hard work promotes a sociology of gender relations whereby food, as a symbol of communal identification, serves as an indicator of the sexual division of labour that maintains the "dynamics of the food politic" within society. Consequently, cooking follows the cycle of domestic duties to provide a weekly schedule of meals based on the particular household chores that a woman has to perform on any given day to maintain her home. As the memoir affirms: "Monday, therefore, was not the best day to cook food that required a lot of time for the selection and preparation of ingreasements. Busy with washing, the woman of the house would resort to a meal of cou-cou or 'dryfood,' mainly because of the short time it took to prepare it" (32). In other words, the preparation of meals follows a daily ritual of labour-intensive domestic patterns that establish a "calendar of events" to regulate the women's household activities. This regulation confers a level of respectability on the women to determine their status in Barbadian society where communal standing rather than money confers social status. The scheduling of meals is therefore dependent on a woman's social status whereby "with status, you had all that money could buy; but if you had no status in the village, you could not 'trust' [buy on credit] the rice, peas and slat meat you needed for cooking your food" (37). The inability to conform to the scheduled weekly meal plan brings about a corresponding social disordering through a lack of "trust" as a violation of the ethos of care and communal accountability. As Brown and Mussell explain: "Foodways bind individuals together, define the limits of the group's outreach and identity, distinguish in-group from out-group, serve as a medium of inter-group communication, celebrate cultural cohesion, and provide a context for performance of group rituals" (5). In other words, attitudes toward food production are based on gender ideologies that are deeply rooted in historic perceptions of culture, as a basis for identity formation. This paradigm locates the kitchen as a paradoxical venue of women's agency and tireless industry where their social identity as the purveyors of culture and family life leads to a situation whereby "cooking, for these women, was drudgery, a serious function of daily family life" (17).

Paradoxically, Clarke's evocation of the kitchen as a gender-based utopia flies in the face of the socio-cultural dystopia faced by Bajan women in everyday life. The author's sense of nostalgia for the women's culinary prowess creates a gap between imagined ideal and concretized reality, leading the reader to question the author's intentionality in terms of gender roles. Does nostalgia mask the tendency to position women's domestic roles as prescriptive of ideal womanhood irrespective of the ways in which the pressure to cook often harmed and oppressed Barbadian women through unreasonable working conditions or through their simple refusal to devote time to cooking in favour of educational pursuits? Even as Clarke points out the power that Bajan women have derived from their culinary knowledge, he also seems quite "retro" in his celebration of how a man should immediately marry a woman who can cook well, thereby reducing a woman's value solely to her cooking skills. On the one hand, he gets away with such claims because they seem to be about how things were in the past; yet he generally makes these assertions using the present tense. In addition, gender dis-symmetries encourage binary distinctions that place men in an active position as income earners and providers of food, and women in a passive stance as cooks and servers of food.

At the same time, the memoir attempts to disrupt misconceptions about women's perceived passivity in food production when the women in Clarke's narrative reorganize the distribution of labour through a redefinition of roles that reveal their managerial skills in the kitchen. The narrator highlights the structural adjustment initiated by the women in his family to create a more complementary social economy based on the equitable participation of men and women. He describes his culinary apprenticeship in the kitchen that leads to his passion for cooking and his desire to participate in this woman-centred cultural legacy. He states:

> My mother never had any great respect for my smallness
> or youth as a determiner of the amount or bigness of
> the tasks she gave me to do. So, from the time I could
> hold a fork, I had to help her mash English potatoes.
> With the other kind of fork, the agricultural fork,
> she made me help her prepare her kitchen garden. ...
> This distribution of labour, not only in the cooking
> of food but including all household chores, is what
> brought me closer to cooking. It prepared me for my
> great fondness for food ... learning everything about
> it at the apron-strings, so to speak, of my mother and
> other women. (6).

Cooking, as a form of primary education, becomes a tool
for self-creation by opening and defining the horizons of
a child's life while, at the same time, grounding him in
the stability of cultural culinary pride and self-sufficiency.
Consequently the author/narrator's participation in
kitchen chores leads to the interruption and reformula-
tion of the male's gender identity formation as mere
wage earner into a more bi-sexual occupational input.
Rigid gender hierarchies based on role differentiation
lead to a subsequent "suspension" of absolute notions of
Caribbean masculinity whereby the male's contribution
to woman-centred kitchen labour temporarily feminizes
the inviolability of Caribbean manhood and its exemp-
tion from domestic work.

This state of suspension is counterbalanced by the
groundedness of cultural permanence that highlights an
enduring tradition of Afro-Caribbean female self-reliance
based on women's subsistence farming skills. The memoir
indicates the importance of the mother's kitchen gardening skills that enable her to plant "cucumber, 'punkin,'
pigeon peas, tomatoes, lettuce, sweet potatoes and yams"

(6). The vegetable patch has constituted an autonomous space for women whereby successful cultivation, as another domestic skill, has enabled them to earn some financial profit through the selling of their products in the local market. The critic Marvalene Hughes evokes the sense of personal and spiritual fulfilment that women experience when they cultivate and produce a garden. Describing her own feelings, she admits: "My garden gave me a sense of pride and took me back to my family roots. When I could dig into the earth, observe the growing results of my cultivation of the soil, and become an active participant in my food production, I became reconnected with my African culture in a private, intimate, historical sense. My garden represented a regeneration of the earth, a spiritual connectedness that allowed me to pay homage to the earth; it provided me the channel to relate my African respect for land and living things to my African spirituality" (Hughes 274). Representing the soul of the community, the kitchen garden reflects a woman-laboured economy in which women demonstrate their domestic and extra-domestic labor that is linked to their spiritual attachment to the land as well as to their intimate knowledge of the land's productivity. As the memoir states: "Because Barbados was a labouring society, most of its inhabitants, including women, worked in the fields" (24). The familiarity with the physical landscape leads to a certain mastery of the cultural landscape when homegrown foods and indigenous cooking styles provide the base for several local "Bajan" dishes that promote a sense of culinary chauvinism and cultural pride. The memoirs establish the superiority of the Barbadian method of preparing blood pudding and souse by stating:

> In St. Kitts and the Bahamas, two countries that
> pretend to be experts in this dish, souse is served hot
> or warm. Barbadians regard this custom as barbaric.
> We pride ourselves on being the inventors of pudding
> and souse, and we have taken it to its culinary elixir.
> We regard serving souse warm as evidence of the
> enormous cultural chasm that separates St. Kitts and
> the Bahamas from Barbados. (27)

Clarke's Bajan disdain for souse served hot or warm in
St. Kitts and the Bahamas indicates the "cultural chasm"
that separates his culture from that of the other islands.
However, the fact that African-Americans have always
served souse cold could, in fact, indicate an important
diasporic culinary link that implies less of a cultural
chasm between African-Americans and Bajans. On the
other hand, Clarke could also be using the preparation of
souse not as an actual indicator of cultural difference, but
as a marker of disdain for Africans on other islands who
do not do things the Bajan way. He engages in a shared
practice of discursive representation that uses warm or
cold souse as cultural signifier of felt superiority and dis-
tinctiveness. In other words, the cultural chasm he notes
is one imputed by his society and him; it may or may
not actually exist, but the imputation is itself a political
act of ranking his version of Caribbean culture against
other ones. In this way, Barbadians determine the status
of their own cuisine within the Caribbean by reversing
bourgeois social norms that equate status with money
and the ability to afford and indulge in the decadence
of haute cuisine. Through a process of ironic reversal,
chicken feet and pig's blood, as examples of food "pure
and simple and good" (2), achieve a certain ascendancy
over other regional and colonial specialities.

The memoir stressed the importance of cooking with natural and wholesome products and ingredients to establish an ethic of health care for the community as opposed to the unnatural nature of the colonial culinary trade and its dietary imbalances. The emphasis on nutrition guaranteed both by the freshness of the product and a balance between meat and a seasoned pro-vegetarian diet endowed Bajan food with a certain tropical earthiness as compared to the blandness of the colonial delicacies. The mother attributes the "nervous conditions" of the colonials to the insipid nature of their food characterized by a lack of spices and other flavourful seasonings, as the following passage indicates: "But it is a well-known fact in Barbados that Plantation people most of whom were white, did not put 'enough seas'ning, nor salt and pepper in their food!' My mother used to say, 'Their food too damn bland. Enough to give a person the belly! As if they're suffering from *low* blood pressure!'" (19-20). The mother seems to indicate that hypertension and gastric disorders are a direct result of sodium deficiency and a deprivation of healthy "seas'nings" that lead to chemical imbalances in the body. The mother prescribes spices as a remedial cure to rectify "first world" eating habits, thereby positioning herself as a folk doctor who possesses an intimate knowledge of the body's chemistry. The healthy ingestion of spices permits the body to purge itself of its neurotic disposition through an effective sweating away of its infirmities whereby "eating food that is piping hot brings out a delicious sweat on your face and opens up all your pores. My mother tell me so. So, is so!" (111). In other words, spices provide a natural cure to automatically regulate the body's temperature without resorting to institutionalized medication. The mother consequently resurrects a strong female-centred tradition of indigenous healing practices that were later eclipsed by the advent of colonialism and the white man's "cure."

In addition, the narrator's mother subverts the culinary hegemony of new age eating fads that advocate a purist disavowal of meat by inverting dominant food habits. Equating vegetarianism with a form of disease and pecuniary deprivation, the mother's culinary ethos offers an alternative to expensive health food crazes. The memoir confirms this attitude: "In my mother's book, a vegetarian is somebody who is not concern with his or her diet and health. 'Someone who prefer bush and grass, as if they is sheeps and cows, is somebody who don't have enough food to put in his mouth,' she always say" (68). In the "first world," the ability to afford a diet of organic vegetables is a sign of bourgeois privilege. However, in the mother's estimation, a vegetarian meal plan symbolizes cattle fodder that is not fit for human consumption. In other words, vegetarianism is not a signifier of status but a misunderstanding of the basic principles of nutrition. The mother's knowledge of food as fuel for the body is inscribed within the historical context of slavery whereby enslaved Africans were forced to intuitively familiarize themselves with foods and eating habits that would provide them with optimum energy and endurance to withstand hard labour on the plantations. Moreover, accessibility to food in order to survive barely was a priority over preoccupations with the actual fat content or nutritive value of particular foods, such as pork, that establishes its primacy in the memoir. At the same time, it is important to indicate that, while Clarke celebrates the traditional butcher (based on his mother's claim), his nostalgia allows him to avoid confronting current industrial practices for producing pork such as hog lots. Nor does he make any specific reference to the excessive use of salt, in the form of cured and fried meats, as the source of cardiovascular degeneration among Blacks or the efforts of modern-day cooks to adapt traditional recipes for a more healthful diet in a fast-paced stressful world.

On the contrary, the mother ironically transforms first world privilege into a sign of severe financial need and misinformation to further reveal the psychic imbalances inherent in western life styles based on individualistic extremes rather than on the complementarity of experiences. In terms of culinary production, this balance is achieved through the process of blending and combining seemingly disparate ingredients into a synthesized culinary richness. Christine Mackie highlights the wholesome nature of the Afro-Caribbean ethic of food preparation that is based on "blending together the African seasonal vegetables and coconut milk—two or more of these combinations in nearly all their dishes, which so typified Afro-Caribbean food" (73). The wholesomeness of food is achieved through a holistic balance between various food combinations that are structured according to a system of binary classifications between spicy and sweet, raw and cooked, hot and cold to produce a "grammatology of food habits" whereby balanced meals ensure society's equilibrium. Consequently, Barbadian food offers itself the "privilege" of culinary distinction through the preparation of balanced poor man's food that is, however, fit to titillate the palate of a king. It is therefore no coincidence that "privilege" becomes a national Bajan dish that transcends the boundaries of class through its inscription in local cultural memory. As the narrator states: "Privilege, like other kinds o' slave food, was the backbone of existence for we. It was consumed regularly all over Barbados …" (66). The narrator creates an ironic reversal by transforming class privilege or entitlement into the local privilege of sharing a wholesome meal to be enjoyed by all.

If financial prosperity does not necessarily symbolize healthy eating, the mother's culinary paradigm exposes the illogic and the racism inherent in first world/third world food production and distribution activities by revealing how the production and consumption of food is linked to the unequal distribution of global wealth, as indicated by Ron Scapp and Brian Seitz. The two authors highlight the structure of culinary colonialism in their remarks: "For some people, the range of eating possibilities has never been better. But for hundreds of millions of others, it remains as empty and bleak as it ever was" (2). Binary disproportions in levels of accessibility to food between the hegemonic centre and its colonies create a hierarchy of discrimination where the third world becomes the site for first world rejects. The memoir exposes this disparity: "Flour does not change. Not unless you buy your flour in countries that are members of the Gee-Sevens economic club. If you buy your flour in the First World countries, it won't have weebulls in it" (50). The third world becomes an official dumping ground for inferior food products that are deemed unacceptable for the western palate. The dehumanization of colonial subjects is reinforced through their forcible ingestion of food that is not fit for human consumption, reducing them to a level of bestiality that justified the colonial "civilizing mission." As the memoir reveals:

In colonial times, which followed the days of slavery, practically all the food we uses to eat had to come from Away—from England, Canada and Australia. Since colonized people was considered second-class people of Away, the food was also second-class, or of an inferior quality. Some of it, like the meat, had to be cured in brine. (62)

The intersections of race, class and culinary discrimination fortified the colonial power play through the politics of food control that designated the quality and quantity of "appropriate" food distribution for select populations whose levels of acceptability were determined by colonial racial hierarchies of difference. For this reason, Jessica Harris describes African and African-inspired cooking as "a cooking of adversity—even in plenty there is necessity and no waste. Little is discarded, and frequently the discards from one meal serve as the basis for another" (xxi). Harris' statement does not imply the substandard nature of African food. On the contrary, Harris highlights the capacity to convert leftovers into a special meal through the survival-oriented skills of the black woman who, according to Marvalene Hughes, trusted "her creative skills to make something out of everything" (276). Cooking, as a form of cultural resistance, demonstrated the women's powers of resilience to maintain their dignity in the face of racism and social denigration. Their transformative culinary capacities were a sign of their pride in themselves and their families in the same way that enslaved African women were able to affirm their feelings of selfhood despite the dehumanizing aspects of slavery and, thereby, acquire the necessary strength to organize and participate in various slave revolts, sabotage plots, labour disputes and strikes. Their voices and actions of protest and rebellion temporarily humanized them from their daily degradation on the plantations and dispelled any misconceptions about their passivity and subservience to male and female colonial dominance. Similarly, the presence of black female cooks in the colonial kitchens subversively "creolized" the colonial palate through culinary hybridizations that affirmed ethnic identity through food preparation. Through her domination of the white kitchen, the black woman was able to create an informal black kitchen network that subtly penetrated and influenced the white politic, according to Hughes (275). The subversive culinary activism of women was both a response and a reaction to the dangers of assimilation and cultural annihilation.

For this reason, food was endowed with a special religious sanctity of meaning as a symbol of the individual's will to live amid exacting circumstances. Hughes associates food preparation with a particular black spiritual ritual (276) as a way of humanizing the gods through communal food preparation. Communal feeding becomes a way of preserving a communal ethic through a collective feeding of gods and humans. In the context of slavery and colonization, personalized contact with the gods was of special significance as a strategy of self-preservation and as a guide to divine intervention. As the memoir states: "So, this is pudding and souse, the food of the gods and of the slaves of Barbados" (162). Food symbolizes a form of worship of the ancestral gods who, in turn, provide protection and guidance as part of a reciprocal pact to sustain ties of intergenerational solidarity and continuity: "Pudding and souse is the sweetest thing handed down by our ancestors, African slaves, to each and every one of us present-day Wessindians" (162). The connection between food, spirituality, and cultural pride constitutes basic guiding principles to maintain a sense of self through an acknowledgement of one's heritage where food becomes "an expression of pride in the cultural forms created out of and articulated through a history of black oppression" (Witt 260). Consequently, a history of disenfranchisement transforms itself into a lesson in cultural empowerment through a subjective re-claiming of blackness.

The mother asserts her blackness through her refusal to follow a recipe: "So there were no recipes and no cookbooks. You might well ask, how then did these women provide the splendour of meals that could be smelled and remembered and yearned for from long distances away from their kitchens?" (15). The memoirs stress the link between food, expressivity and memory as a method of preserving cultural culinary authority that resists objectification in a cookbook. The black cook remembers with pride the ingredients she requires and their relative proportions, but she does not always remember how to make the same food taste exactly the same all of the time. Despite the fact that she is after a certain taste, there is still some variation. Her range of measurements of ingredients is a measure of her creative expressivity as she may vary the measurements with the availability of ingredients and also with her mood. She can express her discontent by making some food not taste so good for certain people. Her blackness is confirmed this way not simply in a refusal of relying on recipes, but also in her recognition that doing so confines her creative expression and range of optional usage during food preparation. Recipes, in other words, epitomize the static controls of whiteness. Consequently, the mother's recipes cannot be replicated through appropriation and converted into multicultural ethnic cuisine that adds local flavour to a predominantly white menu. The oral transmission of culinary knowledge between generations of Barbadian women circumvents the commodification of their cuisine in colonial cookbooks where they are often presented as reproductions of a colonial ideal. The women can thereby guarantee the authenticity of their dishes by protecting them from colonial make-overs in which they lose their flavourful seasonings to become a mere mimicry of the original product. Colonial re-presentations alter the specificity of indigenous foods through caricatural alterations that eliminate culinary differences by assimilating them to a dominant model.

In addition, first world marketing strategies have led to a subsequent devaluing of traditional food preparation through their emphasis on processed goods and ready-made meals that have deprived women from demonstrating their culinary creativity. Marvalene Hughes states that, by defying the "rules of measurement and scientific cooking precision," the black woman uses her "common senses of taste, smell, sight and touch and her soulful intuition ... to reject scientific progress in food in favour of her basic cultural knowledge and intuition" (273-74). Women invest food with a corporeality of expression through a sensory celebration of the taste buds to produce a meal with "feeling." The memoir describes this feeling: "Taste is the thing. And touch. Tasting and touching. So, we are talking about cooking food with feeling" (3). Cooking involves the exploration of the body's geography through tactile movements where "the fingers and hands are the implements for measurement"

(3). Likened to sex, food preparation enjoys an expansiveness of expression that transcends the restrictions imposed by precise measurements or the meticulous reproduction of a particular recipe. The narrator draws a parallel between food and culinary experimentation that is seasoned over time through practice and repetition: "Cooking food is not characterized by strict attention to ounces and grams, cups and litres. A pinch of this and a pinch of that added to a pot, first by trial and error, and then perfected through history and constant usage, from one generation to the next, is the way I remember food being cooked" (2-3). The women raise cooking to an art form through a sense of cultural continuity between several generations to bring it to a level of perfection. The work of these culinary artists resembles the creations of a master sculptor who carefully moulds his clay into a finished product in the same way that the women manually knead flour into a perfect dough for bakes, bread and other essentials: "And when we come to flour and the making of bread, then the hands do all the work. There is no heavy-duty electric mixer, just the heel of the palm of the hand, which is enough to knead the flour into dough" (3). Resisting automation, the dough carries the imprint of a woman's body that infuses it with a particular sweetness comparable to the sweetness of lovemaking where "feeling is stretched to include feeling-up the food: touching the fish …—not using a gadget that ensures precision of cut and duplication of each slice" (3). The traditional association of sweetness with the power of the European sugar economy and the (instant) gratification of the western palate is subverted in favour of a Bajan woman's seductive powers of cooking that leave an endurable mark on the satiated belly.

At the same time, modernization has not been entirely bad for contemporary Barbadian women and their culinary traditions. Modern-day food technology has, in fact, relieved women from the backbreaking work of grinding or kneading by hand, thereby transforming cooking into a time and energy effective enterprise. Consequently, the possibility of not having to engage in cooking everything from scratch could be liberating for women, depending upon their ability to afford modern-day gadgets and packaged produce. Clarke's resistance to technology and its potentially liberating consequences for women creates a definite tension in the narrative which suggests that he unconsciously supports their exclusion from the public despite his overt glorification of their domestic roles. Consequently, the memoir raises the crucial question of whether women can be political only in the domestic sphere. Clarke's attitude confirms Valerie Hoyte's statement about the contemporary situation of women in Barbados: "Times have changed but the attitudes of people have remained static. Women's place in this world is still to be subservient to the man regardless of her position in society." Questioning the double-edged consequences of independence on women in terms of their liberation from colonial and neo-colonial patriarchal structures, Hoyte asserts: "Things have changed from slavery to the present but the change has not been that impressive. Our women have suffered then and are suffering now." Within this context, how can the memoir mediate its location between immortalized stereotype and actualized prototype? Perhaps by serving as a catalyst that collapses symbolic action as revealed in the narrative into instrumental action through organized feminist activism to create an empowering future for

Bajan women and to provide a more politicized reading of Clarke's text. Consequently, the memoir could provide the necessary point of motivation to initiate and engage in more enabling dialogues on women's issues in spite and because of its ambivalent representations of gender.

In conclusion, a feminist reading of gender roles in *Pig Tails 'n Breadfruit* positions the women in Clarke's family as proactive subjects through their culinary distinction. Their negotiations of identity through food preparation engage them in complicated journeys that are marked by their success or failure. Whatever the outcome of these journeys, it is important to emphasize the reality that women have always negotiated change by elaborating indigenous forms of resistance to domination and cultural denigration. Cooking reveals its insurrectional powers of subversions to destabilize the status quo that awards marginal recognition to women. Through their domestic and extra-domestic labour and their collective feeding of their communities through food and oral culture, the women make their mark on the Barbadian landscape as autonomous agents who claim their right to personal subjectivity in a pre-independent context. Continuing the tradition of hard work and resilience demonstrated by their enslaved ancestors, these women nevertheless create the necessary interventions for cultural decolonization and culinary/historical self-determination. Their personal stories of struggle and affirmation illuminate a larger struggle of Caribbean and pan-African resistance to colonial domination as a springboard to contemporary struggles for feminist self-determination in Barbados.

Works Cited

Algoo-Baksh, Stella. *Austin C. Clarke: A Biography*. Barbados: U of the West Indies P, 1994.

Bate, Barbara. "Themes and Perspectives in Women's Talk." *Women Communicating: Studies of Women's Talk*. Norwood, NJ: Ablex, 1988.

Birbalsingh, Frank, ed. *Frontiers of Caribbean Literature in English*. New York: St. Martin's, 1996.

Brown, Linda, and Kay Mussell, eds. *Ethnic and Regional Foodways in the US: The Performance of Group Identity*. Knoxville: U of Tennessee P, 1984.

Clarke, Austin. *Pig Tails 'n Breadfruit: Rituals of Slave Food*. Kingston: Ian Randle, 1999.

Counihan, Carole, and Penny van Esterik, eds. *Food and Culture: A Reader*. New York and London: Routledge, 1997.

Freire, Paulo. *The Politics of Education: Culture, Power and Liberation*. Trans. Donaldo Macedo. New York: Bergin & Harvey, 1985.

Harris, Jessica. *Iron Pots and Wooden Spoons: African's Gifts to New World Cooking*. New York: Atheneum, 1989.

hooks, bell. *Teaching to Transgress: Education as the Practice of Freedom*. New York: Routledge, 1994.

Hoyte, Valerie. "Race, Class and Environment in Barbados." History 101/051, Professor Seenarine: April 13, 1999: 1.

Lévi-Strauss, Claude. "The Culinary Triangle." *The Partisan Review* 33 (1996): 595.

Mackie, Cristine. *Life and Food in the Caribbean*. New York: New Amsterdam, 1992.

Mennelle, Stephen, Anne Murcott, and Anneke Otterloo, eds. *The Sociology of Food: Eating Diet and Culture.* London: Sage, 1992.

Mintz, Sidney. *Tasting Food, Tasting Freedom.* Boston: Beacon, 1996.

_____. *Sweetness and Power: The Place of Sugar in Modern History.* New York: Penguin, 1985.

Mohammed, Patricia, and Catherine Shepherd, eds. *Gender in Caribbean Development.* West Indies: UWI Women and Development Studies Project, 1988.

Nasta, Susheila, ed. *Motherlands: Black Women's Writing from Africa, the Caribbean and South Asia.* London: The Women's Press, 1991.

Reddock, Rhoda. *Women, Labour and Politics in Trinidad and Tobago: A History.* London: Zed, 1994.

Scapp, Ron, and Brian Seitz, eds. *Eating Culture.* Albany: State U of New York P, 1998.

Smith, Sidonie, and Julia Watson, eds. *De/Colonizing the Subject: The Politics of Gender in Women's Autobiography.* Minneapolis: U of Minnesota P, 1992.

Caribbean-Canadian *Reifungsroman*: The Aging Female in Austin Clarke's Later Novels

CAMILLE A. ISAACS

As Austin Clarke has aged, so, too, have his female protagonists. Idora, the struggling mother of *More* (2008), could be seen as the reincarnation of a fifty-ish Bernice or Dots from the Toronto trilogy (*The Meeting Point*, 1967; *Storm of Fortune*, 1973; *The Bigger Light*, 1975). No longer a domestic, she lives in a one-bedroom, basement apartment with her wayward son, BJ, recently renamed Rashan Rashanan. Like Bernice and Dots, she is still downtrodden and overlooked, however, working as a cook at the University of Toronto and subsisting on meagre wages. Much like Boysie does in the last book of the trilogy, her husband has abandoned the family and disappeared into the United States. In another later novel, *The Polished Hoe* (2002), Clarke revisits the Barbadian sugarcane-plantation setting of *The Survivors of the Crossing* (1964) and imagines what life could have been like if we had followed the characters into old age through the voice of the almost-sixty Mary-Mathilda. As was the case for some of the women in *Survivors*, she is forced to use her body to support herself. The story takes place over one night as she confesses to the murder of Mr. Bellfeels, the plantation manager, her former lover, and as it turns out, also her father. By the end of their respective novels, both women have been reborn, of sorts. But their resurrection is short-lived, as Idora and Mary-Mathilda emerge from their periods of despair to face further hardship. Barbara Frey Waxman describes this literature of senescence as *Reifungsroman*,[1] or a "fiction of ripening" (1), wherein aging women characters learn to embrace their invisibility, oftentimes reduced sex life, and declining body as they ripen toward increased self-knowledge, independence, and an understanding of past injustices. This ripening is often accomplished through a physical or mental journey, hence the title of Waxman's book, *From the Hearth to the Open Road* (1990). But for the black, sometimes poor, women of Clarke's later novels, their movement toward the fully blooming self-knowledge of their senior years takes a slightly different path from that described by Waxman. These women's racial and class status limits the very ripening that is supposed to be characteristic of the genre. Idora and Mary-Mathilda do take stock of their lives and are able to reflect on past relationships at the close of their narratives. But unlike their white counterparts, this stage of life is not entirely a space of openness for them. They continue to be relatively poor, invisible, and restricted in their movements. Neither woman takes a trip outside her town/city, although they both take mental journeys. What this suggests is that, if the *Reifungsroman* is going to be accepted as a literary genre, such as the much more well-known *Bildungsroman*, it must take into account the way that race and class affect one's journey into old age, and, in this instance, particularly the way that the genre shows itself in Caribbean-Canadian literature.

In the same way that the traditional *Bildungsroman* has come under critique by many scholars for excluding certain groups,[2] a similar comment can be made against the *Reifungsroman*. Although Clarke's later fiction in many ways fits the category as Waxman describes it, the way it diverges from the genre speaks to a lack in the way the genre is currently conceptualized. Certainly, Waxman's aim in her study was to promote the positive ways aging women have been depicted in the literature. Of the authors she discusses, she says that they "have created a whole new genre of fiction that rejects negative cultural stereotypes of the old woman and aging, seeking to change the society that created these stereotypes. This new genre has been created by women writing about aging women for receptive readers in a rapidly aging society" (2). Her book provides a thorough survey of the field and she provides chapter-length studies of Doris Lessing, Alice Adams, and Paule Marshall, among others. She describes the genre as follows, and some of these characteristics show themselves in Clarke's work:

- Confessional tone/structure, often in a rambling style
- Passion and candour in disclosure
- Emphasis on naming
- Themes of pain (physical and psychic), unreliable, deteriorating body
- Loneliness and alienation
- Self-doubt, feelings of uselessness
- An opening up of time/possibility
- A journey often present as a theme

- Quest for self-knowledge
- Often first-person narration, or limited third-person omniscient
- Stream-of-consciousness style
- Use of dreams and/or flashbacks
- A coming to term with decisions made as youths
- Reviewing of past relationships/sex
- Anger at the past and/or history
- A resolution reached where an identity is reasserted
- Usually written by women (16-17)

But Clarke's work differs from the above list in significant ways. He is a bit of an anomaly in being a male writer in a female-dominated field. While Waxman does refer to a few male authors working in the genre,[3] she writes that "feminist literary critics have also shown that female accounts of life-cycle experiences recorded in fiction differ markedly from male accounts" (14). Clarke has, however, historically always had significant female characters in his fiction. He writes the female voice well in part because of his own history of being raised in female-dominated households (Personal Interview, 2012). More importantly, Clarke has always undertaken to portray under-represented voices in his works. If, as Waxman contends, older female characters outnumber men simply by outliving them (9), and if Clarke continues to wish to give the marginalized a voice, then it should not be surprising that he would take up another discriminated group in his work. In addition to racism, classism, and gender-bias, that Clarke would next tackle ageism in Idora's and Mary-Mathilda's aging marginalization is a fitting progression in his work. So many of his male characters do not live into senescence. Boysie and Barrington disappear into the States. Henry, of the Toronto trilogy, commits suicide. The men of the short-story collection *Nine Men Who Laughed* appear only in sketches, and we do not have fully-drawn portraits. And, of course, Mary-Mathilda kills her "husband." Because many of Clarke's male characters do not survive into old age, the aging black female is a fitting character set in his continued interest in marginalization as he ages.

In considering the aging female in Clarke's work, how-ever, it is critical to examine how race and class affect the aging process. Zoe Brennan, another critic examining the older woman in literature, like Waxman, shies away from class issues in part because the feminization of poverty could be conceived of as another topic altogether: "[T] he poor are marginalized in literary discourse, and so to be female, old and impoverished renders you even more invisible and less likely a participant in representational practices" (33). But this is exactly the subset that Clarke considers in his fiction, in addition to racial factors. Sociologists have long considered the way that race, gender, and age intersect, resulting in what Ketayun Gould calls "multiple jeopardy" (82). If we are going to consider the way that age is represented in fiction, we must also examine how race and class affect that aging process. Gould writes that "racism, sexism and ageism have to be viewed in an interactive framework to analyze the person-environment interaction of the older minority woman" (82).

Where Clarke's work converges with Waxman's is in the invisibility that they both describe as being signifi-cant in the literature of the aging woman. In discussing Lessing's work, Waxman portrays the invisibility of aging women as a potentially positive characteristic. Lessing's

Jane Somers writes that she "likes being invisible" (qtd. in Waxman 55) because of the liberating quality of not being seen as *just* a sexual object. In Lessing's novel, the older woman is free to assert her identity on things outside of sex, such as intelligence, for example. Idora, on the other hand, has yet to realize that she has stopped being seen as a sexual object, that she is no longer visible to the "rapists and molesters" she sees everywhere (*More* 14). She walks around downtown Toronto with a child's toy cellphone, which she pulls out and speaks into loudly whenever she thinks she might be subject to a sexual assault. But the truth is that the aging Idora has stopped being seen as a sexual object, if she ever was. One of the three men she fears calls her the age-defining "ma'am" and she responds: "Good night, son" (14), clearly placing her in a maternal role, rather than a sexual one. Mary-Mathilda, similarly, although she has been seen *only* as a sexual object for most of her life (the "polished ho(e)" of the title), is also, for the most part, now past sexual attraction in the eyes of some of the male characters. The police constable who comes to take her statement after the murder describes her as "a woman past desire; a woman who wears her dress below the knee; a powerful, rich, 'brown-skin' woman; a woman to fear" (30). Even Sarge, her old schoolmate, who vacillates in his attraction to her, describes her as "really not a very attractive woman" and "ugly" (352). In age, it appears that both Idora and Mary-Mathilda have become crones in their invisibility. Because they no longer have any sexual appeal, they fail to register in the eyes of the males around them.

But in the North American setting, the black woman has long been invisible, especially in comparison to the model-esque, size 6, white woman marketed as the norm in mainstream media. They are thus somewhat inured to the further blindness to their condition that accompanies aging. The black aesthetic that emphasizes broad hips and a firm, mighty backside has only recently become popular, in part through rap videos. Although Idora does not seem to realize the extent of her invisibility, she does not hold herself to a North American standard of beauty either. While she chides herself for putting on a few pounds, she still looks in the mirror and likes what she sees: "[I]f she could see behind her, she would notice that the light from the windows has drawn the lusciousness and the size of her hips and her thighs through the thin white imitation silk nightgown to look more sexy and magnificent" (30). But as the sole breadwinner in the family, Idora has had to rely on her visibility as a service-industry worker, which often depends on her physical might, rather than on her physical appeal. This is in contrast to Mary-Mathilda, whose currency, whether she liked it or had any input in it, has always depended on her beauty.

A black North American woman, then, must approach aging differently because her currency has not always depended on her looks. This is what could cause critic Susan Sontag to write that "[e]conomically disadvantaged women in this society are more fatalistic about aging" (32). Perhaps a better word would have been realistic. If one is used to being invisible, being more so because of the added factor of age shocks the system a little less. What Sontag fails to realize, however, is that this "fatalistic" attitude toward aging can be further stigmatized by being the negative factor against which white women judge their own aging: "How women are psychologically damaged by this misogynistic idea of what is beautiful parallels the way in which blacks have been deformed in a society that has up to now defined beautiful as white" (37). Sontag fails to consider the case of the woman who is already on the lowest rung of the beauty ladder—and then ages.

But this emphasis on beauty highlights the importance of mirrors and photographs in Clarke's characters' perception of themselves as they age. They exist somewhere in the space between the photograph and the mirror, in the interplay between how they remember looking in the past and how they actually look in the present. As Sarge prepares to take Mary-Mathilda's confession, he is torn between the woman who sits before him and the various pictures of her that surround him in her parlour. He imagines her much younger than she actually is, as if seeing the aging woman in front of him through the reflection of the photos: "[H]e sees her as a woman he can still love, and want to foop right now; and this madness of desire transforms her, and makes her desirable, even younger and more satisfying than Gertrude [the maid]" (130). He carries with him the fifty-odd years of love he has always felt for her. But this is not necessarily the actual woman who sits in front of him.

> Sarge sees this confrontation with Mary-Mathilda as facing the truth; her new truth, and his, in terms of light, the light reflected in the pictures surrounding him.
>
> The very light in the colours he sees in these pictures, is the light he places her in. Pictures that are strange and foreign and inexplicable to him. But he likes the colours, nevertheless.
>
> The colours he sees, and the colours he paints her in, in his mind, are those same colours which were used by painters whom her son, Wilberforce, had told her about. (131)

Kathleen Woodward argues that, in old age, one is caught between two images of oneself, the "now" and the "then" as it were, and when the view of another is added, it creates a triangular pattern, within which one may exist. The mirror stage of the aged "is inherently triangular, involving the gaze of others as well as two images of oneself" (69). In being attracted to Mary-Mathilda, Sarge is uncertain which view of her he is actually attracted to, hence his "confusion" (130). This would also explain why he vacillates and later calls her "ugly."

Idora similarly vacillates between various images of herself, caught between what she sees in the "looking glass" (32) and what she images herself to be: "In her imagination she is a model, and she goes back to jerking her left hip, hearing the corresponding snap of leather from her high heel; [...] And sadness of self-deception rattles her body, and touches her gait and posture. So she ends her parading" (32-33). Unlike Sarge, who does not realize the source of his confusion, Idora is fully aware that she is deceiving herself, which is the source of much of her sadness. Although she is pretending to be model Naomi Campbell, she knows she is merely playing a child's game of make-believe.

Idora's game of pretense speaks to the larger strategy of passing that many aging characters (and people too) use to stave off the aging process. Instead of passing as one race or another, aging characters are literally trying to pass themselves off as younger than they are. Brennan writes that "[p]assing, the mask of ageing and the assertion 'I don't feel old' are strategies (albeit risky ones) evolved by older individuals to cope with ageist discourses that do not speak realistically about them or their lives" (24). This is essentially what Sarge is doing in imagining Mary-Mathilda as her younger self, and what Idora does in imagining herself as a supermodel. It is not just Naomi Campbell's size and catwalk strut that Idora admires, but her youth. Models appear perpetually young, which is, perhaps, part of their allure. And so we find these characters, Idora primarily, donning the accoutrements of youth (hair dye, a certain style of clothing, and make-up) to appear younger, to be either less invisible as an old lady or more visible as an attractive, and seemingly productive, member of the community. Idora's makeup technique, for example, does touch on the traditional notion of passing in making her skin tone lighter than it is. But because she cannot get the right tone, her attempt borders on farce and she looks like a "professional clown" (75):

> Now she stands in front of the mirror, closing one eye and then the other, to get the correct sightline, to see the colour of shade she must use. [...] And when she has painted her face, leaving a mask of whiteness on her face, like the faces of African women she has seen in books about Africa, she takes her powder from another container and subtracts some whiteness from the sharpness of the white face powder from the colour already applied. She has painted her face too white. She wants a tint, a colour, a complexion that would make a white woman look at her two times, on the subway, to make certain if she is really white, almost white, could be taken for white, could pass. But with Idora it is not a matter of passing, of fading from one culture into another. She always wants to look sharp. Yes, sharp! (76)

Idora's desire is not so much to pass for white. As Clarke writes, she does not want to fade from one culture into another. She's trying to find the right shade that she thinks will make her be seen, primarily by the other white women on the train, and to be seen looking "sharp." What she really wants is to be visible and not overlooked, which she thinks her black skin causes. She says later that, in applying her makeup, what she was attempting to achieve was to be seen as "more acceptable" (111). For in wanting to appear more acceptable, given the rules of the society in which she lives, she wants to continue to assert her usefulness and productivity, and she thinks she can do this by appearing younger and whiter.

If one overdoes it, however, and the hair dye, clothing, or make-up do not quite work, one has the potential to actually become hypervisible and thereby highlight one's age, rather than hide it. Consider the older woman whose grey roots are showing, whose tight-fighting clothing hugs too snugly, or whose make-up gets stuck in the creases and wrinkles, rather than covering them. Her age is thereby made hypervisible, rather than invisible. As Woodward writes, "the social codes of dress and behavior in relation to old age are strict and confining" (150), especially for women. "[H]ow we dress conveys age-related messages, and any deviation from the conventional norm is regarded by others as an offense that borders on the obscene" (150). Inadvertently, Idora does exactly that. In her attempts to pass herself off as younger and thereby visible, she takes it a step too far and highlights her age. She is not fooling anyone in her attempts at passing as younger.

Idora similarly attempts to find a hair style and colour suitable to her age, one that does not make her hypervisible or invisible. She and the hairdresser, Kameel Azan, discuss what hairstyle to give her that "could be worn by women of all ages" (257). She is searching for a style that denotes vitality and not obscenity. As she travels on the subway, she wonders if she found the right space between the two poles: "She tries to see, in her reflection in the windowpane, how her hairdo looks. Did she allow Kameel Azan to put too much colour in her hair? Was she looking more—or less—like a woman of easy virtue?" (258). And as she ventures to church, she is also sporting a pair of high-heeled, patent leather, red shoes, shoes that make it look "as if she was going to a dance; and not to the house of God" (261-62). The correct tone that Idora is trying to find is a space that many aging women have difficulty navigating. There are limited roles for women in youth, and this limitation increases in senescence. "The paradoxical portrayal of the old woman as grandmother/spinster is an extension of the virgin/whore dichotomy that recurs throughout Western culture. In old age, the virgin turns into the respectable and sexless grandmother, and because old age is constructed as a period devoid of an expressible sexuality, the whore transforms into the crone-like spinster" (Brennan 2). In many ways, this novel can be seen as an extended exercise in Idora's attempts to forge an existence between the grandmother and the crone.

Not surprisingly, then, we find Idora contemplating the place of sex in her aging life. She had flirted with the idea of a lesbian relationship with her good friend, Josephine.[4] But despite not knowing in which direction her life will go—spinster or sexless grandmother—Idora decides that sex is a healthy occupation, regardless of age: "It is all right, she thinks, even on a Sunday morning, on the way to church, to think about sex. Sex is such a natural thing. Sex is life. Is blood. And the body needs life. [...] 'It is all right, on a Sunday, to think of the flesh. So long as the flesh you are thinking about is not the piece that belongs to thy neighbour!'" (259-60). Mary-Mathilda, however, is not so fortunate. Perhaps because of her being of a higher class than the majority of the inhabitants of the village, her reduced sex life is a decision that has been made for her. Not only is she now a woman "past desire," but her sexual currency, her only currency, has been downgraded. As she says, the father of her children "no longer had any uses for me" (275). And despite both Mary-Mathilda and Sarge seeming to desire to be intimate, the act does not happen. Her position (class and age) seems to prevent him from acting on his desire: "Is it her age? Is it her station in life? Is it Mr. Bellfeels? Or is it this house? This Great House, which stands for place, for richness, for wealth, for power, and fear ..." (322). But in this way, she is more aligned with the other women of the *Reifungsroman* that Waxman discusses: "The unsexed older woman can separate herself from her appearance, that which has in the past brought her validation from society" (55). But in Mary-Mathilda's case, this separation from appearance is not entirely desired. She leads Sarge to her bed (319) and fantasizes about their being intimate. But Sarge is made impotent by "deep, terrifying, deadly fear" (322). The liberation that Waxman describes may have resulted in increased power for Mary-Mathilda due to wealth, wisdom, and an increased position, but it has also had the unintended result of making her the "sexless grandmother."

Although Clarke's *Reifungsroman* differs from Waxman's account as it relates to race and class issues, it is remarkably similar in narrative style and in the idea of a rebirth. Both *More* and *The Polished Hoe* engage with the

Easter theme of resurrection as symbolic of both women's increased self-knowledge after periods of despair. Idora spends three nights locked away in her basement apartment contemplating her life and the decisions she has made before rising on the Sunday morning with a new energy and a new outlook. She even lies prone in bed as if crucified: "She even thought of her bed as a cross on which she had been hanging for three days and three nights. She decided once again to lie low, to remain 'dead,' for the intended four days and four nights. Cover herself in sackcloth and ashes. And repent" (191). When she finally leaves her apartment on Sunday morning for church, she has come to terms with her estranged husband, missing son, and the limitations that have been placed on her: "She knew all along that she had to wear white on a day like today. For white is the colour of coming out. Coming out, like a new mother, from the days and nights of labour, in severe pain, fighting with her conscience and her body, a pain that refused to be appeased" (246). She is resurrected, like Christ on Easter morning, with a renewed spirit, determined to be productive. Similarly, Mary-Mathilda, before starting her confession, reminisces with the constable about Easters past and a favourite scripture: "*and that through the grave, and the gate of hell, we may pass to our joyful resurrection*" (10). She kills her father, who is also the father of her children, in what she deems a "sacrifice" (461), not a murder, including the severing of his penis. This "sacrifice" recalls, of course, the period of lent and what she has chosen to give up. While Mary-Mathilda's journey takes place in the space of one night, rather than three, she emerges the next morning with a clear conscience, "Clean and pure" (462). This rebirth that both Idora and Mary-Mathilda experience is characteristic of the *Reifungsroman*. Waxman writes that the "narrative structure for these works, then, is commonly a journey, frequently a meandering one, in quest of self-knowledge, self-development, and a role for the future" (16). Certainly the women emerge with a better sense of themselves at the end of their journeys, but their isolation continues.

It is precisely because of the isolation that so many aging women experience that the rambling, stream-of-consciousness narrative is so fitting for the field: "*Reifungsromane* are frequently confessional in tone and structure. They are also usually characterized by great mobility, recursiveness, or rambling in narrative structure, and passion as well as candor" (Waxman 16). A long-winded, stream-of-consciousness narrative structure has long been characteristic of Clarke's style, regardless of the gender or age of his narrators. But he has used it consistently in part because he is so often giving voice to characters who have no one to speak to, to whom no one wants to listen, or who are so low down on the ladder that their opinions appear not to matter. Both novels have long passages of repetitive, divergent, stream-of-consciousness. Even though Mary-Mathilda is confessing to murder and both the constable and Sarge are there to take her statement, both officers fall asleep at various points during her account. She is literally talking to herself at times: "'I am talking this way because I am really talking aloud to myself, and nobody is present.' And even so, you are here and yet you are not here" (68). Idora, on the other hand, is entombed in her sepulchre with no one to talk to, in part because her son is missing. The majority of the novel, with the exception of flashbacks and imaginary conversations, shows Idora talking to herself, and as there is no one there to interject or ask questions or even to argue, there is no self-editing function in her dialogue. "She talks to herself, aloud, as if she is conducting a conversation, a dialogue; and she changes her voice to answer the question she poses to herself, and reverts to her original voice, her natural voice, to ask another question, or to give another opinion, in these arguments she is having with herself" (16). Stream-of-consciousness shows itself in Clarke's work to be the narrative structure of the unheard. Waxman writes that this style of narration is particularly characteristic of the genre:

> *Reifungsromane* about the aging woman create their vividness and intimacy with readers by generally favoring first-person or third-person limited omniscient narratives that float over and through the heroine's memories, often accumulating strings of complex sentences, blending the past with the present, breaking down barriers not only between time and space, but also between rationality and fantasy, feeling and logic, wellness and illness, sanity and senility. (185)

Although stream-of-consciousness is a technique that Clarke uses quite often, its usage for Idora and Mary-Mathilda highlights his continuing interest in under-represented voices.

That Clarke would resort to techniques in his *Reifungsroman* that he uses in his earlier fiction suggests that what all these characters (young and old) share in common is "othering." Clarke has long concerned himself with the immigrant voice in Toronto in order to highlight its marginalization. The focus on the aging Idora and Mary-Mathilda can be seen as a continuance of his interest in discrimination. Critics such as Simone de Beauvoir, Kathleen Woodward, and Zoe Brennan have all pointed out that the aged constitute another category of "Other." Woodward writes that, "like sexism and racism, ageism is prejudice rooted in physical difference as well as in discrepancies in social power" (70). This similarity of discrimination would also explain why so much racial discourse appears appropriate to discussions of aging: passing, the "Other," marginalization, giving voice to under-represented groups, etc.

But while viewing the aged as yet another group to be added to the long list of the marginalized seems to be growing in acceptance, what has not yet been acknowledged are the "Others" within that "Other" category. Woodward argues that "in western culture age takes precedence over and may swallow up gender" (16). That assertion only holds true for a certain category of the aged. For the Idoras and Mary-Mathildas of the world, race and class certainly take precedence over age and gender. Waxman, similarly refers primarily to a middle- and upper-class woman in her description of the *Reifungsroman*: "[T]here is [...] an opening up of life for many of these aging heroines as they literally take to the open road in search of themselves and new roles in life" (16). In the novels she examines, it is largely a white, middle-class woman who is the focus, who may have lost her looks and her husband, but is still able to maintain a certain lifestyle. Neither Idora nor Mary-Mathilda face an "open road" as their novels come to a close. They are both limited by financial constraints and circumstances to an internal journey only. Idora returns home from church to the police and ambulance outside her door, and her dead son beneath a white sheet on a stretcher.

Mary-Mathilda awaits Sarge's accompaniment to the police station, although he seems unwilling and unlikely to prosecute. One cannot imagine "an opening up of life and new roles" for either woman. This racial divide in the *Reifungsroman* category is the same split that threatened the feminist movement of the 1960s. Audre Lorde, in her seminal paper, "Age, Race, Class and Sex," writes that "[i]gnoring the differences of race between women and the implications of those differences presents the most serious threat to the mobilization of women's joint power" (117). The *Reifungsroman* cannot survive as a category unless it acknowledges the very real differences among women of different races and class brackets. Again, this is a point that Canadian sociologists have already realized when working with the aged. Barry McPherson argues that for "those who are now old, the indigenous, racial or ethnic subculture appears to have a significant influence on lifestyle. These elderly people have historically had less access to the life chances that were available to many of their age peers. Their disadvantaged situation does not improve, and indeed may worsen" (65).

One positive difference the *Reifungsroman* may take from the black woman's experience is the relatively robust body image that Idora and Mary-Mathilda continue to hold as they age. As Susan Castillo has argued, it is often in "ethnic" literature that positive self-images of aging women can be found: "In our own century, however, it is curious that female protagonists who actually manage not only to survive but actually to prevail and even prosper can be found in significant numbers in popular fiction and in fiction by so-called 'ethnic' or minority writers" (13). Perhaps because they have been invisible for so long, these women have learned to not as readily tie one's self-worth to others' interpretations. What equally needs to be reconsidered is the idea of the *Reifungsroman* as a "fiction of ripening," because as Idora's and Mary-Mathilda's stories have shown us, not every bud becomes a flower. Some fail to open. Others are overshadowed by showier flowers. Spring fails to come for many aging black women in literature. Very rarely does a full ripening occur in Clarke's works. The women are able to reflect and perhaps come to terms with their lives, but they continue to be limited by race and class, and restricted in their movement.

Endnotes

1. Waxman distinguishes between the *Reifungsroman*, the literature of older men, and *Reifungsromane*, the literature of older women (3). For the purposes of this paper, the term *Reifungsroman* will be used.

2. For various critiques of the *Bildungsroman* genre, see Jed Esty, "The Colonial Bildungsroman," Mary Gosselink De Jong, "Romola: A Bildungsroman for Feminists?" and Maria Karafilis, "Crossing the Borders of Genre."

3. She specifically mentions John Garner's *October Light* and I.B. Singer's *Old Love*.

4. This is a technique Clarke defaults to often in his relationships between women when men are not readily available. Readers of his works will remember he also had Dots and Bernice engage in an affair when they were not satisfied with the men in their lives. It is a technique that Clarke, perhaps too often, resorts to with his female characters.

Works Cited

Brennan, Zoe. *The Older Woman in Recent Fiction*. London: McFarland & Co., 2005.

Castillo, Susan. "Women Aging into Power: Fictional Representations of Power and Authority in Louise Erdrich's Female Characters." *Studies in American Indian Literatures* 8.4 (Winter 1996): 13-20.

Clarke, Austin. *The Bigger Light*. Boston: Little Brown, 1975.

_____. *More*. Toronto: Thomas Allen, 2008.

_____. *The Meeting Point*. Toronto: Macmillan, 1967.

_____. *Nine Men Who Laughed*. Toronto: Penguin, 1986.

_____. Personal Interview. 18 December 2012.

_____. *The Polished Hoe*. Toronto: Thomas Allen, 2002.

_____. *Storm of Fortune*. Boston: Little Brown, 1973.

_____. *The Survivors of the Crossing*. Toronto: McClelland & Stewart, 1964.

De Beauvoir, Simone. *The Coming of Age*. 1970. Trans. Patrick O'Brian. New York: G.P. Putnam's sons, 1972. Print.

Esty, Jed. "The Colonial Bildungsroman: 'The Story of an African Farm' and the Ghost of Goethe." *Victorian Studies* 49:3 (Spring 2007): 407-30.

Gosselink De Jong, Mary. "Romola: A Bildungsroman for Feminists?" *South Atlantic Review* 49:4 (November 1984): 75-90.

Gould, Ketayun H. "A Minority-Feminist Perspective on Women and Aging." *Aging and Inequality: Cultural Constructions of Differences*. Ed. Robynne Neugebauer-Visano. Toronto: Canadian Scholars' Press, 1995. 81-100.

Karafilis, Maria. "Crossing the Borders of Genre: Revisions of the *Bildungsroman* in Sandra Cisneros' *The House on Mango Street* and Jamaica Kincaid's *Annie John*." *Journal of the Midwest Modern Language Association* 31:2 (Winter 1998): 63-78.

Lorde, Audre. "Age, Race, Class and Sex: Women Redefining Difference." *Sister Outsider: Essays and Speeches*. Freedom, CA: Crossing Press, 1984. 114-23.

McPherson, Barry. "Aging from a Historical and Comparative Perspective: Cultural and Subcultural Diversity." *Aging and Inequality: Cultural Constructions of Differences*. Ed. Robynne Neugebauer-Visano. Toronto: Canadian Scholars' Press, 1995. 31-77.

Sontag, Susan. "The Double Standard of Aging" *Saturday Review*. September 23, 1972: 29-38.

Waxman, Barbara Frey. *From the Hearth to the Open Road: A Feminist Study of Aging in Contemporary Literature*. New York: Greenwood Press, 1990.

Woodward, Kathleen. *Aging and Its Discontents: Freud and Other Fictions*. Bloomington: Indiana UP, 1991.

Review: "A Plea of Love and Blood": Social Justice in Austin Clarke's *Where the Sun Shines Best*

MAGGIE QUIRT

Austin Clarke's contemplative new offering, *Where the Sun Shines Best* (Guernica Editions, 2013), has arrived—and it is exceptional. Robust and heartbreaking in turn, Clarke's latest work takes the 2005 murder of Paul Croutch in Toronto's Moss Park as a starting point for questioning larger issues of systemic oppression and brutality. Shaken by the death of a homeless man in civic space, Clarke's sorrow is boundless, as wide as the country that he holds to account for such violence. In his grief, he offers up a lament that is at once prolonged and restrained. It is prolonged because there is much to grieve here, from war, to absent fathers, to class inequalities. It is restrained because, as the white space haunting each successive page indicates, there is so much more that could be said. Tackling issues ranging from international military efforts and local violence, to the plight of street workers and homeless men, to the daily ennui of working mothers and immigrant babysitters, Clarke turns his ever-probing eye to the fault lines in our stratified society, interrogating the nation and all of its pretensions, and finding Canada wanting.

The poem opens onto a microcosmic war zone, the vista that the narrator surveys from his "window two floors above" (53). It is this reality of "War; and the intention for war declared upon Moss Park" that both shocks and galvanizes the narrator. On one side, there are young men training for deployment to Afghanistan, aggressive and ready for a fight; on the other, there are old men shuffling through the fallen leaves in the park, searching for cigarette butts amidst the refuse of city life. It is to this latter group that the victim belongs, and while Paul Croutch is not the only casualty in the cityscape that Clarke depicts, in the summer of 2005 he was, perhaps, the most infamous. Labelled in the news stories of the day as a homeless man and a victim, Croutch is redeemed by Clarke, imagined back into a full and productive life. As a makeshift funeral procession winds its way through the park in the wake of the murder, protesting the violence, the narrator remembers the man killed, "an editor, a man of words, silenced now / unable to write his own obituary" (38) and rails against Croutch's death.

The narrator's full invective is levelled at three soldiers from the Moss Park Armouries, two of whom, after a night of drinking, beat Croutch into a coma as he lay sleeping on a park bench—ostensibly defending their right to claim the park as their own. It is not incidental that soldiers are the cause of violence. Patriotism is a shadowy presence here and the young settler nation recurs as a place where inequity and intolerance prevail. That Canada is culpable seems irrefutable; the imagery of dying maple leaves pervades these pages, indicting the nation and its pretence towards tolerance. Indeed,

the first words of the poem describe "the yellow leaves
... trampled over by the black boots of three soldiers"—
decay overlaid by violence. These same yellowing leaves
recur, at turns "rotting" (3) and "dying" (6), but rarely
in a state of vigour. Canada's star, it would seem, is
tarnished and fading, reduced in no small part by the
occurrence of hate crimes within shared civic space. Even
the Maple Leaf flag flying at half mast during the funeral
is ashamed, "lowered to half its dignity" by the need to
mark a deeply problematic violence where the "haves"
of society—young men from the suburbs training for
deployment to Kandahar—take out the full measure of
their anger on the "have nots"—epitomized by a defence-
less man sleeping under a blanket of garbage bags.

While the two white soldiers who carried out the
assault receive the narrator's harshest censure, he is also
wounded by the involvement of a black soldier, "the
descendant of slaves" (47), noting that "we who wear
the same uniform of brotherhood / are left to mourn for
your cowardice" (50). History weighs heavy here, and the
author's rebuke is unmistakable:

> Didn't he think of weeping mothers
> like his own, recent from Africa, survivor of the crossing,
> her memory crammed full of the creaking of ropes
> in sails, monotonous as the thick green waves running
> in the opposite direction, going back to Africa? (48)

It is, perhaps, an undue burden to place on one young
man; the forced migration of blacks out of Africa is a history that seems almost too overwhelming and expansive
to bear. Yet bear it we must, Clarke seems to be saying,
bear our "fact of dignity" (49), and the responsibilities
we have to "do the noble thing" (49) by categorically

rejecting the atrocities, large and small, that mark our lives as citizens in shared space. In this, the poem is vintage Clarke. As Rinaldo Walcott has observed: "Clarke requires us to think and act on what we can do about injustice" (Walcott 13), and this has remained true both across genres and down through the many decades of Clarke's cultural production.

Where the Sun Shines Best is a complex and, at times, unsettling poem. The title, for instance, is taken from an Al Jolson song and additional lyrics, including that haunting, repetitive entreaty to "Mammy, my Mammy" structure the work's dying pages. Naming a poem that contains, among other things, a meditation on black slavery, after an Al Jolson lyric may seem confusing, if not problematic. Surely an entertainer who dressed in blackface represents an era we might choose to forget, rather than immortalize through verse? That would be the easy reaction, the expected reaction. But taking the easy route has never been Clarke's style. On the contrary, he is a writer who dwells and delights in the complexities of human nature and interactions; in much of his work, Clarke makes connections between oppressed communities across space and time, teasing out alliances and postulating bridges to bring us closer to, not away from, understanding. In *The Polished Hoe*, for instance, Mary-Matilda demonstrates the proximity between the struggles of Jewish people and blacks labouring as slaves, musing that "it was the same suffering, historically speaking, between living on this Plantation and living-through the War in Europe. Much of a muchness" (Clarke 18). Marginalization may divide us, but our oppressions intersect. Much of a muchness.

And that, I think, is why Jolson, himself the victim of anti-Semitism and a proponent of equal rights for all, sings his way onto these pages. In the end, long histories and injustices notwithstanding, Clarke weighs in on the side of human contact and good intentions, urging the reader to "take this plea of love / and blood even from the reddened lips in a face / of black shoe polish." It is quite possible that the writer at the window has seen Moss Park cycle through enough seasons to know that our victories are often won in small, sometimes misguided acts, the stumblings of well-intentioned people that open up our eyes to new possibilities. So Jolson surfaces here, because he sings Clarke's truth and knows "where the sun shines best"—it is in that corner of the city where people resist, march, and come together to denounce senseless violence of any kind. It is not a place where the sun is shining brightly, for that might be too much to ask. It is only where, for the moment, the sun shines best.

Works Cited

Clarke, Austin. *Where the Sun Shines Best*. Toronto: Guernica Editions, 2013.

_____. *The Polished Hoe*. Toronto: Thomas Allen, 2002.

Walcott, Rinaldo. "'Tom Say ...': A Preface." Preface. *The Austin Clarke Reader*. Ed. Barry Callaghan. Toronto: Exile Editions, 1996. 11-13.

Selected Bibliography

Space and time do not allow for an exhaustive list of all of Austin Clarke's writing, including newspaper columns, reviews, interviews, letters, and unpublished manuscripts, among other items. A complete list of his writing can be found at the Austin Clarke Papers held at McMaster University in Hamilton and online at http://library.mcmaster.ca/archives/findaids/fonds/c/clarke-a.htm.

Novels

The Survivors of the Crossing. Toronto: McClelland & Stewart, 1964.

Amongst Thistles and Thorns. Toronto: McClelland & Stewart, 1965.

The Meeting Point. Toronto: Macmillan, 1967.

Storm of Fortune. Boston: Little Brown, 1973.

The Bigger Light. Boston: Little Brown, 1975.

The Prime Minister. Don Mills, ON: General Publishing, 1977.

Proud Empires. London: Gollancz, 1986.

The Origin of Waves. Toronto: McClelland & Stewart, 1997.

The Question. Toronto: McClelland & Stewart, 1999.

The Polished Hoe. Toronto: Thomas Allen, 2002.

More. Toronto: Thomas Allen, 2008.

Short Stories

When He Was Free and Young and He Used to Wear Silks.
Toronto: Anansi, 1971.

When Women Rule. Toronto: McClelland & Stewart,
1985.

Nine Men Who Laughed. Toronto: Penguin, 1986.

In This City. Toronto: Exile Editions, 1992.

There Are No Elders. Toronto: Exile Editions, 1993.

Choosing His Coffin: The Best Stories of Austin Clarke.
Toronto: Thomas Allen, 2003.

Poetry

Where the Sun Shines Best. Toronto: Guernica, 2013.

Memoirs

Growing up Stupid Under the Union Jack: A Memoir.
Toronto: McClelland & Stewart, 1980; Thomas
Allen, 2005.

*A Passage Back Home: A Personal Reminiscence of Samuel
Selvon,* Toronto: Exile Editions, 1994.

*Pigtails 'n Breadfruit: The Rituals of Slave Food, A
Barbadian Memoir.* Toronto: Random House, 1999.
University of Toronto Press, 2001.

Love and Sweet Food: A Culinary Memoir. Toronto:
Thomas Allen, 2004.

Nonfiction

The Confessed Bewilderment of Dr. Martin Luther King: And the Idea of Non-Violence as a Political Tactic. Burlington, ON: Al kitab Sudan, 1968.

Public Enemies: Police Violence and Black Youth. Toronto: HarperCollins, 1992.

The Austin Clarke Reader. Ed. Barry Callaghan. Toronto: Exile Editions, 1996.

Books and Articles about Austin Clarke

Algoo-Baksh, Stella. *Austin C. Clarke: A Biography.* Toronto; Barbados: ECW; U of the West Indies P, 1994.

Antwi, Phaneul. "Rough Play: Reading Black Masculinity in Austin Clarke's 'Sometimes a Motherless Child' and Dionne Brand's *What We All Long For*." *Studies in Canadian Literatue/Etudes en Littérature Canadienne* 34.2 (2009): 194-222.

Baena, Rosalia. "Gastro-Graphy: Food as Metaphor in Fred Wah's *Diamond Grill* and Austin Clarke's *Pig Tails 'n Breadfruit*." *Canadian Ethnic Studies/Etudes Ethniques au Canada* 38.1 (2006): 105-116.

Bailey Nurse, Donna. "Austin Clarke: A Barbadian Abroad." *Publishers Weekly* 250.32 (August 11, 2003): 250.

Balestra, Ginafranca. "In Barbados Evening Shadows Are Blue: An Interview with Austin Clarke." *Caribana* 5 (1996): 19-37.

Baugh, Edward. "Friday in Crusoe's City: The Question of Language in Two West Indian Novels of Exile." *ACLALS-Bulletin* 5.3 (1980): 1-12.

_____. "Friday in Crusoe's City: The Questions of Language in Two West Indian Novels of Exile." *Language and Literature in Multicultural Contexts*. ed. Satendra Nandan. Suva, Fiji: Univ. of South Pacific, 1983. 44-53.

Birbalsingh, Frank. "Austin Clarke: Caribbean-Canadians." *Frontiers of Caribbean Literatures in English*. Ed. Frank Birbalsingh. New York: St. Martin's, 1996. 86-105.

Boxill, Anthony. "Austin C. Clarke." *Canadian Writers since 1960: First Series. Ed.* W.H. New. Detroit: Thomson Gale, 1986. 124-29.

Brown, Lloyd W. "The West Indian Novel in North America: A Study of Austin Clarke." *The Journal of Commonwealth Literature* 9 (1970): 89-103.

Brydon, Diana. "Caribbean Revolution & Literary Convention." *Canadian Literature* 95 (1982): 181-85.

Bucknor, Michael A. "'Voices under the Window' of Representation: Austin Clarke's Poetics of (Body)-Memory in *The Meeting Point*." *Journal of West Indian Literature* 13.1-2 (2005): 141-75.

Carmona Rodriquez, Pedro M. "Men Don't Have Nothing Like Virginity: Migration, Refraction, and Black Masculine Performance in Austin Clarke's *The Question*." *Revista Alicantina de Estudios Inglese* 16 (2003): 21-34.

Casteel, Sarah Phillips. "Experiences of Arrival: Jewishness and Caribbean-Canadian Identity in Austin Clarke's *The Meeting Point*." *Journal of West Indian Literature* 14.1-2 (2005): 113-40.

Chanady, Amaryll. "The Trans-American Outcast and Figurations of Displacement." *Comparative Literature* 61.3 (2009): 335-45.

Chariandy, David. "That's What You Want, Isn't It?: Austin Clarke and the New Politics of Recognition." *Journal of West Indian Literature* 14.1-2 (2005): 141-65.

Cerutti, Ornella. "From Barbados to Canada: A Metropolitan Route through Austin Clarke's Stories." *Routes of the Roots: Geography and Literature in the English-Speaking Countries.* Ed. Isabella Maria Zoppi. Rome, Italy: Bulzoni, 1998. 545-560.

Clarke, George Elliott. "Clarke vs. Clarke: Tory Elitism in Austin Clarke's Short Fiction." *West-Coast Line* 22.1 (31) (1997): 110-28.

Craig, Terrence. "Interview with Austin Clarke." *World Literature Written in English* 26.1 (1986): 115-27.

Dance, Daryl. "'I Going Away. I Going Home': Austin Clarke's 'Leaving This Island Place.'" *Journal of Caribbean Literatures.* 6.3 (Spring 2010): 1.

Edwards, Whitney B. "'Migration Trauma': Diasporan Pathologies in Austin Clarke's *The Meeting Point,* Edwidge Danticat's *The Dew Breaker,* and Cristina Garcia's *Dreaming in Cuban.*" *Dissertation Abstracts International, Section A: The Humanities and Social Sciences* 70.3 (2009): 877-788.

Fabre, Michel. "Changing the Metropolis or Being Changed by It: Toronto West Indians in Austin Clarke's Trilogy. *Recherches Anglaises et Nord-Américaines* 24 (1991): 129-35.

Goddard, Horace L. "The Immigrants' Pain: The Socio-Literary Context of Austin Clarke's Trilogy." *ACLALS Bulletin* 8.1 (1989): 39-57.

_____. "One Griot Speaks Out: The West Indian-Canadian Connection: Interview with Austin Clarke. *Kola.* 20.1 (Spring 2008).

Hamner, Robert D. "Overseas Male: Austin Clarke's *Growing Up Stupid Under the Union Jack.*" *College Language Association Journal* 36.2 (1992): 123-33.

Henry, Keith S. "An Assessment of Austin Clarke, West Indian-Canadian Novelist." *College Language Association Journal* 29.1 (1985): 9-32.

Kamboureli, Smaro. "Signifying Contamination: On Austin Clarke's *Nine Men Who Laughed.*" *Essays on Canadian Writing* 57 (1995): 212-34.

Lacovia, R. M. "Migration and Transmutation in the Novels of McKay, Marshall, and Clarke." *Journal of Black Studies* 7 (1977): 437-54.

Laigle, Genevieve. "Toronto et les immigrants antillais dans *Nine Men Who Laughed* d'Austin Clarke." *La Ville plurielle dans la fiction antillaise anglophone: Images de l'interculturel.* Ed. Corinne Duboin and Eric Tabuteau. Toulouse, France: PU du Mirail, 2000. 94-114.

Lopez-Ropero, Lourdes. "Ethnographic Engagement and Autobiographical Practice in Austin Clarke's Culinary Memoir *Pigtails 'n Breadfruit.*" *World Literature Written in English* 40.2 (2004): 77-90.

_____. "The Pleasures of Slave Food: The Politics of Creolization in Austin Clarke's *Pigtails 'n Breadfruit.*" *A Sea for Encounters: Essays towards a Postcolonial Commonwealth.* Ed. Stella Borg Barthet. Amsterdam: Rodopi, 2009. 81-91. *Cross/Cultures: Readings in the Post/Colonial Literatures in English* 117.

Mehta, Brinda. "The Mother as Culinary Griotte: Food and Cultural Memory in Austin Clarke's *Pigtails 'n Breadfruit.*" *MaComere: Journal of the Association of Caribbean Women Writers and Scholars* 5 (2002): 184-203.

Misrahi-Barak, Judith. "The Cityscape in a Few Caribbean-Canadian Short Stories." *Journal of the Short Story in English* 31 (1998): 9-22.

———. "Tilling the Caribbean Narrative Field with Austin Clarke's *The Polished Hoe*." *Cultures de la confession: Formes de l'aveu dans le monde Anglophone*. Ed. Sylvie Mathé and Gilles Teulié. Aix-en-Provence, France: PU de Provence, 2006. 127-42.

———. "Skeletons in Caribbean Closets: Family Secrets and Silences in Austin Clarke's *The Polished Hoe* and Denise Harris's *Web of Secrets*." *CDS Research Report* 23 (2005): 53-64.

Ramraj, Victor. "Austin C. Clarke." *Twentieth-Century Caribbean and Black African Writers, Second Series*. Ed. Bernth Lindfors and Reinhard Sander. Detroit: Gale, 1993. 29-34.

———. "Temporizing Laughter: The Later Stories of Austin Clarke." *Short Fiction in the New Literatures in English: Proceedings of the Nice Conference of the European Association for Commonwealth Literature and Language Studies*. Ed. Jacqueline Bardolph. Nice, France: Fac. des Lettres & Sciences Humaines de Nice, 1989. 127-31.

Riemenschneider, Dieter. "Intercultural Communication: Minority Writing in the Post-Colonial World: The Caribbean-Canadian Connection." *Crabtracks: Progress and Process in Teaching the New Literatures in English*. Ed. Gordon Collier and Frank Schulze-Engler, Amsterdam, Netherlands: Rodopi, 2002. 383-400. *Cross/Cultures: Readings in the Post/Colonial Literatures in English* 59.

Robertson, Patricia. "Austin Clarke in Conversation." *Wasafiri: The Transnational Journal of International Writing* 40 (2003): 45-50.

Sanders, Leslie. "Austin Clarke." *Profiles in Canadian Literature*. ed. Jeffrey M. Heath. Vol. 4. Toronto: Dundurn, 1982. 93-100.

Stolar, Batia Boe. "Building and Living the Immigrant City: Michael Ondaatje's and Austin Clarke's Toronto." *Downtown Canada: Writing Canadian Cities*. Ed. Justin D. Edwards and Douglas Ivison. Toronto: U Toronto P, 2005. 122-41.

Walcott, Rinaldo. "Dedans et dehors: Nations, nationalisme et désirs de la Diaspora/Within and Without: Nations, Nationalism and Diasporan Desires." *Revue LISA/LISA e-journal* 3.2 (2005): 199-213.

Weiss, Allan. "Austin C. Clarke: Overview." *Reference Guide to Short Fiction*. Ed. Noelle Watson. Detroit: St. James P, 2003.

Contributors

Michael A. Bucknor is Associate Professor/Senior Lecturer and Head of the Department of Literatures in English at the University of the West Indies, Mona Campus. He has co-edited with Alison Donnell *The Routledge Companion to Anglophone Caribbean Literature* (2011) and is currently working on a book length manuscript entitled "Performing Masculinities in Jamaican Popular Culture."

George Elliott Clarke, revered poet, playwright, novelist, and literary critic, is the E.J. Pratt Professor of Canadian Literature at the University of Toronto. The Windsor, Nova Scotia, native (1960 vintage), is a seventh-generation Canadian of African-American and Aboriginal heritage. A recipient of multiple laurels, his most recent books are *Directions Home: Approaches to African-Canadian Literature* (2012) and a poetry collection, *Red* (2011). He is also currently the fourth Poet Laureate of Toronto (2012-15).

Daniel Coleman was born and raised in Ethiopia where his Canadian parents worked as missionaries. After undergraduate and graduate studies in Regina and Edmonton, he now teaches and writes on Canadian literature at McMaster University in Hamilton, Ontario. He has published books on his upbringing as well as on migration, masculinity, whiteness, and the spiritual and cultural politics of reading. He has co-edited books and special issues of journals on postcolonial and Canadian masculinities, early

Canadian literary culture, race in Canadian cultural history, Caribbean-Canadian diasporic writing, the retooling of the humanities in Canadian universities, and the resilience and creativity of displaced peoples.

Camille A. Isaacs is an assistant professor at OCAD University in Toronto, specializing in postcolonial, Black North American, Caribbean, and diasporic literatures. Her current research considers the Black diaspora in interwar Europe, the connections between the Gothic literary tradition and some Canadian diasporic writing, and aging.

Smaro Kamboureli is a professor at the School of English and Theatre Studies (SETS), University of Guelph, and Canada Research Chair (Tier 1) in Critical Studies in Canadian Literature. Her publications include *in the second person* (Longspoon 1985); *A Mazing Space: Writing Canadian Women Writing*, co-edited with Shirley Neuman (NeWest 1986); *On the Edge of Genre: The Contemporary Canadian Long Poem* (University of Toronto Press 1991); and *Scandalous Bodies: Diasporic Literature in English Canada* (Oxford 2000), which received the Gabrielle Roy Prize for Canadian Criticism. Her most recent book is *Trans.Can.Lit: Resituating the Study of Canadian Literature* (Wilfrid Laurier UP 2007), which she co-edited with Roy Miki.

Linda MacKinley-Hay is an instructor in the English Department and the School of Education at the University of Northern British Columbia. Her dissertation considered the role of education in postcolonial narrative and featured a chapter on Caribbean education and the part this British export played in shaping such authors as Austin Clarke. She has reviewed and co-authored for both literary and educational publications and at an upcoming CONGRESS session will present a paper examining one of Austin Clarke's Barbadian teachers.

Brinda J. Mehta is the Germaine Thompson Professor of French and Francophone Studies at Mills College in Oakland, California where she teaches postcolonial African and Caribbean literatures and Francophone studies. She is the author of four books, two co-edited volumes on Indo-Caribbean and Afro-Caribbean thought, and numerous articles on postcolonial literature. She has just completed her fifth book on dissident creativity in Arab women's postcolonial writings.

Sarah Phillips Casteel is an associate professor in the Department of English and Institute of African Studies at Carleton University, Ottawa, Ontario. She is the author of *Second Arrivals: Landscape and Belonging in Contemporary Writing of the Americas* (U of Virginia P, 2007) and the co-editor of *Canada and Its Americas: Transnational Navigations* (McGill-Queen's UP, 2010). Her current SSHRC-funded book project examines how Jewishness figures in the Caribbean literary imagination.

Maggie Quirt teaches in the Department of Equity Studies at York University. Her work explores issues of social justice, with an emphasis on racialized and diasporic communities in particular. Her current research, a work of creative non-fiction, explores the relationship between teachers and Inuit staff at the Shingle Point residential school. She is also an award-winning poet working on her first collection of poetry.

Victor J. Ramraj is Professor of English, University of Calgary, was editor of *ARIEL: A Review of International English Literature* (1990-2001) and past President of CALJ (Canadian Association of Learned Journals), and of CACLALS (Canadian Association for Commonwealth Literature and Language Studies). He has given numerous lectures and plenary addresses at various institutions and conferences. His publications include a book on the Canadian writer Mordecai Richler and an anthology, *Concert of Voices: An Anthology of World Writing in English*. He is currently working on a study of the politics of differences and affinities in International English literature.

Marquita R. Smith is a third-year PhD candidate (2013) in English & Cultural Studies at McMaster University in Hamilton, Ontario, where she is working on a dissertation on hip-hop feminism and black womanhood in the public sphere. She has published articles about feminism, critical race studies, and popular culture in journals such as *Postcolonial Text* and *Michigan Feminist Studies*.

Batia Boe Stolar teaches literary and film studies at Lakehead University in Thunder Bay, Ontario. She has published articles on the representations of immigrant experiences in Canadian literature and film. In collaboration with Clara Sacchetti, her work also explores the intersections between photography and multicultural dance.

Acknowledgements

Sections from Batia Boe Stolar, "Afro-Caribbean Immigrant Experiences in the White City: Austin Clarke's Toronto" were originally published in "Building and Living the Immigrant City: Michael Ondaatje's and Austin Clarke's Toronto," published in *Downtown Canada: Writing Canadian Cities*, edited by Justin D. Edwards and Douglas Ivison, © U Toronto P, 2005, pp. 122-41. Reprinted with permission of the publisher.

Daniel Coleman, "'Playin' 'Mas,' Hustling Respect: Multicultural Masculinities in Two Stories by Austin Clarke," was originally published in *Masculine Migrations: Reading the Postcolonial Male in New Canadian Narratives*, by Daniel Coleman, © U Toronto P, 1998. Reprinted with permission of the publisher.

Michael A. Bucknor, "'Voices Under the Window' of Representation: Austin Clarke's Poetics of (Body)-Memory in *The Meeting Point*," was first published in the *Journal of West Indian Literature*, Vol. 13, Nos. 1 & 2 (April 2005), pp. 141-174.

Smaro Kamboureli, "Signifying Contamination: Austin Clarke's *Nine Men Who Laughed*," was originally published in *Essays on Canadian Writing* 57 (Winter 1995), pp. 212-34. Reprinted with permission from Smaro Kamboureli.

Sarah Phillips Casteel, "Experiences of Arrival: Jewishness and Caribbean-Canadian Identity in Austin Clarke's *The Meeting Point*," was first published in the *Journal of West Indian Literature,* Vol. 14, Nos. 1 & 2 (November 2005), pp. 113-140.

George Elliott Clarke, "Clarke versus Clarke: Tory Elitism in Austin Clarke's Short Fiction," was originally published in *West Coast Line* 22.1 (1997): 110-28, and revised and reprinted in *Odysseys Home*, by George Elliott Clarke, U Toronto Press, 2002, pp. 238-52. Reprinted with permission of the author.

Brinda Mehta, "The Mother as Culinary Griotte: Food and Cultural Memory in Austin Clarke's *Pigtails 'n Breadfruit*," was originally published in *MaComère: Journal of the Association of Caribbean Women Writers and Scholars* 5 (2002), pp. 184-203. Reprinted by permission of the author.

Special thanks to Michael Mirolla, Joseph Pivato, and Guernica Editions for allowing me to add Austin Clarke to the Canadian Writers Series. Thank you to the essayists for their contribution to the scholarship on Austin Clarke. And my sincere appreciation goes to Jude Polsky and Selmin Kara who gave me valuable feedback on my sections.